THE TRUE STORY OF THE WORLD'S MOST POPULAR AUTHOR
. . . is a story that rivals any of her novels.

It seems there is something inside Danielle herself, some high-speed motor, that drives her on to work into the night, every night.

So when you hear that she buys things, enjoys picking out presents for people, has a love for jewels, that her fourth husband gives her wonderful sparkling gifts, you want to cheer her on. Someone needs to encourage her to have more fun with the money she's worked so hard for.

But you have to remember that to Danielle, the sheer act of writing herself into that dream world every nine months may probably be more fun than any afternoon on a spree with a credit card at Tiffany's.

Danielle Steel

NICOLE HOYT

PINNACLE BOOKS
WINDSOR PUBLISHING CORP.

For my mother, who taught me wonderment, and my father, who gave me the courage to stay with it, with a heart full of love.

PINNACLE BOOKS are published by

Windsor Publishing Corp.
850 Third Avenue
New York, NY 10022

First Printing: July, 1994

Printed in the United States of America

Acknowledgments

With immense gratitude for the spellbinding books of America's premiere novelist, Danielle Steel.

The author wishes to acknowledge the invaluable assistance of Ashley and Bill; her dear friends Belinda and TM; and the wonderful librarians at the DeWitt Wallace Periodicals Room, The Central Research Library of The New York Public Library; The Elmer Holmes Bobst Library at New York University; and the Goethe Institute Library.

And my dear husband, Tom.

Permissions Acknowledgements

Grateful acknowledgment is made to the following for permission to reprint previously published material:

HarperCollins Publishers, Inc. and Faber & Faber Limited for permission to reprint an excerpt from "Getting There" from *Ariel* by Sylvia Plath, © 1963 by Ted Hughes.

"Paris Report" by Diana Vreeland, Courtesy *Vogue*. Copyright © 1963 (renewed 1991) by The Condé Nast Publications, Inc.

Charles Hamden-Turner for permission to quote from *Sane Asylum*, © 1976, San Francisco Book Company.

Cyra McFadden for permission to quote from "Passion's Profitable Prose," *San Francisco Magazine*, © 1983.

HarperCollins Publishers, Inc. for permission to reprint excerpts from *Supergirls: The Autobiography of an Outrageous Business* by Claudia Jessup and Genie Chipps, edited by Betty Baer Krieger, © 1972 by Claudia J. Jessup, Genie Davis Chipps and Betty Baer Krieger.

The Velveteen Rabbitt by Margery Williams, Doubleday & Co., Inc.

And very special thanks to *Publishers Weekly* for permission to use reviews of Danielle Steel books © 1973-1994, Cahners Publishing Company, A Division of Reed Publishing USA.

I shall bury the wounded like pupas,
I shall count and bury the dead.
Let their souls writhe in a dew,
Incense in my track.
The carriages rock, they are cradles.
And I, stepping from this skin
Of old bandages, boredoms, old faces

Step to you from the black car of Lethe,
Pure as a baby.

—From "Getting There" by Sylvia Plath,
Ariel.
The poem Danielle Steel chose as
the epigraph for her first big novel,
Passion's Promise, 1976.

Prologue

Tonight, she entertains eighty guests for a dinner-dance in the ballroom of her new house. It's a first look at the revamped, sparkling Spreckels Mansion for many of her friends.

She leans cozily on the strong arm of tall, dark, and handsome John Traina, as she welcomes her guests. A figure-caressing Dior gown wraps her petite body and sets off her tiny 5'1" Victorian figure. Her skin is young and vibrant, eyes a strong green-gray, lips sensuous and smiling, cheekbones strong. That famous silken dark hair swirls up, behind her ears, to set off a lovely profile. At her ears, twinkling jewels gather up the starlight and sprinkle it out generously among her guests.

Like novelist Edith Wharton before her, she asked that her writing career be fitted in around her social life, and her wish has been granted. Her husband John Traina is dressed in the sort of formal evening clothes he seems born to wear, the crisp white linen setting off his warm tan, lively eyes sparkling at the guests. He looks lovingly at his beautiful Danielle beside him, his black hair touched lightly with gray. They have much to be proud of—a long, strong marriage, and between them, nine happy, healthy children.

John Traina laughs softly as the black-tie guests extravagantly admire their new place, astounded at his beautiful wife's transformation of this huge old mansion.

The limousines and cars roll up and the sparkling lights of San Francisco society step grandly out, making their way past Danielle and John's welcoming warmth, and into the interior of this lavishly restored local landmark. The Mansion was erected by sugar baron Adolph Spreckels in 1913, and until recently, nearly deserted and bereft of loving human companionship.

Now, Danielle has pulled off another miracle, and the mansion opens again to the full and happy family life it was designed for.

Danielle had set her sights on this famous San Francisco landmark. Now, after a brief scuffle, it is in her possession. This brilliant evening is the glittering apotheosis of all her work, her hopes, her reveries: the one love of her life on her arm, the one house of their dreams at her feet, surrounded by her loving children, and, some say, looking barely older than her daughter Beatrix, now in her mid-twenties.

The crème de la crème of San Francisco society is here in all its glory—couture gowns, fine dinner jackets, jewels from Tiffany and Cartier and Gump's, spit-polished shoes, and elegant minaudieres. The vaults of Wells Fargo, Crocker, the Bank of America—all the old banks with all the old San Francisco money—are giving up the family jewels for this evening, jewels that had been lining their coffers since the days when the first one-room banks were opened, when the rush of gold nuggets clattered into instant riches over a century ago.

The heavy bronze portico that had once flanked the front entrance, with its dual stone pillars and carved urns, once gave the visage of the Spreckels mansion a look more municipal than homey. The original owner, the formidable Alma Spreckels, had torn it off in the 1930s. Now the Spreckels Mansion looked less like the Opera House and more like a home, a transformation at which Danielle excelled. Did anyone guess at Danielle's secret, that the ball-room they were entering was Danielle's re-creation, from two bedrooms and a bathroom?

The place is buzzing with heat and excitement as the beautifully gowned ladies and their escorts find their place cards and sit down for the dinner-dance. Not one woman can believe that Danielle completely remodeled this fifty-five-room mansion in six months. One day Herb Caen, the longest running columnist in San Francisco, spotted a dumpster outside the house, and before you knew it, the deed was done.

But then San Francisco had already seen Danielle, in her marriage with John Traina, give birth to one daughter, Samantha; another, Victoria; another, Vanessa; then a son, Maxx; and lastly another daughter, Zara; all while writing a string of best-sellers. But this? To take over the old Social

Landmark of the Bay Area? And then to move in so fast. And pull it off so brilliantly!

The stylish Dodie Rosenkrans lived in this very house as Mrs. John Spreckels in 1960. She's full of delight: "They turned a mansion into a cozy, beautiful large house," she tells a reporter. "The house is used almost as it was designed."

Peering up into the newly gilt ceiling of the ball-room, another couture-clad woman sighs and figures Danielle could have squeezed in even more than the guest-lined eighty swells for dinner and dancing. And socialite Frances Bowes simply murmurs "beautifully done, beautifully done."

The French connection in San Francisco society—the de Limurs and the de Guignes, as well as Danielle's own Lazard daughter—were as impressed as perhaps Danielle's friend President Mitterand of France might be. He'd visited her old mansion, but the hospitality of the new would surely boost the international reputation of the City by the Bay.

Of course Gordon and Ann Getty also have a marvelous house. But as Gordon's father, J. Paul Getty, the oil Midas, once said, "Money doesn't necessarily have any connection with happiness. Maybe with unhappiness." And the money now invested in Danielle's new house was surely bringing happiness. The city, and the grand old fortunes around the bay, were favorite topics in Danielle's books; now she had her very own splendid mansion.

The gossip is that Danielle had been working right through the evening before the grand ball.

That her hand is personally to be seen from stem
to stern of the huge mansion—in the dining room's
beautiful eighteenth-century-style mosaic tile
floor, on the lovely ballroom's hand-gilt ceiling, in
the dreamy clouds drifting across the blue sky of
the children's bedrooms.

When the restless guests finally sit, the polite
social roar turns to a buzz. Guests are charmed
anew by the custom-made Schmidt chocolate doll-
house-sized reproductions of the mansion at each
place setting.

Those guests who'd told their cooks to cut back on
expenses during the recession of the early 1990s are
impressed by the eggs, served by the formal waiters,
eggs overflowing with the richest, blackest caviar.

Sleek young waiters, trying to suppress laughs
of amazement, joyously pop the corks on endless
bottles of Cristal champagne—French, $110 a bot-
tle—and the room buzzes again with the arrival of
the centerpiece production, something like a huge
wedding cake, but no. It is a replica, again. Of
Danielle Steel's Mansion.

"She's at the HEART of the hardcore social
scene . . . wearing Dior couture . . . the Ann
Getty crowd . . . the 'real thing' socially in San
Francisco," murmurs a San Franciscan who keeps
score of these blue bloods by the bay.

"There are people out there with money who
can do anything they want," says a top San Francisco real estate man, Vincent Friia.

* * *

San Francisco society dances to a new tune tonight, the tune of a Danielle Steel novel come to life. It is almost twenty years from her first shaky days in San Francisco, as a struggling single mother, forced to work to support her tiny family, living in a small apartment, afraid, but refusing to give up on the novel-writing.

Chapter One
Crossings: 1947-1963

"I try to protect my children . . . maybe because nobody ever protected me."
                                                    —Danielle Steel

A biography issued by Danielle Steel's public relations firm, the prestigious Rogers & Cowan, claimed that she "grew up in Europe" and also mentioned "an education in France," and "a background in public relations and advertising."

One cannot blame the PR writer for getting things wrong. Over the years, interviewers and publishers have emerged from encounters with Danielle Steel convinced that they have the truth, only to discover that the details conflict just a bit with other stories she has told.

There are those who have written that her father was a scion of Munich's Löwenbräu beer dynasty and her Portuguese mother the daughter of a diplomat, while some are convinced her father was a German nobleman, whose family seat was a moated castle in Bavaria. Others believe that she was educated in European private schools, or at French lycée and a snooty Swiss boarding school. There are those who believe that she was at one time head of a public relations firm.

None of this is exactly true. For reasons known only to herself, Danielle Steel has chosen to obscure and romanticize the facts of her life. Perhaps she wanted to protect the material so that she use it in her own books, for, as this writer has discovered, the real life of Danielle Steel is far more dramatic and romantic than any fiction even she could invent.

Danielle-Fernande Dominique Schulein-Steel was born in a Manhattan hospital on August 14, 1947, the product of an unlikely marriage of stone and steel, the only child of John Schulein-Steel and Norma Da Camara Stone Reis Schulein-Steel.

Life on the Upper East Side of Manhattan in the late forties and early fifties was a charmed round of strolls through Central Park, fathers working regular workdays at the office, and mothers who stayed home with the children.

On the weekend, mommies and daddies spent time with their children and each other, sent a child's sailboat flying across the still waters of the park's pond. At Christmas, fathers set up great blinking Lionel train sets in the library or one of the guest bedrooms, where the kids could scream with delight as the gigantic locomotives roared and clattered round the curved tracks, the crossing-guard bells rang out, and the whistle tooted a warning. Daughters would be taken to the great merchants like Best & Co. for children's clothes, and then maybe run over to Rumpelmayer's for a special dessert, *mit schlag*.

Neighbors nodded at each other, passing up and down the tall apartment buildings along Fifth Avenue, and stopped to chat for a while on lazy weekends while taking the children's little dogs for a stroll. The doormen, with their shiny brass buttons and taxicab whistles, seemed to be the only security system a family needed back then.

The nannies would gather in the Central Park playground, sitting in the dappled sunlight of the birch, beech, and oak trees, rocking their little charges in navy blue English baby carriages or watching them on the seesaws in their baby Princess Margaret outfits.

But as F. Scott Fitzgerald once observed, "Let me tell you about the very rich. They are different from you and me." For one thing, they often have a hard time playing the less glamorous, more demanding role of mother and father when their own social life spins from nightclub to ballroom, continent to continent. Danielle's magazine interviews and biographies have painted her parents like this. "My father, John Steel, was very gregarious, very social, an international roué," she explains. "My mother was an international beauty. Together they were two very spectacular people."

They were the kind of international glamour couple—from the impression formed by her portrait of them—who might dance to the popular tunes of the era at the St. Regis Roof, see their pals at Shemmy Billingsley's Stork Club, or the El Morocco, and stop by the Plaza during a beautiful winter snowfall to watch the young debutantes on the arms of their college-age beaux, rushing off to smaller parties after their coming-out balls, commenting on the beauty of one, the fast reputation of another.

The rich themselves were often raised by nurses
and nannies and housekeepers and cooks. So unless
they were very lucky, they missed out on the wonderful warm chicken-soup servings of parental love
that gives any young child a booster shot into life.

Danielle's parents, she says, were such social but-
terflies, two very "flamboyant" people. She once
confessed that she was so emotionally neglected
that they sometimes even forgot her birthday, was
raised by nannies and maids, and told an early
interviewer that instead of parents, she was looked
after by relatives and servants. "I got very attached
to the cook," she recalls.

"My father was a gay blade who was fun but not
fatherly . . . ," she explained.

Her mother was the beautiful and soignée Norma
Da Camara Stone Reis, the daughter of Gil da
Camara Stone Reis, director of "Casa de Portugal"
(now the Portuguese Tourist Office) from 1949 to
1953. Interviewers have emerged from chats with
Danielle under the impression that Norma Stone
was "the daughter of a high-ranking Portuguese
diplomat." Bill Toth, Danielle's third husband,
claims he was told that Norma Stone was related by
birth to King Juan Carlos and the Spanish royal family. But, although Gil da Camara Stone Reis had a
diplomatic passport, the Portuguese Embassy in
Washington insists "he was not a career diplomat."

"My parents were very visible in the press,"
Danielle says, although a close scrutiny of New

York newspapers of the period yields no mention of either John Schulein-Steel or Norma Da Camara Stone Dos Reis.

Life at home for little Danielle was very noisy, full of the arguments and threats of two people, once madly in love, now decidedly at odds. Danielle today speaks very little of her mother, though she did include Norma Stone among the fourteen people to whom she dedicated her first book *Going Home,* in 1973.

Danielle's family myth, told to early interviewers and her third husband, paints a picture of her father as a dashing playboy, a lovable roué who relished a glittering evening at the opera in white tie and tails.

Danielle's ex-husband Bill Toth described John Schulein-Steel's appearance as the epitome of 1930s Berlin. A blond, blue-eyed Aryan type, about 5′6,″ and beautifully put together.

Danielle's father spoke four or five languages. He was a genuine man of the world, according to Bill Toth. His style, Toth told us, was to travel to the Adirondacks, far north of New York, rent himself a lodge, and invite a handful of guests for a weekend. If he were charmed by a young woman, he'd choose a special present for her. This would help explain Danielle's taste for choosing the perfect present. It is the ultimate expression of love.

But are we to believe these family myths, as passed on by an ex-husband? We will talk further about the fascinating historical reality of the Schuelein family of Munich (John Schulein-Steel changed the spelling) in just a few chapters.

Danielle's mother was equally colorful. "I remember my mother," she says, "as being absolutely beautiful and very flirtatious. She took it as normal that when she walked into a restaurant, everyone would stop eating and look at her. That wouldn't happen to me unless I yelled, 'Fire.' My father was sort of a great international playboy; that was his work—even after he got married. They didn't stay married for long. My mother was very young and wanted to be free. She split when I was six or seven."

When the marriage of stone and steel came to an end, they divorced "politely," according to Danielle, and the custody arrangement was civilized: "they flipped a coin and he won." Danielle stayed with her father and her mother went to live in Europe. "I saw her over the years," she recalls. "I didn't see a lot of her, but I saw her."

Danielle frequently describes romantic travels with her father. "We'd spend parts of summers in Capri, parts in Rome," she recalls. "He'd give two or three parties a week—big, wild, wonderful bashes with lots of food, lots of music—gypsy violinists—and a hundred or so guests. An international group of equally indolent people.

"It was always very dressed up. My father's idea of an informal evening was black tie for dinner. They wore white ties, tails, top hats, even capes. He was completely crazy, but wonderful—a scholarly man, and a big lady chaser, with a great knack for bringing people together. Of course, with all these parties, I never had the typical life of a child."

Where once she'd been a small child, lonely in

the midst of a noisy marriage, Danielle now sometimes found herself in the oppressive silence of her German grandparents' household. Her grandmother Omi was a rigid taskmaster.

The children of divorce may have looked the same during these years on the Upper East Side, they may have lived in the same houses near the same park, but the emotional tenor of their childhood was entirely different. They did not see the world through rose-colored glasses.

"I was very impressed by her apartment on Fifth Avenue," recalls a little boy who visited her in her childhood. "It was extremely large . . . a many-windowed corner living room; a plush carpet; the living room perhaps 50 or 60 feet long, large enough that there was one seating area and then another [seating area] in another corner, old paintings in gilded frames—the things in my mind I associate with her."

Did her daddy enjoy taking her through the Metropolitan Museum, within walking distance of the apartment? Taking impressionable Danielle past the grand tombs of Egyptian kings? Through rows of imposing suits of armor sold by an English earl to brash American robber barons? (Today she keeps a battered suit of armor in her country house. The kids even have a nickname for it.) Did Daddy let her stare in wonder at the baubles once belonging to Madame Pompadour, or the delicate sixteenth century etched glass from Germany?

Perhaps. But we do know from Danielle that John Schulein-Steel preferred travel and exploration to a stationary fatherhood: riding by camel through the wilds of Manchuria, tromping through the Amazonian rainforest.

He was, indeed, the black sheep of this high-achievement family, she admitted later. Something of a disappointment. "This was a matter of great concern to his family," she emphatically told a reporter.

While her father continued a life with less than the normal load of responsibility, Danielle became a quiet, studious child of eight going on thirty. She was responsible. She was self-disciplined. She was an excellent student. A high achiever. She was a child forced to be old and wise before her time, a child left underfoot for her grandparents' generation, and an extra responsibility for the household help. Was she sometimes perceived as simply more clothes to iron, an extra mouth to feed, more linen to launder, and an intrusion on an older, stately Germanic household?

It was stiff German training she got, both from her father and in that older household on Fifth Avenue. She ran her father's house from the age of eight, making his appointments, keeping things running smoothly. She never realized that *that* wasn't a little girl's job. She would write about such daughters in *Loving*, where the daughter of an internationally famous author, organized her father's life and ran his dinner parties then took on his debts after his death. In *Thurston House*, a daughter has similar chores.

But since Danielle's father was a brilliantly organized man who could accomplish more in fifteen minutes than another could in an hour, she learned some lessons. But did she ever get to be just a kid?

As the only child of only children, she remembers being very lonely. "I grew up an only child, and it was very lonely," she says.

She wrote about a figure that could have been partly her grandmother in some early fiction, her first book *Going Home*. This grandmother was a terrifying, formidable figure; a master of the verbal put-down; a cold and sometimes cruel woman.

As a child, Danielle lived a very grown-up life. She says she was sometimes allowed to take a role in formal dinner parties. Can you imagine the highly polished silver and rich white linens, eggshell-thin Limoges and burning candles, and Danielle, all of eight or nine? She listened to political conversations, experiencing the ebb and flow of argument around a passionate guest list of exiled Europeans and sophisticated Americans. And despite her guardians' desire to protect her, she saw illicit romances blossom in the hothouse European atmosphere of postwar Manhattan.

"I was very shy. Besides, no one was going to talk to an eight-year-old. So I became a sort of fly-on-the-wall observer at an early age," she remembers. "Looking back on it now, it's probably what made me a writer."

Beyond what she saw, there was what she read. There was always the reading. There were the ro-

mances of Colette. She read widely and well in the
wise, sensual writings of Colette.

When it came time for little Danielle to go to
grade school, a nearby school was chosen that was
within walking distance of her grandmother's apartment on Fifth Avenue. The Lycée Français of New
York prepared children from grade school through
the end of high school to take the French Baccalauréat examinations for entry to French universities.
It gave students an exact duplicate of the curriculum
studied by all public school students in France.

Finally, Danielle shyly walked up Fifth Avenue to
her first class in the first grade, dressed in her
school uniform. At last, school with kids her own
age! A break from the distant doings of a beautiful
father and his problems, and the mother she only
very, very occasionally caught a glimpse of.

And school was right up the street, a structured
yet friendly second home.

It was wonderful!

Most of the lively children at the French-speak-
ing Lycée thought Danielle was just swell. But they
were quite aware of her status as the only child of
a broken home, an awareness that never quite left
their perception of her.

They were charmed by their first introduction
to Danielle: Even then, they remembered how well-
mannered she was, her little-girl charm, her
grooming. She felt the responsibility of running
her father's household from the age of eight. It

wasn't much of a childhood. But her classmates were totally unaware of the realities of the newly broken home that Danielle walked away from when she came to school every single morning.

From time to time, Danielle has claimed that classmates tortured her by calling her *"sale boche"*— filthy German. Another Lycée student familiar with those explosive postwar years explains that *"sale boche"* was what Parisians called the Germans tramping through their streets during the Second World War. "It was a term heard from the parents in France . . . in speaking, people in France always referred to the Germans who occupied France and mistreated the people as *sale boche*, but I can't imagine why they'd call *her* that."

Yet she was registered in a French school with that German last name, Schulein. Any lingering pride she may have had in Germany, any sense of the family's former splendor she may have imagined from Omi, or discovered in her reading or daydreaming, may have gotten her in difficult arguments with other American kids on the block. Certainly in her later books, like *The Ring* and *Jewels*, one comes across many, many good Germans. In the black-and-white mentality of the immediate postwar era, there simply were no good Germans.

The students at the Lycée were a cosmopolitan lot: a Frenchman could pop his children in and out of a Lycée any place in the world and the education would go on as if nothing had changed. The curriculum never wavered around the globe, and the schools were recognized by the French

Ministry of National Education and the French Ministry of Foreign Affairs.

This particular Lycée, at 3 East 95th Street, was established in 1935, by an actual French nobleman, Count Charles de Ferry de Fontnouvelle, with the support of several rich Americans.

The count acquired a splendid American robber-baron-style mansion for his school, the former Amory S. Carhart residence, built in 1919—even later than the grand mansion Danielle now owns in San Francisco—and designed by another Beaux Arts influenced architect, the stately Horace Trumbauer.

By the end of the Second World War, there were many emigrés like the Schuleins who had escaped from Hitler's Germany, war-ravaged Eastern Europe, and Stalin's Russia, to start over in New York. The city was now the capital of the world.

These literate, sophisticated exiles re-created in Manhattan the worlds of art, music, literature, and fine conversation they had known in Europe. Many Europeans, not only Frenchmen, viewed French as the *common language* of diplomacy and upper-class conversation. It was only fitting that the children of these immigrants should study in the French language.

The children often reflected the questioning mood of the immigrant parents. The European intellectuals were gripped by the hard questions asked by the existentialists, of Camus and Sartre and de Beauvoir. Arguments that had raged through the Left Bank of Paris (*Rive Gauche*) after

the Liberation now made their way through the
Lycée. Students, aping their parents, started asking
the forbidden question: Did God exist?

Danielle Schulein-Steel was not questioning the
existence of God: He was a Father that she deeply
needed.

Danielle, as a serious Catholic, worshipped Him.
At the Lycée, a priest from the nearby Catholic
church gave Catechism classes.

She took to traditional Catholicism. She also
took to the traditional, classic lines of the Lycée
education. Conservative, orderly progression of levels of instruction. Monthly report cards, graded on
a scale of one to twenty. At the end of each of
three terms, her father or guardian reviewed her
exact ranking in class, grade averages, and results
on her examinations.

The teachers were certified French teachers, the
language in the classroom French. And in French,
she learned what the Lycée set out to teach: that she
read French fluently, that she express herself well,
speaking with proper pronunciation, and that her
vocabulary, spelling, and grammar be beyond re-
proach.

The school stressed, over and over, the myster-
ies of French grammar and syntax through writing practice and the study of classics of French
literature. Each year, from what we'd call first
grade on, she studied all the required courses.
These were French, English, mathematics, history

and geography, a science, and art. At night, she'd
often bring home a heavy dose of homework: five
hours.

Although the Lycée was in the heart of New York
City, French was the language heard in the school
halls. After school, of course, the children
switched quite nimbly to English.

Each summer, according to a classmate, many
students would sail back to France in utter bliss
with their parents on the *Île de France* luxury liner
or the *France*, traveling in style, first-class. Many
were the offspring of parents in the diplomatic or
consular service, posted in New York, and the government would foot the bill for their travel.

Danielle might imagine them tucking their favorite summer cottons and linens—red, white, and
blue—into their small leather suitcases from Hermès or Vuitton—they'd be driven in their limousine
or the big old New York Yellow Cabs down to the
bustling excitement of the New York piers, where
the luxury liner lay at berth, tooting of grand ad-
ventures to come. The food was sublime; the staterooms très chic; the ambiance in the dining rooms
and smoking rooms, bars and lounges, the height
of Parisian sophistication. She caught the flavor of
the great liners in her novel *Crossings*.

The only way you'd catch the parents of a Lycée
student taking the United States line would be
when the French line had a completely booked
summer cruise schedule. American was good,
French was the best, thought the children, the
crème de la crème, the tops, the Eiffel Tower!

* * *

Already, by the age of eleven, Danielle's mind was trained to self-discipline and clean-rigorous logic by her organized education. It may have saved her from the pull of yearning for her mother, yet being left with her father. Or of yearning for her father, yet being left with her stern grandmother Omi. Of wanting a childhood, and finding Omi, a rigid, serious taskmaster.

The hours of concentration required by her homework gave her training for her future career. Work was an escape into the timeless, hourless realm of the mind. It was better than a drug, better than the sought-for, longed-for but perhaps impossible love of a mother or father. It was a drug that was totally under her control: the drug of concentration.

Classmates don't remember Danielle Schulein-Steel as a bookworm. No, by all accounts, she had good social skills in the midst of this very literate, verbal group. Everybody liked her.

But there was always that subliminal awareness that Danielle was the first girl in their school whose parents were divorced. And perhaps along with that awareness, a subliminal fear that her story might portend a similar story in their own family. And one classmate did note a certain "moody" quality to Danielle because of the divorce.

Danielle Schulein-Steel was the first person with two last names, a "hyphenate," that the students classmate did note a certain "moody" quality to Danielle because of the divorce.

Danielle Schulein-Steel was the first person with two last names, a "hyphenate," that the students knew of at the Lycée. It was something the upper classes in England did quite often with their double-barreled family names, but she wasn't English. And yet why did her father decide to call himself "Steel"? Or, again, why her father had changed the spelling of his last name to Schulein, by dropping the "e" in the Americanized spelling of the Schuelein family name, or why he added the "-Steel," while leaving Danielle registered in school under a different spelling at times, as Schuelein-Steel. So there was further mystery attached to Danielle.

Children of the successful, the intellectuals, and those of humble means could all attend the Lycée. The French Ministry of Education was actually quite liberal with scholarship assistance for the students who were planning to continue on to University in France. But the now-retired Headmaster, Monsieur Brodin, is adamant that Danielle was not a scholarship student, that she came from quite an important family.

The other parents packed up their kids into the country wagon for weekends in the Berkshires, Hampshires, Adirondacks, or Hamptons. According to stories she has told reporters, one imagines Danielle's father polishing his opera pumps for an evening out on the town with a new, even more a Manhattan under Maxfield Parrish's mural at the King Cole bar at the St. Regis Hotel, an elegant pile built in the early years of the century in the French Beaux Arts style.

The Lycée was both sophisticated and studious. It's just that Danielle's home turf was a little less predictable, and sounded a little more stylish.

One classmate remembers a telling incident: When his parents gave him his ninth birthday party, Danielle presented him with a very special Danielle-style gift. It was his very first "designer" T-shirt: a Lacoste polo shirt. The other children gave toys and books. Danielle was already aware of the status distinctions that mean so much in the adult world. It was a fond gesture, he believes, for her to choose a Lacoste polo shirt, with its tiny green alligator logo, to educate him in the arcane importance of small details.

Despite the money at the Lycée, the enthusiastic egalitarianism of childhood cut across class and nationality. One was envied for the wealth of one's learning, argumentativeness and imagination rather than the number of mink coats one's mother hung in her cedar-lined closet.

The only boys who raised eyebrows during Danielle's stay were the infamous Marx brothers. This is not to say the Marx Brothers of Hollywood, but the children of the Marx toy dynasty. "Every week a new toy and showing off," recalls Danielle's classmate. "But no, there was no discrimination against the Marx brothers because they were Americans but because of the showing off . . . we were interested in variety in the school, all countries, all religions, the Cambodians, the Vietnamese."

Danielle's grandmother Omi might take her out into the sparkling winter snow scenes of New York's Fifth Avenue. They'd travel down to the German wonderland of stuffed Steiff teddy bears at F.A.O. Schwartz. Then they'd plow on through the glistening, pristine snowbanks to the glorious Plaza Hotel, with the huge Christmas tree set up outside.

The Plaza seemed to be one of Danielle's favorite places. She writes of it often in her books, beginning with the first, *Going Home*.

Then, on very special occasions, the children would go for formal tea at the Plaza Hotel, with violins and harps, perhaps a pianist, and rich white table linens, Victorian potted palms and air of timeless fin-de-siècle elegance. A child could listen quietly, while teacups clicked politely on china saucers and sugar cubes plunked gently into the fragrant brew—listen and look. After school, the children from the Lycée would swarm in a lively, hyperactive gang to the delicatessen on the southeast corner of Park and 96th Street . . . they'd throw down their schoolbags, gossip and argue excitedly, and sip Cokes through straws, American-style.

Elementary school soaked up all of Danielle's energies from the ages of six through ten.

Then she made the great leap into secondary school.

* * *

Danielle Steel in junior high. Can she ever have been so young? As an August child, she was always ahead for her age.

"I remember her as being very outgoing, always a smile . . . always positive," says one classmate.

"And laughing a lot," says another.

A third classmate adds, "She was part of the parties all the time—she loved to dance!"

In Danielle's high school photographs, she looks quite jolly and very young. Smiling directly at the camera in her *Classe de Seconde* photo (something like our senior year in high school), she stands out as the only girl in the front row wearing white. Every other girl is wearing a navy blue top. Just the year before, her face was only partially visible: The girl sitting in front of her blocked her from the camera's eye. She has learned to become more central in her senior year. Her legs are demurely crossed at the ankles and tucked under her chair. She is wearing bangs. She is only fifteen, we must remember. And unlike any of the other girls in the photo, she has crossed her arms on her chest rather than delicately resting her hands in her lap like a debutante-in-training. She looks sweet . . . and determined.

No one remembers that she had any particular steady boyfriend, but that was a time when the kids went places in groups.

The girls could get their excess energy and anger worked off during recess; she could get her gossip quota worked off with her girlfriends on the phone. She was good friends with several girls in her class.

They'd go in groups to dancing parties at each other's houses: Back then, the hot dance coming out of a discotheque on Times Square was by Chubby Checker. It was called the Twist.

They no longer went with their grannies to Rumpelmayer's, down Central Park South. They were now too sophisticated for the dollops of whipped cream, the steaming hot chocolate *mit schlag,* in their perfectly groomed skirts and shirts and blazers, perfectly polished flat pumps, and warm stockings. With the Twist around, fattening desserts were definitely out.

Danielle's first published writing was probably the poem that appeared in French in her school yearbook, in 1961, when she was thirteen. Roughly paraphrased, it is a sweet and gentle salute to her school,

> "a happy place," where
> the boys are bored, the girls are happy,
> and the teachers are gentle and sweet
> "like our mothers."

Even then, Danielle was observing the difference between the boys and the girls. And talking of her teachers as being as sweet as her mother . . . a mother that didn't exist in her life then.

No matter how French the education was, these kids were Americans in their teenage hearts. Still,

even then her schoolmates remember Danielle for
her distinct chic—her almost palpable air of self-
control and self-contained style. She was not a
Jayne Mansfield, recollects a classmate, but a
Grace Kelly.

The uniform during the entire Lycée experience
never varied: a navy blue blazer, a white blouse, a
gray wool skirt. Yet one of the boys pointed out
Danielle's decided "allure." Of course, a Grace
Kelly would look divine in a blue blazer and white
shirt and gray skirt. But how is it possible for a girl
to mobilize such allure in such a strict uniform?

Danielle Schulein-Steel didn't seem to have to
work very hard to keep her figure svelte and lithe.
She was one of those human beings blessed by the
fates with a high metabolism that kept her weight
low, and in later years, enabled her to work twelve,
fourteen, sixteen, even twenty hours per day.

During the winter, the gang from Lycée Français
would grab their ice skates and head for Wollman
Rink, in Central Park at 65th Street near the Children's Zoo. Wollman Rink later made an appearance in her novel *A Perfect Stranger.* (A young girl,
whose parents didn't give her enough spending
money to go skating at the much safer private rink
at Rockefeller Center, is brutally raped there.)

The classmates would go to dancing parties at
each other's houses, up and down the East Side,
with parents playing strict chaperones. The classes
were small, only twelve in most, a large class run-

ning fifteen or twenty, so they all knew each other well. By the time Danielle left the Lycée, there were only about twenty-four students in her entire school's coed class of 1963.

They'd stop by Stark's, an upscale coffee shop on Madison Avenue that served cocktails, where they dined with their parents on cook's night off.

And without their parents, they'd head off to the dark and smoky bistro called The Left Bank, one of those places designed to lure in prep school students hoping to pass for a grown-up drinking-age eighteen. There, an occasional student would light up a fragrant Gauloises cigarette (Danielle smoked an American brand), and try out their existential poses for each other, as if they were sitting at the Deux Magots on the Left Bank of Paris.

Secondary school demanded much more of all the students. Everyone studied the same curriculum for the first two years, from the sixième (sixth grade) to what would be the end of an American junior high school. Secondary school ended with *terminale* (the next to last grade, almost the equivalent of an American's freshman year in college).

Her required courses: mathematics, Latin (or classical Greek) and French, English and American history, world history and geography, physics, chemistry, biology, art and music, and of course physical education.

In the American freshman year, Danielle and the other students began to study a third modern language, either German, Spanish, Italian, or Russian. Their once-feared Latin or Classic Greek classes became electives.

In what would be her American-system junior and senior years (troisième and seconde), she finished the equivalent of an American high school education.

She had mastered the "logical and disciplined form of thinking" and the "critical examination of data" the Lycée prides itself on.

But she was missing one crucial element of her education: the wild, unruly world of the emotions.

Chapter Two
Kaleidoscope

Ah, but you see, explained Danielle's old headmaster, she didn't graduate from the Lycée. She didn't complete her course of study. The headmaster was sorry to see her leave early because she had been such an exceptional student.

Danielle chose to leave the Lycée Français before her final year. She had already qualified for an American high school diploma. Did she need the French Baccalauréat degree when she was going to become . . . the next Coco Chanel?

During high school she discovered that her heart's desire was to become a fashion designer. Surely, she could become as famous as, or more famous than, the gifted Coco Chanel, the Frenchwoman as famed for her tart sayings as for her classic suits.

"Chanel," said fashion editor Diana Vreeland of the 1963 collection, "never so gala, riveting, and young—every suit has the *mystère* that's meant for private life: the look that's prone to romance and adventure.

"As always Coco Chanel believes in the woman first, the costume that best answers her needs. . . . The rigorous magic of Chanel is felt in every lining, every binding, every fitting. . . ." Today, the only remnants of that dream are in her books, especially *To Love Again,* the story of a ravishing Italian fashion designer, the poor little rich girl, Isabella.

In 1963 Danielle chose to enroll at Parsons School of Design, which was located on elegant Sutton Place, just a brisk walk and a bus ride to the bustling center of New York's garment industry, at 42nd and Times Square.

And by studying at Parsons, she qualified for a dual program with New York University. Courses at Parsons would add up for units at NYU.

Here, studying at Parsons and walking through the garment district, Danielle would sometimes pass the tall buildings in the garment center that housed the showrooms and offices of Norman Norell and Teal Traina, even Pauline Trigère.

That beautiful New York fall she also had a chance, between classes, to see fashion at work. The Parsons fashion students would even skip classes . . . unheard of at the solemn Lycée Français . . . to watch the glorious runway shows of the New York couture.

Impossibly tall and impossibly thin models made their hip-jutting way down the T-shaped runways, turned imperiously, and slid back up to a hail of popping flashbulbs, to the polite applause of elegant clients in white gloves, their escorts, and the all-important buyers.

Jo Hughes, the couture buyer at Bergdorf Goodman, was sure to pull rank to get her rich customers, her "girls," front row, center at the fashion shows. But sixteen-year-old Danielle Schulein-Steel, without a Jo Hughes forging the way like a general leading her troops, probably made do as a guerrilla with her classmates. Classmates peeked through the pages of the *Fashion Calendar* to discover which shows were scheduled for which grand hotel, zipped past the doormen, then nimbly dashed to the back row to be near the spectacular scene unfolding under bright klieg lights. Fashion! At last! An up-close and personal look at this precious heavenly scene . . .

1964. All hell was breaking loose. The Beatles were mobbed when they touched down at La Guardia Airport. Their sound had something to do with it.

But basically, it was the whole package, the LOOK. They had long hair. They had mod clothes. They had everything American youth wanted and demanded that the American fashion industry give them.

It was a brilliant position for Danielle Schulein-Steel: a talented, driven, organized, and creative young woman. Beautiful as well. And speaking the language of fashion: French.

Danielle was the perfect person in the perfect time at the perfect place to become a fashion star: designed by luck to become a youthful translator of the extraordinary Mod look from Swinging London, a jazzy reinterpreter of the Courrèges mini look that had swept in from Paris.

* * *

And yet she was stopped dead in her tracks.

Devastating was the word for her first year at Parsons. Taken from the security and structure of her classes and friends at the Lycée, she became quite ill.

But it seemed then that she had all the time in the world. There was nothing to compare with the insane amounts of homework the Lycée heaped on her tiny, slim frame. A classmate of hers said he almost flunked during his first year in college. It seemed like such a breeze after the rigors of the Lycée, he couldn't bear studying anymore. He was so happy to have escaped!

Danielle's taste of freedom, if only to skip off to Parsons, was tantalizing. But then, suddenly, the freedom was too much for her body, and she collapsed.

She told different versions of this year at fashion design, but it seems that the pressures of the new school and the whole new world of Manhattan, wild and untamed, led to an ulcer.

Danielle-Fernande Dominique Schulein-Steel was a very serious Catholic. But getting so sick led her to explore a new sort of religion, Christian Science. It was a faith that might grant a young girl a sense of control over the uncontrollable: the series of medical tragedies that plagued her. First, she developed an ulcer. The condition threw her off her pace. Danielle's superb self-confidence, her burnished young presence, and her extraordinary

French sense of style at first faltered, then fell. Her zest for life fizzled.

She said she then switched her studies to New York University.

Another medical emergency then ground her to a crashing halt: Women who have suffered from it mention an almost unspeakable pain, and then the fear of never being able to bear children.

Danielle had an incredible pain on her left side.

Checked into a nearby hospital, she underwent a serious surgery and lost an ovary, a terrible blow for a sixteen-year-old girl. Surgery for the tumor was followed by a bout with hepatitis. She almost died.

She had to trust in the knowledge and expertise of her surgeon, but beyond that, she prayed to the God of her childhood that she would live, and that she would be able to marry and bear children.

She slowly recovered from these medical emergencies, a pale young slip of a girl weighing under one hundred pounds. A white-uniformed nurse tucked her into the white sheets of her hospital bed. Perhaps she listlessly picked up the recent issues of *Harper's Bazaar, Vogue* and *Women's Wear Daily* dropped on the bed by a visiting school friend from Parsons. And an old "Paris Collections" issue, the student's Bible. There she would find the words of Diana Vreeland, an American from Paris who was galvanizing the young fashionables in America. . . .

"Fashion is the zest we live on—the idée fixe of Paris," wrote Diana Vreeland in *Vogue,* September 1963. "From the concierge in the rue du Bac to the portier who receives us on our return from an opening, to the little parfumeurs on the Faubourg, the cheese sellers at Fauchon, the chasseurs who deliver the bundles of French roses and lilies, Paris is alerted . . . suspended in projecting the glories of the ateliers of the couture." Vreeland's prose fed Danielle's sensual images of Paris, the sights, the sounds, the smells, that inspired the designer in her, and inspired the French.

"Never has Paris been more green and golden—hot days and cool evenings . . ." continued Diana Vreeland. "The air was charged with pinpoint bubbles of anticipated success as we entered the door at St. Laurent. . . . He began by amusing us with a flurry of cops and gamines, a West Side Story de luxe, parading the far-flung heroines of science fiction—a space queen with a Japanese face, graceful as a lily in black kidskin . . . crocodile boots zipped up as high as waders."

The nightclubs and discotheques exploding in Manhattan in 1963 and 1964 were awash with such scenes and Danielle was inspired by it all, energized by the streets of New York.

"On and on they came" Mrs. Vreeland continued from her ringside seat at the couture collections in Paris, "like a rush of trippers from Mars, wearing jerkins and overblouses of checked wool and suede and mink with slack gold chains circling their waists, under their collars; chains rimming jaunty porkpie hats with wiglets of thick, curvy, bent Chinese hair arranged inside each one. Then came the couture. . . ."

These fashion magazines, with their brilliant photographs by Richard Avedon and David Bailey; the incredible beauty of the towering, skinny, superstar models of the day; the designs of Courrèges, St. Laurent, and Dior . . . all these were wonderful. But she would have to brush them to the side.

Her energy and her focus was not diamond-hard enough now, not concentrated and clear enough to absorb all these fashion explosions, with this scary weakening of her health.

Still to read, after she'd studied the fashion magazines, the *Vogue*s and the *Harper's Bazaar*s, was the little twenty-eight-page newsprint-smudged issue of *Women's Wear Daily*, with its industry gossip of who was in, who was out, who was lunching with whom. . . . Maybe this could be her future life, in the second-by-second box scores of New York City's youngest socialites, celebrities, and fashion designers . . . her future world.

If she could not conquer Manhattan as a fashion designer, perhaps she would explore Manhattan as the fashionable wife of a rich young man. If she could not design the clothes, she could at least wear them.

For the devotees of the fashion parade like the Parsons students, there was the glorious afternoon stroll from Henri Bendel on West 57th Street, down to Bergdorf Goodman on 57th and Fifth, perhaps across the street for a peek into Tiffany's astounding windows, then a hop, skip, and a jump down to a little serious business with the serious stones at Harry Winston.

Farther down, the blandishments of Saks Fifth Avenue wooed the mod young girls with cash burning a hole in their Gucci wallets.

There were scads of French restaurants to provide a luscious meal for the ladies who lunched, wonderful old hotels at which to take tea, and the grand French culinary shrines like Pavillon and Lutèce where one could pay gustatory obeisance to the high priests of French cuisine . . . and perhaps delight in a stolen sideways glance at the new woman on the arm of Aristotle Onassis.

Aside from the wonderful shops, grand old stores, and heavenly French restaurants, New York had even come up with its own Boswell, its own social chronicler: Truman Capote.

She didn't know it then, but Danielle Schulein-Steel was soon to pull up a typewriter next to Truman, and make her own name in the process.

"I was very bored and disenchanted with the comfortable world I grew up in," she says. "I saw the hypocrisy."

Restless to break away from that world, Danielle contracted what looked to be a brilliant marriage.

At various times, reporters have emerged from their interviews with Danielle Steel under the impression that "at age eighteen she married a wealthy French banker."

There is no doubt that it was a "glamourous marriage," even a brilliant one, but the "wealthy

French banker" came from a French-American family with roots back to the California Gold Rush.

She had met Claude-Eric Lazard when she was thirteen, he was eleven years older. She married him four years later. "It just seemed like the thing to do," Danielle explains. "I wasn't pregnant, contrary to what everybody was hoping to discover at the wedding. As we were standing in the receiving line, I remember hearing these two old bags say, 'I want to see her in three months.' "

It certainly seemed like the only reason a beautiful, promising future fashion designer of seventeen would want to marry a staid, buttoned-down investment banker more than a decade older.

In any case, the wedding itself is cloaked in mystery. While Claude-Eric's two sisters were married in lavish weddings in Paris, Danielle herself seems to have wed under a shroud of secrecy, and almost nothing is known about the time, place or circumstances of the wedding. All we have are Danielle's words.

But why would she marry at all? Perhaps the reason lies in the story of the Lazard family, a family full of characters and stories that could have been created by a novelist, a novelist such as Danielle Steel.

Chapter Three
Fine Things

"She wanted to be rich . . . she wanted to meet people with money."
—A former in-law of Danielle Steel

In becoming the bride of Claude-Eric Lazard, Danielle was marrying into a distinguished San Francisco family with strong roots in California, New York, and France.

The great Lazard banking empire originated with the three Lazard brothers who left what is now the Saar region of France in the middle of the nineteenth century to set up shop as dry goods merchants, first in New Orleans, then, drawn by the California Gold Rush, in San Francisco. The Lazard brothers specialized in French, Swiss, and German imports and were enormously successful.

From 1850 to 1860 California's population swelled from less than one hundred thousand to almost four hundred thousand. A flood of raw gold poured into San Francisco and from there into the international financial markets. The Lazard brothers saw the future, and it was banking. They formed Lazard Frères and by 1856 they had opened a Paris branch, Lazard Frères et Cie.

The Lazards became part of the California "Our Crowd," a tightly knit, intellectual, and cosmopolitan group of Newmarks, Hellmans, Weils, and others who lived on a lavish scale, traveling frequently between California and the great cities and spas of Europe. Like the characters in Danielle's *Thurston House,* these families had the will to tame a new land and the riches to build splendid mansions.

An 1884 letter from one of the Lazard girls to a cousin gives some hint of their life-style: "Yesterday Marco Hellman was bar mitzvahed . . . he got a hundred dollars from his mother to buy a horse, four lots from his father . . . diamond cuff buttons . . . a gold locket with an immense diamond . . . a diamond scarf pin and an index dictionary . . ."

At the wedding of Mr. Stern to Miss Meyer, other Lazards presented the newlyweds with a "royal size solid silver tea set."

By the time of Christian Lazard, Claude-Eric's grandfather, his branch of the family was living in France and had also abandoned Judaism and become Roman Catholics. They had kept their ties to San Francisco and that was where Claude Lazard married Esther Ehrman in a 1932 wedding that *The San Francisco Chronicle* dubbed "one of the brilliant social events of the year." A few months after the wedding, the bride was presented to Paris society at a reception given by her new in-laws, Mr. and Mrs. Christian Lazard at their estate, Château Couharde, outside Paris. Among the guests was a former president of France.

Esther Ehrman was the daughter of Florence Hellman, whose father controlled Wells Fargo, and Sidney Ehrman, a lawyer with Heller, Powers & Ehrman, a firm that would be closely entwined with the growth of post-Earthquake San Francisco, and the development of the water systems, the Golden Gate Bridge, and new towns outside the city. One Heller, Powers & Ehrman partner started Atherton next to Hillsboro, another developed Carmel-by-the-Sea near Monterey, a location in two of Danielle's books, *Summer's End* and *Crossings*.

Sidney Ehrman, son of a wholesale grocer, graduated from the University of California at Berkeley and spent a year in University in Munich (home of the Schueleins). He became a director of the San Francisco Opera and the San Francisco symphony and a patron of the arts. Among the artists he supported was the young Yehudi Menuhin (who attended the reception for the newlyweds at Château Couharde). He acquired an estate at Lake Tahoe which had become a summer colony for the rich of San Francisco. Nestled in the High Sierras along the California-Nevada border, Sugarpine, as the Ehrman house was known, epitomized the riches and sophistication of the resort.

When Sidney's daughter Esther Ehrman married Claude Lazard at the Ehrman mansion in the Presidio Heights section of the city, it meant the union of two great San Francisco-based fortunes. The rich and social young Claude Lazards took up residence in New York, then lived in Paris until the rise of the Nazis made the city dangerous. By then, the Lazard family was no longer associated with the banking firm that bore its name.

By 1937, Claude Lazard, concerned about Hitler's plans for expanding the Third Reich, had sent Esther and their four children: Sidney, Florence,

Christiane and Claude-Eric back to live with her father in San Francisco while he stayed on in Paris,
becoming an officer with the French army. After the
Nazi occupation, he joined the French Resistance
and was wounded. By summer of 1944, he was Lieu-
tenant Lazard and lay in a military hospital in
Naples, recovering from wounds incurred when an
eight-inch shell burst in front of his foxhole.

These dramatic events would provide rich material for several of Danielle's novels, including *Crossings* and *Jewels.*

Immediately after the war, Claude Lazard served
with the French Consulate in New York, and the
family continued to divide its time among San
Francisco, New York, and Paris. Of Claude and Esther's children, Sidney married and was posted to
Rome by the ABC network in the 1960s. Florence
married Barnard Lasnier de Lavalette at St.
Clothilde's in Paris, in 1959, wearing the lace gown
her mother wore in 1932, although it had been "remodeled" by the house of Dior. Five years later,
her sister Christiane wore the same gown to marry
Andre-Paul Peyromaure de Bord at Notre Dame
des Victoires in San Francisco. (Note the great-
granddaughters of the Jewish merchant bankers
were educated in the Convent of the Sacred Heart
in San Francisco and New York and were married
in Roman Catholic ceremonies.)

Yes, in marrying into the Lazard family, Danielle
Schulein-Steel was joining a family that would
eventually inspire some of her best work.

But the circumstances under which she joined

the Lazard family remain lost in the mists of time. Unlike the weddings of Claude-Eric Lazard's two sisters, which were described in detail in the press, there is no public record of the wedding of seventeen-year-old Danielle Schulein-Steel to twenty-eight-year-old Claude-Eric Lazard.

It is known that after their marriage, the newlyweds moved into Claude-Eric's suite at the Stanhope Hotel on Fifth Avenue, opposite the Metropolitan Museum of Art. They kept a low social profile. Unlike the Claude Lazards, whose social schedules were chronicled in society columns, there is no mention of the young couple in columns of that era.

Perhaps Danielle was busy with her classes. She had switched her course of study from Parsons to New York University downtown at Washington Square, in the heart of Greenwich Village.

NYU was no place for the St. Laurent couture Danielle was reading about in *Vogue*, the "jewelled buttons made by fantasy jewelers, flat medallions, stones bursting with light mounted in huge squared Byzantine pins in the Empress Theodora manner . . . gala night looks . . . slightly medieval, and so ravishing that even the press, wrote Diane Vreeland, dropped pencils and joined in the clatter of applause."

Nor could Danielle wear the latest Paris fashion on the Lexington Avenue IRT that took her downtown. But she had started wearing her hair à la Vreeland in the evenings: "Very subtle, very chic . . . pulled back in a tight oval with height behind the crown of the head and a coiled figure-eight chignon low on the neck . . ."

A reporter who interviewed Danielle in 1979 emerged with the impression that "as a newlywed she had homes in New York, Paris, and San Francisco." But it was not a life that Danielle found fulfilling.

A friend remembers that she wanted security, she wanted to meet people with enough money to make her feel secure.

Colorful shards of Danielle's early married life flash by, as if in a kaleidoscope, in her early books: the brilliant dinner parties, the wonderful restaurants, the magical city of New York she describes in *Going Home* and *Passion's Promise*.

But she also describes a less than bubbly, rather buttoned-up and emotionally distant figure, especially in *Summer's End,* a young French-American husband and the family behind him.

Still, there were some compensations. Life at the Stanhope included a splendid restaurant downstairs, the services of a concierge and a Telex, a nimble-footed doorman to summon a taxi, and the sense of always being able to pick up and go at a moment's notice.

And there was the Lazard fortune. The young husband was clearly smitten with his even younger bride. According to family lore, Claude-Eric bought her a perfect diamond ring. She always loved shopping. And when she was married to Claude-Eric, the Lazard family told her to charge things to their account. That was the beginning of her jewels, said a friend.

Eventually, Danielle did become pregnant, and the couple moved to an apartment with room for their infant daughter, Beatrix, and a nanny. But by this time the world of the Lazards had become too stuffy and constraining for Danielle, and she began to look for new challenges everywhere.

Chapter Four
Daddy

Danielle came from a cultured family, but they had lost their money. That, and the fact that her parents were divorced, concerned the now-Catholic Lazards, according to a friend.

What of Danielle's father, John Schulein-Steel, the enigmatic man who has variously been described as a "scion of Munich's Löwenbräu beer dynasty" and a "German nobleman"? This mysterious figure, so lovingly recalled in the epigraph to *Wanderlust* and in myriad interviews, is not an easy man to get a handle on.

We can begin with the Schuelein family of Munich, Germany. Germany has more breweries than the rest of the world put together, and Bavarians brew and consume more beer than any other part of Germany. Of the 825 breweries in Bavaria, two such businesses were owned by Josef Schuelein, Danielle's great-grandfather.

Josef Schuelein, was born in Thalmassing, in Mittelfranken, in 1854. He married Ida Baer, born in Nordlingen, Bavaria, in Munich, where he operated the Union and the Kindl breweries. Julius, their first son, was born there in 1881, and was followed by five more children. The family prospered, and Josef Schuelein got into the food import and export business as well.

Julius Schuelein obtained a Doctorate of Laws degree entitling him to be addressed as Dr. Schuelein, and married Minni Laura Kahn. Their son John was born in 1914 and would one day become the father of Danielle. Julius joined the family food business, Presco-Vegex, while his younger brother, Hermann, took over management of the Union and Kindl breweries. After World War I, the breweries were combined with Löwenbräu AG, and in 1919 Hermann Schuelein became a director of Löwenbräu. Between 1921 and 1935, he served as General Director of Löwenbräu and also as a director of the Deutsch Bank.

Danielle, it seems, is descended from the somewhat less glamourous Julius Schueleins, rather than the Hermann Schueleins.

But that does not mean that the family is undistinguished. Julius and Hermann's siblings were equally illustrious. Franziska Schuelein Heinemann, born in 1882, a year after Julius, became a successful New York art dealer specializing in European canvases. Another sister, Elsa Schuelein Haas, born in 1886, married a surgeon and also emigrated to the United States, as did the two younger Schuelein brothers, Fritz, also born in 1886, and Kurt, born in 1892, who both died in New York in the early 1960s.

So successful was Josef Schuelein that he acquired a *schloss* outside Munich. A comfortable country house, it was far from the "moated castle" sometimes described in interviews with Danielle. Rather than the collection of racehorses one Lazard relative kept in his stables, Herr Schuelein kept cows. But in pictures and family stories, it must have seemed wonderfully romantic to the young Danielle and would one day provide source material for her books.

The comfortable, *haute-bourgeois* life the Schueleins enjoyed in Munich came to an end with the rise of Adolf Hitler. As assimilated Jews, they were regarded as undesirables. As businesses were confiscated, as the Nazi government took over operation of important companies like Löwenbräu, the Schuleins knew it was only a matter of time before they were targets for extermination.

Josef Schuelein, widowed in 1929, chose to stay behind in Munich, where he died in 1938. But his children resolved to make their escape from Germany. An affidavit from one of Hermann's friends in America helped them get into the United States the following year.

Julius Schuelein set up the food company Presco-Vegex in New York. But for reasons that remain bafflingly obscure, John changed his name to Steel, perhaps because of anti-German sentiments. He dropped the first "e" and added "Steel," becoming John Schulein-Steel.

But as for the playboy gadabout that Danielle has described, a Schuelein relative insists nothing could be further from the real John Schulein-Steel.

"I don't think it's very kind to call [John Schulein-Steel] a 'playboy,' " says the relative.

"He didn't work an awful lot, that's true," the

relative admits, "but a 'playboy' usually implies a lot of money, which he didn't have. . . . He worked all right, he wasn't terribly successful, but he worked. He worked for his father. Presco-Vegex Food Company, that's right."

Although the noble relatives are tenuous at best, Danielle has a genuinely colorful relative whose life could be the basis for a Danielle Steel novel. She is Danielle's cousin, Annemarie Schuelein Utsch, daughter of Danielle's great-uncle Hermann and thus someone with a closer claim to the Löwenbräu connection.

But Annemarie's life is more than banks and breweries. Born in 1915, she joined her father Hermann, her uncle Julius, and her cousin John when they made their escape from Germany. By August 1935 she had reached London. The following year she rejoined her parents in the United States. The Hermann Schueleins had taken an apartment on Fifth Avenue not far from the rest of the family.

The dashing Annemarie went to work for the Office of War Information, the OWI, in Washington, D.C., in 1941. In six years she worked her way up from secretary to writer and editor, then became a broadcaster, beaming German-language programs into Nazi-occupied territories. Although she never traveled behind enemy lines like the heroine of Susan Isaacs's novel, *Shining Through,* she was there in spirit, and most especially in Munich.

In 1947, after the German defeat, Hermann Schuelein was again named a director of the Löwenbräu breweries. He did not visit Germany until 1950, however, and eventually gave up the position, saying he did not have the proper time to devote to it.

Hermann Schuelein went on to become head of the New York-based Rheingold Brewery. Among the numerous honors bestowed on him later in life were a medal from the National Conference of Christians and Jews and a Golden Key to the City of Munich.

In annexing Hermann Schuelein's biography for her own, Danielle was demonstrating the storytelling skills that would later win her fame and fortune.

But first, Danielle would have to find that storytelling was where her future lay. In the mid-1960s, disenchanted with fashion design, restless in her role as the pampered wife of a rich man, Danielle must have known that she had to find a new challenge for herself. And in an amazing coincidence, this future superwoman found her niche in a new and innovative company called Supergirls.

Chapter Five
Changes: Supergirls

The springboard of German gentility, Portuguese beauty, and a classic French education had landed Danielle in her storybook marriage. But she did not live happily ever after. On the contrary, she began to face some basic realities. She was an American girl, living in the New York City of the sixties. Here, all hell was breaking loose, no matter how fancy your relatives were in Europe! And Danielle was itching to escape the constraints of her conservative marriage, at least in spirit. "I changed so radically between the ages of 17 and 21," she later told a reporter.

Danielle has rarely discussed her first marriage, but when she has she has always shown sympathy for her first husband. She acknowledges that he had no way of knowing how much the woman he married in her teens would change as she reached her twenties. "It's like you buy a puppy not quite knowing what it is and you take it home and it turns out to be a giraffe," she told one interviewer. "When we met, I was going to school. I was very well behaved. And then I did everything to the poor man but grow two heads."

Against her husband's wishes, Danielle went to work, at around twenty-two, for a feisty little all-girl company called Supergirls.

The Lazards weren't people who needed to work. Their wives, especially, weren't people who needed to work. In fact, they were expected NOT to work.

It was a vast mystery to the family why someone's young wife wouldn't want to stay home and live the life of a properly cossetted Mrs. Lazard. But Danielle Schulein-Steel Lazard was bursting with far too much energy for a quiet life at home, no matter how special the perks.

Since she'd been a schoolgirl, she'd sometimes done as much as eight hours of homework a night. Work wasn't something that made her cringe and run; it was something she relished.

She left her daughter at home with the nanny, and became a Supergirl.

Supergirls, the business, was a reflection of its time: the late 1960s. Two young New Yorkers, frustrated at the entry level jobs available to them, decided to forget the old rules and traditions and do something on their own. They decided to start a business.

The concept was simple: they would sell themselves—their time and energy to people who needed it.

Genie Chipps and Claudia Jessup were prep school pals from St. Anne's in Charlottesville, Virginia, who brainstormed the concept over their dinner table one night, using legal, accounting, and advertising expertise gleaned from various boyfriends. From a stuffy downtown law firm, the friend of a friend gave them thousands of dollars of legal advice for free. From an old-line accounting firm, sharp beginner's lessons in how to keep track of income and expenses. From a beau in advertising, lessons on how to put it all together with flair. And flair was something they had in spades.

As soon as things took off, the two girls rented an office space on Madison and 67th Street in the center of the most expensive boutique strip of Manhattan. With a next-to-nothing start-up budget, they hired a tiny staff of three.

The rough-and-tumble world of a start-up business couldn't have been better for a young mother like Danielle Schulein-Steel Lazard who was just getting her bearings in the grown-up world. The rough-and-tumble women owners shaped the working world Danielle first experienced. It was a world of seemingly wide-open opportunities for women in magazines, fashion, television, and the arts that her readers would come to love.

Danielle was first hired as a temporary fill-in, "eighty-five pounds of beautifully accessorized chic," said her bosses in the book they later wrote about how they started their own business, and made it work.

"Danielle was married to one of those wealthy, prestigious, and familied French," they explained, somewhat inaccurately, "who like to keep their grand old names out of places with suspect names like Supergirls."

In the beginning, according to Genie and Claudia, Danielle had a thing with names.

She was "Danielle Steel" to business people on the telephone. To personal friends, she was "Danielle Lazard." And, wrote her bosses, ". . . there were people to whom she was 'no longer in the country,' and a whole other group to whom she was irreversibly 'dead.' "

Danielle herself was always on the phone—as well she should be, with the grand title of "Director of Public Relations and Vice President in Charge of Marketing." ("Because we couldn't afford to pay much in salaries, we handed out executive titles like so much applesauce," Claudia and Genie explain.) But when into deep gossiping with chums, she switched to French, then neither Genie nor Claudia could understand a word of what sounded like delicious, tempting observations.

Getting out into the working world helped Danielle transform herself from the schoolgirl she was when she married Claude-Eric Lazard—a schoolgirl who'd been terribly ill with an ulcer, the removal of an ovary, and hepatitis.

She may have given her in-laws the docile appearance of stay-at-home wife and mother, content to be at her husband's beck and call. But in reality, she was learning to be part of the new breed of independent, liberated women.

Danielle seemed to be the last person who needed to work. They estimated that her weekly florist bill exceeded her salary, and she was probably paying her daughter's nanny more than she could ever hope to earn at Supergirls. But she was so enthusiastic and devoted to their cause that when Timmie Scott Mason, for whom she'd been substituting, returned, Genie and Claudia decided to keep her on staff.

Betty Friedan's 1962 book, *The Feminine Mystique*, was one of the first rumblings of the movement for women's liberation in the 1960s. In it, Friedan took on the women's magazines like *Good Housekeeping* and *Ladies' Home Journal* for convincing a woman to stay at home, addicted to detergents, floor waxes, and soap operas, rather than venture out into the working world . . . and off the Valium.

Danielle now found herself following the tenets of Betty Friedan.

Danielle found herself in a liberated business created and run by women, complete with an office on Madison Avenue, two new phones with five—count'em—buttons and one for hold. They had a sparkling new IBM Selectric with a clever snap-out typing ball, "While You Were Out" pink phone message pads, invoices, petty cash slips, a row of full-size filing cabinets, an adding machine, gizmos to fit the phone receiver onto your collarbone, an electric pencil sharpener, and—most important—a Rolodex.

Not to mention their brand-new Pitney Bowes postage meter.

And Claudia and Genie never did figure out Danielle's "obsession with typewriters." According to them, when Danielle first came to work for Supergirls, the office had three machines, and Danielle "never failed to change typewriters, always in utmost urgency, at least several times a day. There was never any particular pattern to her quirk. She would just go up to someone and say, 'How much longer are you going to be typing? I need to do this up.' Then she would stand there, tapping her foot and breathing down her prey's neck, while another typewriter would be sitting idle."

What makes this so fascinating is fans of Danielle Steel know that she typed all her books on her beloved 1948 Olympia manual machine. Could she have been searching for the perfect typewriter to begin her writing career?

There was no budget for swanky offices. At first they gathered and refinished some used office furniture, and found a woman carpenter to redesign their space. But still, none of them really had a permanent desk or a permanent phone, for that matter. The staff moved about in a constant state of flux, from desk to sofa to floor.

An office meeting was called to solve the desk situation, according to Supergirls. Everyone arrived at nine with her take-out bag from the coffee shop except Danielle, who did not think it chic to carry in food. It was just not done, in her mind. So the meeting couldn't start until she called for her coffee to be delivered from Mayfair Coffee Shop.

As her bosses explained it, once a call went in,

other orders got loaded on, then the bill had to be split up, jelly spread on bagels, and over the roar of crumpling paper bags and wax paper, desks apparently never did get assigned. (Later, they simply bought another two desks.)

But Danielle was actually out there on the front lines in her own way; working with an all-woman company and seeing this new business world firsthand over the office desk barricades.

What she learned may not have been cozy and reassuring, but it built character. And, of course, she never needed the money.

The Supergirls learned up-close about sexual harassment, before the term had been invented. Back then, Claudia and Genie gingerly avoided situations that might involve the syndrome, and suggested it was a situation women should be prepared for in advance.

Danielle had come onto the Supergirls staff third, after Patsy, the half-day assistant, and Timmie Scott Mason, a former physical ed instructor from the very social Brearley School for Girls. (Timmie was among those Danielle later thanked in the dedication to her first novel, *Going Home*.)

At one point, the owners gave Danielle the job of interviewing women for their freelance Action Staff roster, sort of a hiring agency for creative temps for creative jobs.

Danielle was told to fill in an application form for each, with information on her schooling, experience, references, special strengths, and foreign languages. "It soon became clear," say her bosses, "that Danielle never really liked anybody and, as a result, we weren't building up much of a file."

The publicity for Supergirls had been stupendous from the start, a perfect example of being in the right place at the right time. The baby boom had hit the consciousness of big business, and they were scrambling for ways to speak to the kids, and capitalize on their vast new market.

Supergirls was in Manhattan, the quivering epicenter of the media world, just when the earth-shaking trends of the youth culture and the women's movement were joining forces—and they capitalized on both, with an energizing spin from the English-sounding "super" in their title. The media giants like *Time* and *Newsweek* were thrashing about for stories on this new "youth scene," sending their girl "researchers" out to explore, and Supergirls was what they came up with.

Howard Smith put Supergirls in the must-read downtown *Village Voice* Scenes column.

The midtown media moguls caught on, and *Look* magazine ran an entire feature on them. That brought them TV: *The Joe Franklin Show, Girl Talk, Dick Cavett.*

They made weekly appearances on Cleveland Amory's show dressed in the skimpiest Betsey Johnson dresses.

They appeared twice on *The Mike Douglas Show.*

The *Look* piece brought them to the attention of the biggest of all: Johnny Carson's *Tonight Show.*

Before their *Tonight Show* appearance, they trembled in fear in the green room. Sharing the green room with them was Mama Cass from the Mamas and the Papas. They were terrified . . . but after surviving Johnny Carson, the floodgates opened.

The Supergirls made a name for itself filling impossible requests: they found the man who ate cars for the award-winning Alka-Seltzer account; a rich woman in New England wanted them to help her marry Frank Sinatra; a Supergirls crew scrubbed down Frank Sinatra's jet during a strike at the Washington, D.C., airport.

At first, Danielle made herself useful with her language skills (something like English, French, German, Italian, Spanish, and more) to sell Supergirls to the various Consulates in town. The Italian Consul very rudely returned her note, pointing out several mistakes, and instead of sending off a pipe bomb, fashionable in the sixties, she returned an apology.

But now, with the economic slump of late 1969, they redefined their services. Their strengths: marketing and promotional services slanted toward women. Henceforth, they executed "projects," not jobs, and became creative consultants to big business.

* * *

Who was Danielle Steel in those days? "A constant bundle of energy, always giving the impression her imagination is just about to flash on the best idea since the wheel."

She took a cut in salary to work on commission, presenting the Supergirls story to big businesses around Manhattan.

Danielle, their "social whirlwind," kept her ears open after work, and found terrific leads at dinner parties. She didn't have to wait around in the lower rungs of a stodgy old bureaucracy, stifled by old men muttering about "the way things always were." She was off and running, her scintillating talents zooming her all over the city, day and night. Her new title: "Executive in Charge of Drumming Up New Clients."

In a 1985 interview, she told a reporter that Supergirls "was a fun venture. I did PR for the firm itself. We did things like big corporate parties, PR campaigns with either feminine or youth-minded aspects in mind. That was the 60s; it was the beginning of all the popularity of youth stuff and women's lib."

Supergirls was suffused with camaraderie and team spirit—a self-esteem and enthusiasm that helped them over petty squabbles. When each person was assigned to clean-up tasks, "Danielle's idea of cleaning the office," said Claudia and Genie, "was to breeze out the door, then run back in with a pseudo-earnest wail: 'My God, I forgot. Today's my day.' " She'd then tilt an ashtray into a wastebasket before rushing downstairs to grab a cab, very pleased with herself.

Mayfair, the downstairs coffee shop, was in her thrall. She phoned in five or six phone orders a day for delivery. "Coffee and Danish first thing in the morning, then a little nibble around eleven, lunch at one, a tide-me-over at three, and, finally, lemonade at five. Then she'd leave," said her bosses. "Crumbling beside her pyramiding ashtray: maybe a soggy bagel with cream cheese and usually a couple of coffees that had sprung oil slicks from the cold."

Danielle was the only person in the office who could phone the Mayfair—or had the brashness to pull it off—and ask them to send over a pack of cigarettes or a cup of coffee. They forgot the one dollar minimum order in her case, because they could guarantee another five more from her by the end of the day.

Danielle had to then get out there and sell Supergirls to big business with supreme self-confidence. Supergirls' research proved that the image women most admired and identified with—in 1969—was "the career woman or the housewife active outside the home." Before she knew it, she was both serious and capable in her business life, and one of those most-admired women herself.

How did she get this self-esteem?

What she was doing on 67th and Madison was all

about the unfolding of Danielle Steel, the public
personality, and this coltish young writer-to-be was
learning from the inside out that she was a very
talented and very valuable woman. She was ventur-
ing out into a Brave New World, selling the Supergirl savvy to company CEOs on her own steam:
taking on responsibility, making decisions, becoming a professional, forcing herself to make those
calls, going on despite turndown after turndown.
She was practically a baby herself, and she had a
baby at home. But the things she picked up from
her father John Schulein-Steel, the innate sense of
organization and the inner clock, propelled her into
the work world with a professional, adult attitude.

She learned to mold her public image and her
personal style to further one goal. She dressed as
a sophisticated, young woman should in the business world of Manhattan. And thanks to her marriage, she now had the money to be able to buy
the clothes that even a successful advertising copy-
writer in her thirties could barely afford. And not
just the clothes, but the jewels. But as much as she
loved luxury, how she looked on the outside was
matched by how she was starting to feel on the
inside. As working woman Mrs. Claude-Eric Lazard, she realized she was still feminine—she just
wasn't weak and dependent any longer. She was a
young woman with strength of character.

Learning to stand up alone like this, explained
her bosses, was just like going through a horrible
second adolescence. Once again, you had to feel
like a fifteen-year-old out on your very first date;

only this time you were twentysomething and sitting across the desk from the CEO of a Fortune 500 company. You had to experience the terror, you had to be more than prepared, you had to act as if you weren't afraid, and you couldn't die of embarrassment. You couldn't get stage fright, or if you did, you had to just wait there for it to go away. You learned to survive and grow stronger.

"Danielle carried the Supergirls gospel to Big Business shrines with a religious zeal," wrote her boss Claudia. "In fact, every once in a while, when Genie and I were about to see a client, with Danielle in tow, she would slink into the office like a guilty dog and allow as how this particular client 'somehow has the impression that *I* own the business.' We were not, she said, to be upset if he directed all the questions to her."

This trial by fire, this second adolescence, did take its toll. At one point, Danielle went from her skinny eighty-five-pound frame down to seventy-nine pounds. She was under too much pressure.

Her weight may have been dropping, but her fortunes were rising: John Mack Carter, (who has been editor of both of the feminists' *bêtes noires*, *Ladies' Home Journal* and *Good Housekeeping*) became an early mentor. "Through my PR and advertising work," she told a reporter, "I had done some writing, and the editor of *Good Housekeeping*, John Mack Carter (he was at *Ladies' Home Journal* then), encouraged me. He was one of our clients."

* * *

Danielle's job with Supergirls was worth more to her than getting a degree from Harvard Business School. It taught this tiny young mother about being a strong woman.

And it introduced her to a magical new world. She learned how to edit and write for a magazine. One night at a dinner party, she met Fred R. Smith, about to become the editor of *American Home* magazine.

Hubbard H. Cobb, the summer 1969 editor of *American Home*, had already been sufficiently enchanted with Danielle and her publicity for Supergirls to run her picture, full-page. She was wearing a pair of perfectly cut bell-bottom pants and a tiny cut-at-the-waist jacket, complete with knotted silk scarf at the neck and French cuffs pierced with gold cuff links. She looks as thin and gorgeous as Audrey Hepburn in *Breakfast at Tiffany's*, hiding behind the largest, blackest, chicest sunglasses. She is not smiling, but she is definitely learning.

It was the new editor of *American Home*, Fred Smith, who unleashed Danielle in the writer's den by hiring Supergirls to temporarily take over some of the *American Home* staff while he replaced the old staff.

Fred Smith gave Danielle the opportunity to do *American Home*'s Lifestyle column without using her name—picking up a tidbit of gossip at this dinner party, another at that, a third over the phone. The column found a "Mrs. Entwhistle Thrip," for instance:

Because she doubts that thieves would eat and run, when Mrs. Entwhistle Thrip (whose name has been changed to protect her diamonds) goes away, she tucks her jewelry into hamburger patties and freezes them. Now if Tiffany and Co. were to merge with McDonald's.

American Home found C. Ray Smith, who could project the crash of Niagara Falls on his all-white walls.

Folkway records' sounds of the tropical rain forest of South America was also noted.

The column profiled Dr. Roger Payne, of Rockefeller University and the New York Zoological Society, and his recording of the sounds of the humpback whales off Bermuda; and his warning that we must save the whales.

Danielle's column discovered the new Russian vodka that the Munson Shaw company was importing.

It zoomed in on the computerized Astroflash booth for high-tech astrological forecasts, introduced from Paris to New York's Grand Central Station.

And the column wrote about the down-home folkways of the 1969 "basket social," still alive in San Francisco, where Hillsborough hostess Mrs. Owen Spann invited ten couples—black tie and hostess pajamas de rigeur—to a Gourmet Auction, with a $25 limit.

Danielle's column found a Mrs. Brandon Sweitzer who, instead of throwing the baby out with the bathwater, puts the baby and the high chair into the shower, hops in herself, and when lunch is over, showers down the lot.

The column reported on the hot new footgear: platform-style clogs.

On the promising new kid's program due in November 1969 to be called *Sesame Street.*

She was the Supergirl behind the Lifestyle column—unsigned—keeping her eyes and ears open at cocktail parties, dinner parties, country weekends, and lunch break. In the middle of deadline pressures, she got close to the quirky writers and editors that populate the magazine world. And it took. There was something about it she loved, like reading Colette as a little girl. Something almost addictive. And soon it all fell into place. She was thinking of taking a break in San Francisco, and John Mack Carter, then-president of Downe Communications, owners of *American Home, strongly* suggested she damned well start writing novels: what a novelistic life she was already leading in the midst of all the social upheaval of the sixties. A young writer with a front-row seat on the baby boomers, chauvinistic husbands, stuffy society, French bankers, broken homes, women's liberation, Europe, uptown, downtown, NYU, Parsons, the sixties, working women, single mothers supporting children. And the fear.

The fear of leaving the husband and not being able to make enough money—not being able to type fast enough—to stay independent.

But the password at Supergirls had been along the lines of "figure out what you want and get it."

It had a certain ring.

And Danielle's Supergirls colleague Timmie Scott Mason was an intrepid traveler. She was thinking of taking off for San Francisco. Combined with the push from John Mack Carter, Danielle took off to try her wings in San Francisco with her daughter Beatrix in tow, and wrote her first novel *Going Home* there in a couple of months.

And she's never looked back.

Chapter Six
Summer's End

One doesn't discover new
lands without consenting to
lose sight of the shore
for a very long time

ANDRÉ GIDE

Why did Danielle move to San Francisco exactly? She wasn't very fond of her husband by then. It was the same old story—a woman takes her child and leaves her husband, they fight over custody, child support payments. But why not Paris?

Perhaps because her Lazard in-laws had returned to live in San Francisco. Esther Lazard had died there in 1969.

She probably came because of her family, thought of people she knew back then . . . her Wells Fargo relatives . . . Sidney Ehrman, and his offspring. Sidney's wife had recently died and left the huge mansion and a mile on the waterfront at Lake Tahoe. So Bede would be close to all her Lazard relatives.

Of course the Ehrmans and the Wells Fargo bank and the Lazards were her husband's family, and they did seem to take her in when she left him and came to San Francisco. One of the Lazard relatives even stayed with her in the late seventies after she managed to buy a new house on Russian Hill.

Danielle trailed a wealth of cosmopolitan social connections behind her when she moved to San Francisco and started visiting with her Lazard relatives in the city.

Some of the straitlaced residents of the City by the Bay still perceived San Francisco as a continuation of the 1950s: society matrons in crisp white gloves and ladylike little hats, dressed in well-tailored suits from I. Magnin or Ransahof's, conservative grays, navy blues and beiges; or as summer grew less chilly, some delicate, female pastels. Their well-bespoke men worked in the Montgomery District, and were lawyers or brokers. For a gay night out, dinner at Ernies or the Hawaiian specials at Trader Vic's, a society hangout known for their pu-pu platters, and gigantic drinks like the Mai Tai and the Fogcutter.

And yet just blocks and light-years away, in the section of town called the Haight-Ashbury, the hippie movement had been born, and the journalists of the day had made their visitations to the hippie shrine: Tom Wolfe, to write *The Electric Kool-Aid Acid Test* about novelist Ken Kesey and his gang; Joan Didion, to write *Slouching Towards Bethlehem;* as well as every Tom, Dick, Harry, and Joe from *Life, Look, Time,* and *Newsweek.*

They were all jamming the Haight, squeezing into those few precious square blocks of well-documented San Francisco territory where an entirely new movement was afoot.

And it was Joan Didion that got it right: This wasn't a super new explosion of American youth toward freedom and self-expression. In the Haight, it was the opening wedge of a more terrifying reality: American parents had gotten divorced, and in the process, forgotten about parenting their children.

The nuclear family was no more. These were the lost children in the Haight-Ashbury, a vision of what would happen across America by 1990, druggies, gang members, criminals, and the abused.

They were children of divorce like Danielle, but much less well-educated and well-bred, searching for some primitive form of community among themselves, and creating some primitive form of bonding here in the years following the Summer of Love, through the ritual use of drugs, free love, and rock and roll. They found that everything had its price.

Bill Graham's Fillmore Auditorium was home to all the great acts coming out of San Francisco: Janis Joplin, the Grateful Dead, the Jefferson Airplane.

And acid rock was not just something you listened to, but something you augmented by the ingestion of lysergic acid or tabs of Owsley Blue and the visual assistance of the spectacular light shows for which Graham's people were justly celebrated.

Snaking through the rock and roll and the druggies were the antiwar politicos, based mainly over across the Bay Bridge at the University of California, Berkeley. But the political virus crossed over the Bay Bridge more freely as the draft calls for Vietnam became more intense in the late 1960s and early 1970s. All San Francisco was going liberal now, not just the Haight.

The Movement had already brought down one president, Lyndon Johnson, and was sharpening its teeth for another, Richard Nixon. But it was Nixon's own shortsighted fumbling that got him into Watergate, and out of office.

It was a time of upheaval, shooting creative sparks in every direction as the old rules were forgotten and new rules not yet invented.

And Danielle chose this time to leave New York for San Francisco. She had been writing poetry since grade school, and in the early seventies, started submitting poems to women's magazines. She sold her first poem to *Cosmopolitan* in 1971.

"Payment was not much, $50 or $75," she told an interviewer, but it brought her "sheer delight" and also "the self-confidence that I could sell."

But now she was trying for a novel, *Going Home*.

Her New York had been like the San Francisco of the white-gloved ladies: the New York of grade school and high school at the Lycée Français, and college at Parsons/NYU, and marriage to a conservative man.

Supergirls gave her a taste of what was to come with jobs and power for women, but she was eager to strike out on her own, away from Claude-Eric Lazard.

She wanted to leave it all and pitch her tent of many colors in San Francisco.

She came with something like $2,000-a-month child support for her little child, a friend of those times remembered, finally got an apartment on Pacific and Goff and an old metal Olympia typewriter.

That staked her to an entirely new career.

The place she rented was nothing grand, just two or three bedrooms.

She wrote of an affair with the wrong man in her first book, *Going Home*. And it sold! Published in 1973, the advance was small, reportedly only $3,500, but she was now a published novelist. It was her first glimmer of her heart's desire, her first validation that she could be a creative woman who could support herself.

The story was a simple one: "Divorcée Gillian Forrester flees New York for San Francisco with her five-year-old daughter. She falls in love with Chris, a handsome filmmaker who suffers from a bad case of irresponsibility, and when she becomes pregnant, Chris talks her into going back East. There she begins an affair with responsible, mature Gordon."

It's easy to imagine the heady excitement Danielle must have felt when *Going Home* was published that October. You sense it in the long list of people she thanks (in alphabetical order) at the beginning of the book. They include John Mack Carter, her mentor from *Ladies' Home Journal;* Sidney M. Ehrman, her estranged husband's wealthy grandfather and a leader of San Francisco society; Timmie Scott Mason, her colleague from Supergirls; her father and his Japanese wife, Kuniko Schulein-Steel; her mother, Norma Stone, her daughter "Bede" and her agent, Phyllis Westberg.

It must have been painful, then, to read the review for *Going Home* that appeared in *Publishers Weekly*, the bible of the bookselling industry. "Gillian, for all her beauty, sophistication and use of the proper four-letter words," the reviewer carped, "is not very interesting and neither is her story."

This would not be the last time that a reviewer completely misjudged Danielle's talent as a storyteller. But this book, which, like all her books, is still in print, is a stunning example of a fully formed writing talent. She combines an observant eye, especially when she is comparing life in New York with life in San Francisco, an evocative sense of place and time, with an emotional punch.

She found a "day job" at Grey Advertising. She shared half of a fine old Victorian house—a duplex with a tiny backyard—with her daughter, living a life very much like that of Gillian, the heroine of *Going Home* (although, unlike Gillian, she did not get pregnant).

Yet there was room for neat cookouts with the neighbors, with her daughter Beatrix helping out with all her five-year-old culinary skills.

And every few months, she'd go back to New York, presumably to meet her publisher.

Her house gave visitors a feeling of money.

There was a nice comfortable aura to it, the welcoming arms of overstuffed chairs and well-framed pictures.

But one never knew if it was family money or support money. People who knew her then knew she'd grown up in New York, and thought she was a classic WASP, in Gucci shoes.

To San Franciscans, she was Catholic, or sometimes a Christian Scientist.

Her mother, Norma Stone, came out to visit her.

Like every tenant who's ever lived, Danielle fought with the absentee landlord. In her case, the battle involved long, closely reasoned letters to him up in Mendocino, trying to pin him down on a specific date for needed repairs. She was always pissed off at the landlord, even more so than her husband, it seemed.

How successful was she from her writing?

Five other books written during these years were turned down by the New York editors.

But all the time she was working, just "whaling away on that typewriter," said a friend.

She never brought home her work from the ad agency, or talked about it. The focus was always her books. During the days, she would go to her job at Grey Advertising, extolling the virtues of grapefruit juice or the other little jobs she picked up, and after work, she'd return to the 1948 typewriter in her study.

She had surges of incredible energy, a tremendous amount of élan that would keep her typing away at her work until three or four A.M., then get her up and off to work in the morning.

There was a wonderfully romantic wood-burning fireplace in her Victorian house . . . but Danielle didn't have time for boyfriends really, or much romantic interest, because of that entrancing typewriter and its Circe promise of great riches, a future with a successful novel-writing career.

Her daughter was able to entertain herself a lot, and play with the neighbors. Danielle was a mother who seemed able to juggle a lot of things at the same time.

Did she socialize much? Well, she didn't have the time for it. She was writing, not going to parties. No one remembers ever seeing her in an evening gown or even in a cocktail dress. Danielle's couture in 1972 bore the label Levi Strauss, her shirts weren't silk but cotton, and her shoes less often Guccis than Weejuns. "Casual Junior League," was how a friend remembered Danielle. She continued to wear the diamond ring Claude-Eric Lazard had given her with its perfect color and clarity.

She later told husband Bill Toth that she had married at seventeen to get away from her father, and then ended up with Claude-Eric Lazard, another "control freak," in his words. "She was always terrified of Claude-Eric that he would take Beatrix away from her—because he had more money than she did and she thought money equalled power," he said.

So Danielle in San Francisco wasn't driven by a relationship, by various crushes on various men, but entranced by the sound of the carriage return on her old-fashioned manual typewriter, the click-clack of the keyboard. She knew to follow the California dream like the Lazard brothers before her, finding themselves in the middle of the gold rush. For Danielle-Fernande Schulein-Steel Lazard, the money was not in the gold coming out of the California earth, but in the gold coming out of the deep veins of social upheaval that shook California in these years, social upheaval that was soon to affect the entire nation. The broken marriages, the child abuse, the teen alcoholics. The pregnant teenagers, gays coming out of the closet, the burglars and junkies. The movement for social change. By the end of the seventies, Danielle had immersed herself personally in all of these issues. And most of all, the single mothers continued to be her focus.

Because it was the single mothers who would eagerly pay the price of a romantic paperback to consume the happy-ending story of another single mother who miraculously survived, and finally found her handsome prince to marry and raise her children.

But before finding her prince, Danielle had some life experience to go through. Danny Zugelder was the first man she fell in love with when she came to California.

Danny was taking part in a twenty-eight-day medical experiment for SKYLAB, part of NASA's space program. She later discovered he was living deep inside the walls of Lompoc Federal Penitentiary. But by then, it was too late to stop falling deeply, madly in love.

Chapter Seven
Passion's Promise

The criminals are all interesting to me. To me, when a criminal is forced to talk, you see in purer form than in any other person what is a very distinctive human trait: the capacity for self-deception and rationalization. A criminal has it in purer form.

Nothing is ever a criminal's fault. And for a writer, that's a beautiful thing to watch—to watch someone lie, to watch the ways people lie and believe their lies. And lying is clearly not a trait on which criminals have a patent or a monopoly. It's really what allows each of us to get up in the morning.

—interview with writer David Milch
of *NYPD Blue, New York Times,* 10/26/93

For those who know her as the glamorous Mrs. Danielle Steel Traina of Pacific Heights, former wife of Claude-Eric Lazard, it comes as a surprise to learn that this vivacious socialite had two marriages she never discusses.

But just like the women in her early fiction—like Kezia Saint Martin and Kaitlin Harper—she endured some rough and rocky roads on her trip to the orderly life she now lives with John Traina. Some of that tempestuous past may help flavor her fiction, though her characters—like all fictional characters—are a blend of many people, many observations.

She has always been reluctant to admit to her two marriages in the 1970s. She told Nikke Finke in the *Los Angeles Times* that "Alzheimer's has come on" when asked in 1988 about her third marriage.

The prisoner she may partially have based the fictional men on in *Passion's Promise*, *Now and Forever*, and *Season of Passion* was her second husband, Danny Zugelder.

Danny Zugelder was the handsome young bank robber she met in the early 1970s. He was born January 6, 1950, 2 1/2 years younger than Danielle. She didn't learn he was a felon until after their first meeting. She was not doing research for a magazine article when she met him; she was probably visiting a friend while Danny was engaged in the SKYLAB experiments NASA was performing with some prisoner volunteers, perhaps at the Presidio.

When Danny was paroled, he moved in with her in her little Victorian duplex in San Francisco.

She'd been flying back and forth between San Francisco and New York since the mid-sixties. She visited with Sidney Ehrman, the paterfamilias of the Lazard clan in San Francisco and Sidney's daughter Esther Ehrman Lazard and her husband, Claude-Eric's parents.

Danielle was enchanted with San Francisco. Her novels are love songs to the place, exploring the nooks and crannies from the Marina to the Presidio, its many charms from the sea, the hills, the Golden Gate Bridge crossing to the windswept beaches of Marin, even the funky little restaurants in Chinatown.

She left a string of clues in her books about Danny's existence.

There was the dedication to *Passion's Promise*. She quoted from poet Sylvia Plath's "Getting There." And next to the Plath poem about being reborn from a living death, she wrote a loving dedication to Danny, for making her such a happy woman and such a lucky one. Lucky, because it was the first book of hers to be published after the three-year dry spell after *Going Home*.

Now and Forever was also dedicated to Danny. And in it, she quoted from her own "Poem to

Danny," copyright 1974, which first appeared in *Cosmopolitan* magazine.

Season of Passion involved another tall, strong man who drank, fought, and went to jail.

Soon, with her best-seller *The Promise*, she started selling so many books that her publishers started up The Danielle Steel Fan Club. She was not yet a household name, and she was not yet in Pacific Heights society, but she was on her way.

The fan club's clip-out entry forms printed in the backs of her early paperbacks, promised

- photo of Danielle Steel, personally autographed
- first look at all of the writer's future books
- and last-minute information on her visits to your hometown.

All for free.

But by this time, Danny Zugelder wasn't even getting any autographed photographs of Danielle Steel.

He was behind bars charged with attempted murder and rape in Colorado.

Drop free-fall down the coast of California from San Francisco to Los Angeles, and veer in toward the arid high desert on Interstate 10. You'll soon hit Riverside, near Danny Zugelder's place of birth, the scene of his teen years.

Downtown Riverside has telltale signs of the Great Society spending that Lyndon Johnson initiated in the 1960s. When Johnson declared his War on Poverty, fading cities around the United States with a strong party apparatus and a festering downtown were treated to a rich frosting of federal funds. Never mind that these jolts of new life sometimes didn't take root, it was pump-priming, good for the economy of the towns, good for the sense of civic pride.

Riverside was one of those towns a benign federal government smiled upon. The grand old Riverside County Courthouse, awash with cupids and classic statuary, was the white marble plinth this urban renewal project was built around. The courthouse, put up around 1900, had the gleaming, naive, open charm of a neoclassical Beaux Arts building facing a brand new century, the twentieth. Back then, it was facing a wide-open future with all the enthusiastic civic spirit a jaunty new southern California town could muster.

Towering groves of date palms had been imported from the Middle East to grace this new land of milk and honey. Groves of fragrant orange trees circled Riverside, and promised the easy life and gold in the streets for those who'd been living under the gray wintry skies of the Midwest.

This was the naive, open charm that Danny Zugelder's father, an agricultural worker, hoped to find when he moved here from the chilly Midwest. But by the time his hard-drinking father arrived, the promise was fading.

Danny Zugelder grew up to be a lost soul, a sweet bear of a man, and a vicious bastard. The FBI knew him as #634-105-G. The ex-husband of Danielle Steel, Danielle Lazard back then.

His real father deserted the family when Danny was only three or four . . . leaving his Oregon-born mother Joyce with an armful of kids. Sharon was four years older, Scharlene three years older than Danny. Was Danny the extra child that pushed his birth father into deserting the whole batch of noisy, wailing kids? It's hard to keep a family of five, and feed an alcohol habit, on a farm worker's salary.

His mother remarried a Carl Zugelder, and Danny ended up using his name.

As his mother later told Colorado authorities, "He has emotional problems dating back from early childhood."

The reason was quite simple: His mother's new husband, a heavy drinking child-abuser, beat him with his fists, according to prison records.

Danny was running away from home from the age of seven or eight, maybe even at six.

His little sister was born seven years after Danny, and luckily, his stepfather never beat the girls. But as soon as Danny grew taller than his stepfather, home was hell.

By the time Danny was thirteen, Danny started drinking. Because by the time he was twelve, he towered over his stepfather. And the man, used to whopping Danny, now had to deal with his resistance.

According to his statements in Colorado, he had been dragged into the Riverside Courts by age thirteen on over fifty charges of joyriding, breaking and entering, and grand theft.

Shipped off to relatives back east for nine months, he was paroled.

Heroin was his next stop, at sixteen or seventeen. He was charged with statutory rape.

In 1968-70, his records show he was married, though it seems to have been a common-law marriage, from information in his 1970 court papers.

His mother wrote that "he is a very intelligent, loving human . . . he needs help." But his spirit was beaten out of him.

He made a little money working in construction or driving a truck as a teenager ($115 a week, $460 a month). He went to so many different schools that he refused to fill out his "high school" lines on a resumé. He said there weren't enough lines. There were only three.

In 1969, Danielle Steel had not yet met Daniel Zugelder. But the boy who "becomes a different person when he drinks" started making his appearances here at the Riverside County Courthouse, taking the baby steps in a career of crime that eventually saw him branded a Registered Sex Offender.

And it started in this all-American town. The town, like the family, was starting to tatter around the edges.

* * *

A solitary pedestrian crossing the downtown Riverside Plaza in search of Danny Zugelder's past came upon a hawk, intent on the vicious work of tearing apart a recently captured sparrow. Turning a cold, glinting eye at the unexpected intruder, the hawk clutched the small, dying creature in its talons, and flew behind an escarpment on the flank of the courthouse.

Diagonally across the plaza, Riverside City Monument Number 80, a former funeral home. The Spanish-styled funeral home, with "every necessary convenience," according to the plaque, was now in the service of a more modern manifestation of the embalmer's art: the Riverside County's Coroner's Office.

One could imagine a hapless youth caught up here in the bureaucratic nightmare of Kafka's *The Trial*.

But one didn't hear any echoes of Danny's fifty or sixty arrests.

This being a lazy Sunday afternoon, the only sound disturbing the sepulchral quiet of the vast Presley plaza was the old-fashioned wheeze of the roof-mounted refrigeration unit at the Coroner's Office, keeping the toe-tagged corpses chilled until Monday, and the bustle of a new work week.

The old jail: jail cells on the upper levels, and down a slanting drive, the dark inner courtyard of the building.

Down here was the records section, row after row of beige-jacketed files, stacked five- or six-high, registering the careers of some of the county's less notable citizens. It is here that Danny Zugelder, fledgling felon, can be found.

But it is "United States District Court Case 6985-Criminal" that starts the relentless downward slide of his wasted life.

1970. Danny chose a bank with a camera poised and cocked, sure to capture him on film.

He handed the terrified teller, a Miss Sue Lee, a note that said he was carrying a bomb. If she didn't hand over the money, they'd all be dead at the Mission Boulevard bank.

Hand it over she did, all $608 of it. A pittance. In a strange twist of fate, it was the price for meeting Danielle. But even Danielle's love couldn't save him.

After being identified by four witnesses from his photos in a lineup, Danny admitted his guilt to FBI Special Agent L. L. Blanton.

Records of his bench trial were hidden away in the imposing pyramid-shaped Federal Archives building near Laguna Beach, where they had been bearing silent witness to Danny's early prison years.

On November 9, 1970, the Commissioner of the United States District Court, Central District, State of California, issued his Final Commitment, and Danny was escorted, bound with chained hands and feet, from the Riverside County Jail by a Deputy U.S. Marshal to the Los Angeles County Jail.

Downtown Los Angeles is surely familiar to viewers who have seen old black-and-white reruns of *Dragnet* on television. But the insides of County are like nothing you ever saw in your living room.

Danny was very poor, and on November 30, appearing in court, he was handed over to a court-appointed attorney.

The reason becomes painfully clear when reviewing the court papers. In his small scrawl, with capital letters interspersed with lower-case, the script interspersed with block letters, he filled out his questionnaire: yes, he was employed, at a weekly income of $115 gross, with no other income, savings or investments, and one dependent, a common-law wife.

Yet the signature of the defendant "Dan Zugelder" had an optimistic upward tilt to it and definite marks of high native intelligence.

Perhaps he hadn't yet realized the nightmarish system he'd been handed over to, an endless round of paper forms and bureaucracy. But since he later revealed his real father had been imprisoned in California, he may have known what to expect.

His court-appointed attorney was Richard Kolostian, a lawyer with offices in the warren of buildings surrounding the courthouse, who made a living from the criminal court buildings of downtown Los Angeles.

So within thirty days, Danny had gotten drunk, robbed a bank, gotten drunk and perhaps high on heroin, spent the money, been taken in, transferred to Los Angeles and County Jail, been appointed a court-ordered attorney not of his choosing.

No one had tried to get him out on bail, as far as research indicates, and no one had brought him a lawyer from Riverside.

He had no one . . . and nothing.

He started going through D.T.'s according to later prison records.

By December seventeenth, United States District Judge A. Andrew Hauk had issued the order for a court-appointed psychiatrist to determine the "mental competency and legal responsibility" of Danny Zugelder. His lawyer Richard Kolostian had advised the judge that the defendant "may be presently insane or otherwise so mentally incompetent. . . ." In quick succession, three psychiatrists had a chat with Danny.

There was Dr. Marcus Crahan. There was Dr. George Abe. And thirdly, there was Dr. Harold Deering.

When he came to trial, there was some confusion about Danny's name. Was it Danny Eugene Joslin, or was it Danny Eugene Zugelder? In later paperwork, it seems that his real name was indeed Joslin, but since he'd been checked into his first prison under the name Zugelder, it stuck for life.

He was saddled with the name of the man who beat him with his fists.

For the trial memorandum of January 13, Alan H. Friedman served as the Assistant U.S. Attorney on the case for the plaintiff, United States of America. They figured the trial would take two days, and call six witnesses on the government's side on the one-count felony indictment of bank robbery, section 2113(a). Did Danny have anyone on his side? It seems not.

But there was to be no jury trial. The three psychiatrists all reported that Danny was sane. There was to be no insanity plea.

The lawyer convinced Danny that the sentence might be lighter if he saved the Court's time and money and attention by changing his plea to guilty. The possible sentence for the $608: twenty years.

Five days later, Danny changed his plea to guilty.

United States District Judge A. Andrew Hauk found Danny guilty.

For sentencing, a probation officer must first evaluate the rehabilitation possibilities of the prisoner, and get that report to the judge.

His paperwork was sent to the U.S. Probation officer on January 18, 1971, and the case was continued for final sentencing until Monday, February 8, 1971 at 2:00 PM, about three weeks after the probation people got his life story.

But since he was only twenty-one, he was handled under the Federal Youth Corrections Act as a "Youth Offender."

Unlike the "three strikes and you're out" arguments raging in America in the 1990s, some citizens felt youth should have a second chance with what conservatives would call "kid-glove treatment." Danny got what sounded like the kid-glove treatment.

But in reality, it was a sham. This was not rehabilitation.

Because when he was committed to custody by the Federal Youth Corrections Division, and sent from the Los Angeles county jail to the Federal Community Treatment Center Complex at Lompoc, he was sent to hell.

Lompoc had been built as a maximum security prison for the military. And it looked as forbidding as a prison could look, with thick walls and guard towers and lonely, windswept location.

Lompoc was a nightmare, but luckily for Danny, Vandenberg Air Force base shared the same desolate peninsula in Lompoc. Vandenberg was involved with NASA and the space program, and in 1972 word passed through the prison that volunteers were wanted for medical experiments.

Danny volunteered, and it was as a medical guinea pig for the space program SKYLAB that he met Danielle, probably up at the Presidio's Letterman Hospital, six blocks from Sidney Ehrman's mansion in San Francisco.

Danny was lying flat on his back. The requirement was to stay prone for twenty-eight days, to determine the effect of weightlessness on bone density, to determine why astronauts lost so much calcium in space. And Danielle came in to visit a friend.

It was attraction at first sight.

According to Danielle, she had no idea that Danny Zugelder was a prisoner until later.

She came back to visit him soon. Once the experiment was over, Danny went back to Lompoc, placed in the Medium Security area of the prison.

After visiting San Francisco and her husband's family there, Danielle ultimately decided to leave New York and move to the City by the Bay. After a long-distance phone relationship with Danny, that lasted four months, she moved to San Francisco.

A friend from Supergirls, Timmie Scott Mason, made the switch as well, and of course, she had the Lazard and Ehrman family in the city.

She rented the duplex and started living apart from Claude-Eric Lazard, still her husband.

It was a long, long drive down from San Francisco to Lompoc, which is near Santa Barbara, and more in the orbit of Los Angeles in the south than San Francisco in the north.

But nearly every weekend, she made the trip.

She had a tremendous amount of energy. Her friends all said that.

Passion's Promise, the novel she thanked Danny for in her dedication, was the story of a rich young socialite whose parents both died when she was a child. Kezia Saint Martin was just stepping out into the world by writing a column under another name. (Much like the first magazine job Danielle had when she was working with Supergirls, supervising a column for the magazine *American Home*.) She's sent by her editor to interview a prison reform figure, Lucas Johns (as her friend John Mack Carter, the magazine editor, had suggested she go out and write fiction, perhaps features). They meet, and fall wildly in love. Lucas Johns is almost a spitting image of Danny Zugelder.

"Danielle was about the size of a button, adorable, very serious, very intense, but with a great sense of humor," her former neighbor Dan Talbott recalls. "But she was very focused, very disciplined. All her time was scheduled . . . she didn't spend a lot of time doing nothing."

Falling in love, while she was writing her string of five unpublished novels, may have seemed like "doing nothing" at the time. But falling in love gave her writing a drive and a fire that it lacked before.

She got even more practice writing Danny hundreds of love letters, he claims, some pages and pages long.

Readers of Danielle may prefer to skip the following material on Danny Zugelder. They might prefer to rent the video of the Danielle Steel novel, *Now and Forever*, a romanticized version of what came next for Danielle and Danny.

Cheryl Ladd, the gorgeous blonde on *Charlie's Angels*, made her movie debut in the 1983 motion picture version of Danielle Steel's 1978 book *Now and Forever.* It was a rather strange film. The Australian producers shifted the San Francisco locations to Sydney, to save money. The scenery was different, the accents unexpected. Yet the plot was the same.

It was the story of a beautiful young couple—rich, successful, handsome, envied—and the shock that threatened to break their loving marriage apart.

He was a former ad agency man who was writing fiction, being supported by her boutique.

She was a successful woman who didn't want a child, just him.

And there was a horrible miscarriage of justice: Her fictional husband, Ian Clark, was unjustly accused of rape.

Shockingly, the jury chose to believe the conniving, lying, insane, lower-class seductress rather than Jessie Clark's handsome husband. And they sent him to prison.

She tried everything in her power to stop the wheels of justice, but he was sent to prison all the same.

Just weeks before it had seemed that lovely Jessie, the film's heroine, had everything . . . a successful fashion boutique, wonderful friends, a beautiful husband who was about to write a great novel and start bringing his own money into the marriage.

Now, they're calling her husband a "kept man,"

and she's broken in two as they drag him off in chains for trial.

And beautiful Jessie Clark starts to fall apart without Ian around to make her feel safe.

She's afraid in the house alone at night.

She's hassled by the detectives on the case. They stoop so low as to go through her dirty laundry to find his underpants, with their telltale semen stains.

She is sure that the policemen, the girl who unjustly charged Ian with the rape, all the witnesses at the trial, probably the jury . . . all working-class . . . are simply jealous of her and Ian's beauty and their wealth and their happiness.

Finally, Jessie turns to alcohol and drugs for comfort.

But, as the promo for the movie promises, "slowly, each realizes that the forced separation can make them stronger, and that devotion doesn't always reveal itself in times of happiness."

Their marriage comes back together.

We've warned you.

But if you're interested in reading about what really happened between the time they moved in together in San Francisco, and the time of his trial-by-jury for rape and other crimes, continue reading the next chapters.

Chapter Eight

Season of Passion: Danny and Danielle

The problem is insurmountable . . . three vicious, brutal attacks on unsuspecting women . . .

—The Honorable Donald B. Constine, Judge of the Superior Court of the State of California, In and For the City and County of San Francisco Friday, June 7, 1974
   RE: Danny Zugelder

June 1973. A few months before Danielle's second book, *Passion's Promise*, was published, Danny Zugelder was paroled from Lompoc and moved in with Danielle in San Francisco.

From now on, his address would be 1907 Pacific . . . and he'd rise, phoenixlike, from the depths of the Federal Penitentiary to the top of San Francisco, then plummet again as he got too near the glittering sun. His own abused childhood, self-deception and rationalization would bring him down in a crashing flameout.

Danielle moved to San Francisco to get far away from her family—and to separate from her husband.

Now that Danny Zugelder had moved in, casual friends thought she'd found someone tall and rangy to escort her about town, someone "in banking" as Danny told her social friends.

There were bandwagons of fun New Yorkers who'd come over to visit, like Timmie Scott Mason, Danielle's old colleague at Supergirls.

And Danielle was making new friends among some interesting San Franciscans. Richard Hongisto was one. Hongisto was a very liberal San

Francisco sheriff of the time. Later, he became a supervisor, and finally served briefly as San Francisco's Chief of Police.

Today, Danny Zugelder has been moved to a new high-security Colorado prison. In an interview for this book, Danielle's second husband simply says these friends of Danielle's were "phony." But still, he remembers the fun of going places with her, going to parties and getting crazy drunk.

"What are you into?" they'd ask him, as if just being a human being weren't enough. "It would be stocks, and bonds, and business things," Danny Zugelder said in an interview for this book. And the guest lists were fashionably balanced as well: a token black, a token homosexual, a token priest, and him, Danielle's token ex-con.

Danielle arranged a job for Danny as an "expediter" at an architectural firm Whisler-Patri. It was a good place for a guy without an education to start learning about the more polished members of society, running errands, being a "gofer," getting a look into the way the Other Side lives and works in a big city.

Today, from behind bars, Danny says Danielle worked hard and deserved every bit of fame and fortune that came her way.

"She could make a typewriter go faster than anyone I've every heard," he recalls. When they'd go out for the evening, Danielle would come home and stay up to write into the night.

A friend confirms her work habits—banging

away until three or four in the morning with that incredible energy.

But after only a few months of living in San Francisco, Danny got very disillusioned and very frustrated with his "old lady."

Danny started to perceive things like this: Here's a girl that you think is smitten with you. You're out on parole, she brings you home, introduces you to her friends . . . you start to feel like a novelty.

Why? Because her focus always seems to be on the book that she's typing away on, not on you.

The message, Danny began to figure, was to start learning to function in polite society and stay out of her hair.

Like they say, the criminal always blames things on other people. Danny started blaming Danielle. It was always her fault, not his.

As Danny remembers it in 1994, Danielle read the Bible, and they even searched for a church together. She had been raised a Catholic, as had her husband, Claude-Eric Lazard.

For a while, they tried going to a hip black church, but, according to Zugelder, she ultimately became a serious Christian Scientist.

He started to look at the job Danielle had helped him get with the architectural firm as just a menial job. And he couldn't understand why people were suddenly so NICE to him . . . he'd never met people like this before. It made him suspicious. Again, it was their fault.

But finally the alcoholism got to him: He had no idea that he was an alcoholic and he didn't admit to it until the late seventies, wrote his mother. "He becomes a different person when he drinks," wrote Joyce Zugelder. "Most alcoholics do."

He finally became very jealous and very envious of Danielle, a classic symptom of toxic levels of alcohol abuse.

"She's not giving me enough time," was the feeling he'd get across to Dan Talbott back then.

Or, "She's more interested in her book than in me. I'm just a freak in a sideshow."

At night he'd get drunk and make these pathetic, rambling sob-story phone calls from their house at all hours of the night.

"I don't know if he ever struck her, but he was terribly, terribly unhappy," says Dan Talbott. A friend of hers back then would swing by the house with her husband, and her husband would take out his tools for a little repair work. Danny, when he got angry, had been punching holes in the wall. And a 6'5" man, angry, was frightening. Especially for a 100 pound 5'1" woman.

"She wasn't being a loving, sensuous partner . . . they weren't having loving sex" was Danny's story in these rambling midnight calls of complaint to his friends. Again, nothing was ever his fault.

She never kicked him out.

And Danny Zugelder was proving to be something that no amount of money could help.

* * *

On November 29, 1973, Danny Zugelder was visiting friends in Reno, Nevada. He was away from Danielle for a few days, but still on federal parole.

A woman, a car, a parking lot.

He assaulted the woman in her car in the parking lot, stole her purse, and fled.

When he came home to Danielle's apartment, a felony assault and robbery charge were howling at his back.

Then on February 1, 1974, the same man jumped from the darkness of a doorway in Pacific Heights, armed with a wooden club, and struck an unsuspecting woman. Not just once, to steal her handbag, but repeatedly, like a crazed man, "at least 30 times, primarily in the head area, resulting in serious injuries," according to the district attorney.

The charges were as follows, according to papers filed in San Francisco Superior Court:

Felony assault upon "Miss Y."

Felony possession of a weapon prohibited by law.

Danny was released on $25,000 bail. And his attacks continued.

He offered a ride to a woman waiting at a bus stop. She worked for a company like CBS or NBC. He motioned her to get into the car he'd borrowed from the architectural firm, from the job Danielle had set up.

(Today, he claims it was a 1964 Jaguar that

Danielle had bought him: Their neighbor, Dan
Talbott, says he never saw such a car.)

He drove the woman home and violently raped
her. It was only ten days before Valentine's Day.

"Danielle called us in a very agitated state," says
Dan Talbott. "She begged us to come over.

"We came over . . . and she said, 'I believe in
Danny—what are we going to do?'

"I don't know if he stayed in jail, or whether
she got him out. . . .

"I just ran across a letter that I sent to the courts
for him the other day. . . ."

There were six charges at the trial including
rape and sodomy.

Danielle Lazard, which was the name she went
under in 1974, was convinced that Danny was not
guilty of the charges against him.

The Pacific Heights attack should be overlooked,
Danny should not go to prison.

She was passionate about his innocence, and
convinced her friends that the rape charge was a
setup, that he'd been railroaded, and that this was
a total miscarriage of justice.

Letters that flowed into the judge's chambers on
Danny's behalf confirmed Danny's version of
events: Danielle hadn't been treating him properly,
she'd been working too hard, if she'd done something differently, he never would have attacked,
robbed, raped, and sodomized.

These letters demonstrated the fascinating mind

of a criminal, a sociopath, at work: It's not my fault, Momma, it's YOUR FAULT.

Danielle—guileless, ingenuous—wrote a five-page letter trying to explain away the trouble Danny had gotten himself into, and the pain and terror he'd unleashed on his unsuspecting young victims.

The fictional treatment of the rape trial in *Now and Forever* may be based on the version Danny fed Danielle.

Looking back on this rape trial with the benefit of hindsight, Danielle and all concerned must realize it was yet another step in the inexorable tragedy of Danny Zugelder. It was a tragedy that started when his stepfather beat him with his fists for the first time, and his mother looked away.

Friends tried to sit with her and Danny in the courtroom during the long days of the jury trial, as it went through the five days of slow, nightmarish tedium of hearing the witnesses, looking at the State's exhibits . . . all those horrible photographs. . . .

"It was a testament to her will and persistence that regardless of the testimony and the verdict she not only believed in this guy and his innocence, but she convinced all of us that this was a classic case of justice gone awry . . . ," said Dan Talbott. "I wasn't at the trial every single day, I was working. But I met her there a couple of ties. When the verdict came down, that was a bad day at Black Rock."

Danielle tried to outmaneuver the parole report, desperate to convince the judge that putting Danny back in jail would be the worst thing for him. He should be allowed to stay out on parole . . . even though he'd broken his parole first by the attack on a woman in Reno, and then by savagely attacking the woman in Pacific Heights. Surely he'd change.

How was their friendship played out in the letters to the judge? Danny had her friends convinced that "part of Danny's problem was that he was her SLAVE . . . the only time he got access to her was when she had need of him. The rest of the time was [her work]. It wasn't a loving relationship."

Danielle tried to convince the judge and the parole officer *she* could change. And make Danny happy. All he needed was the love of a good woman and a rehab. Danny's violent attacks on women would stop.

The figures in the case, besides Danielle and Danny, were Assistant District Attorney Robert Dondero, and representing Danny, the lawyer Tom Gee. And the women who'd been attacked.

The rape case went to a trial by jury.

Six counts.

Rape, oral copulation by force, sodomy, false imprisonment, robbery, and assault.

The jury came back with a guilty verdict on each charge. It was a dramatic moment in the courtroom, as the jury foreman read out "Guilty," and again, "Guilty," once more "Guilty," until the word seemed to be crashing from the walls of the court-room and echoing in people's heads.

Nine days before his sentencing on the rape trial, Danny came up before the judge on the Pacific Heights attack, Action No. 88083. Danny "jumped from a doorway in the Pacific Heights District, and struck a woman victim with a wooden club at least 30 times, primarily in the head . . . resulting in serious injuries . . . ," said the district attorney in a later state-ment. "This was, according to the probation report, an unprovoked attack on a stranger, although the De-fendant in his statement to the Probation Office seemed to indicate the motive in this was one of rob-bery," the district attorney continued.

The court noted that a charge of assault with intent to commit rape had already been dismissed in the Pacific Heights attack.

So Danny Zugelder, with the advice of Tom Gee, wisely decided to skip the jury trial on this one, and changed his plea to guilty.

Zugelder's lawyer then made a point of asking the judge to exonerate the $25,000 bail on the Pacific Heights attack, so the cash could be released. The judge did that. And then the lawyer asked again ("for the record, so that it is totally clear . . . order an exoneration of bail") that the funds be released in the rape trial as well. If anyone had money tied up with a bail bondsman, it could be used to better advantage elsewhere. The night Danny Zugelder was convicted he was put in custody.

Now the struggle was organizing the materials for Danny's parole officer, getting people into the courtroom for the sentencing. It was now May 29. There were only nine more days until Danny's sentencing date on Friday, June 7, 1974, at 9:30 A.M.

Sentencing day was the final test of Danielle's committed efforts to keep Danny out of jail.

The judge, Donald B. Constine, opened the proceedings when he reviewed the charges against Danny, repeated the jury's guilty verdicts on every count in the rape trial, and again, Danny's guilty plea on the Pacific Heights Attack.

He continued by talking about the probation officer, Tom Quinlan, who, along with the judge, had been the focus of Danielle's intense campaign to change the course of the trial. Let us hear it in the judge's measured words:

THE COURT: The Probation Officer, Tom Quinlan, a Senior Probation Officer, has submitted a nine-page probation report with numerous attachments, and I have read and carefully examined the report, the nine-page statement attached thereto, submitted by the Defendant, and the psychiatric evaluation of Dr. Lomisaruk, a psychiatric evaluation by Dr. David Kessler, and a psychiatric evaluation by Dr. Owen Renik, three psychiatrists requested by the Defense to examine the Defendant.

I have also examined the letters that have

been submitted on behalf of the Defendant
from friends, employers, interested parties, as
well as a letter and statement of Mr. Keith
Matthews, the Administrator of Walden
House in San Francisco.

And in that connection, I have also read and
examined the statement of the Federal Probation Officer, a Joy Valentine, who indicates
that notwithstanding the three offenses committed by the Defendant, three offenses committed and admitted by the Defendant while
on parole, but because of the Defendant's response to an exposure to the program offered
by Walden House since the last arrest a few
months ago, she apparently is not going to
move for a parole violation, and recommends
that the Defendant not be incarcerated, but be
allowed to remain under the supervision of
the Walden House authorities.

I have also read, let the record show, the
five-page letter and explanation submitted by
Mrs. Lazard [Danielle Steel], who is, as I understand, the fiancée of the Defendant.

MR. GEE: That is correct.

THE COURT: Is this a fair statement of the
background of this case and its present posture, for the purpose of sentence?

MR. DONDERO: Yes.

MR. GEE: Yes, Your Honor.

The judge seemed surprised that the Federal
Probation Officer, with the truly romantic name

of Joy Valentine, was willing to let bygones be bygones, now that Danny had been checked in as a resident of Walden House, the halfway house and rehab Danielle had found for him. Valentine would not call Danny on his parole violation for federal bank robbery and she didn't think Danny should go to jail for the attacks: He would be best left at Walden House.

Next, the judge talked about Danielle, referring to her as "the fiancée of the defendant," and wants the record to show that he has indeed "read the five-page letter and explanation submitted by Miss Lazard. . . ." (According to one report, Danielle wrote the following to the county probation department in her try to keep Danny in Walden House and out of prison: "Everything was 'mine'—my house . . . my friends, my job," she wrote. "I continued to expect him to conform and do all the adjusting. . . . Our attempt to blend our very different lifestyles was hopelessly clumsy, and painful for both of us."

Danielle was convinced by a violent criminal that everything was her fault, none of it was his fault, it just happened, he wasn't thinking, he must have been drinking . . . it must have been all her fault.

After the judge made it clear he'd already read Danielle's five-page "letter and explanation," he heard from the lawyer, Mr. Gee, that Danielle had arranged for Danny. Let the trial transcript speak:

MR. GEE: Now I did all that I could here in hiring three psychiatrists to come and talk to Mr. Zugelder, and I thought too, myself, if anyone was unfavorable, I might not submit it to the Court.

And I told the psychiatrists I wanted a fair report.

I told them I hoped it would be possible for the Court to see a possible 1203.03 evaluation under the Penal Code.

I am not asking for a grant of probation at this time, but I am saying that I don't think that the evaluation by the Probation Department is full or thorough, and I think a proper evaluation can be had by the Department of Corrections.

And each of the three psychiatrists did come back with a favorable finding as far as his progress at Walden House, and recommended that further consideration be given to sending him to an evaluation with the Department of Corrections.

Mr. Gee was bending over backwards to be polite to the judge while asking for the impossible: parole for a convicted rapist and violent felon who is currently a federal parole violator. Perhaps he thought the case would go to appeal. Gee started by implying that although the parole officer had been courteous and polite, he really hadn't done his job well enough:

He did not get up to see the Defendant until the first part of this week, on Monday. He went to see the Defendant, and he got a . . . he got the necessary statistical information.

And then he said to the Defendant, "Do you have anything to say?"

And as the Defendant started talking, he started shuffling papers, and he did listen to the Defendant for approximately five minutes, but then terminated the conversation.

As far as I know, I asked him to go to Walden House to look at the facilities, and he did not do so.

As far as I know, he has not contacted any of the psychiatrists.

His only comment regarding any of the psychiatrists' reports was that he was offended by a rather uncomplimentary reference to the victim in the rape case.

That is all he said to me about the psychiatric reports. I am not questioning the sincerity of Mr. Quinlan, but I think that he simply looked at the offenses here, and did not bother to consider whether these were extraordinary circumstances.

Lastly, Gee pulled his rabbit from the hat: Danielle had paid for three private psychiatrists to talk with Danny; they saw rehabilitation, and thought he was going to change. Therefore, since the probation department didn't have the money for a psychiatric staff of its own, Danny should be sent to prison under Penal Code 1203.03 for an evaluation. Then Vacaville can judge if Danny has progressed, if "Mr. Zugelder is, in fact, a menace to the community."

The lawyer then asked Keith Matthews to speak. Matthews headed up Walden House, a well-known San Francisco rehab, and Matthews was charmed by Danny and pleased with his progress.

But the judge seemed reluctant to hear more pleading:

THE COURT: I might only state to you, I have read the letter of Mr. Matthews. I am aware of the work of Walden House. And you need not convince me of its validity or legitimacy in that regard.

The Court uses Walden House as well as Delancey Street [another halfway house]. I understand what the purpose of it is.

But if you wish to have him make a statement, I will let him do that, of course.

MR. GEE: I appreciate the Court's remarks, but I would like to have him make a brief statement.

THE COURT: Mr. Matthews, no purpose in having you sworn. I will be glad to hear what you wish to say.

MR. KEITH MATTHEWS: Your Honor, you read the report I submitted to you?

THE COURT: Yes, sir. In fact, I read through these documents twice, taken several hours to do so.

MR. MATTHEWS: So I don't need to bore you going over them again.

I wish to say to you, of all the people that we have received in Walden House who come in to us for help, there are very few that progress as fast as Dan Zugelder has, or done as well, or got into the family as quickly.

As you can see, there are quite a few people here today. And they are all here because of Dan, and because of their love for him, and because of his love for them. They know he is hurting, and just want to be here with him.

I would be glad to answer any questions that you have.

THE COURT: I have none to put to you.

I have had very few cases in the last several years that I have had as complete an evaluation as this, with as many letters and documents and evaluations submitted to me. I have sufficient, and I understand your position. And thank you for confidence.

The lawyer then called on Danielle (then Danielle Lazard), after a brief warning from the judge:

MR. GEE: Your Honor, I would also like to call at this time for a very few brief remarks Mrs. Danielle Lazard.

MR. DONDERO: I don't have any objection to her stating anything, Your Honor. I have read her statement of five pages, and I am sure the Court has too.

THE COURT: I really don't understand—at the time of sentencing, there is no right to make such a statement, but I can only assure that I have read her statement with great particularity. It is a single-spaced typewritten statement of several pages.

I do not wish to foreclose her from making any statement, but to agonize over this will not be of assistance to her or the Defendant.

MR. GEE: She would like to address a few brief remarks . . .

THE COURT: But no purpose in a repetition of what you have written, because I have read it.

MISS DANIELLE LAZARD: I merely want to represent to the Court my willingness to stand by Mr. Zugelder. If there were any possibilities for consideration of the suggestions by Walden House, I would appreciate it.

THE COURT: I understand. Thank you.

And finally, after Danielle's few anguished words, Danny Zugelder stood, all 6'5" of him, to make a statement to the court:

THE DEFENDANT: My life in the past has been pretty much of a catastrophe. I was brought up in a strange sort of way. I never had any friends before up until these people here. I love everyone of them, and I have learned an awful lot from everyone of them. And I have never had people like I have now.

My only wish now is to continue on to rehabilitate myself, and go on further and help others that end up in situations like this. I realize the situation and the seriousness of what I have done, and there is no way I can take back what I did do.

The only thing I can do is try to keep on and be stronger, and help myself and others so there will not be any other situations like this.

I don't feel I am a threat to society any longer, and I would appreciate the mercy of the Court.

THE COURT: Thank you. Anything further, Mr. Gee?

MR. GEE: I would like to make some closing remarks.

And now, Danielle's lawyer made his last-ditch attempt to keep Danny out of prison, questioning that Danielle's private "psychiatrists' reports were taken seriously into account" and trying desperately to get Danny on a 1203.03. If you will notice, the lawyer had made Danny's case an "extraordinary circumstance," because of the letters, the support, the friends in the courtroom, the positive private psychiatrists' reports. . . . It would seem Danielle's strategy was beginning to bear fruit.

MR. GEE: Again, Your Honor, I don't want to minimize the seriousness of these offenses, and the fact that the Defendant is not eligible for probation unless the Court finds extraordinary circumstances.

I am very distressed about this probation report. I know it was prepared at the last minute. I went in yesterday morning at 9:30, and the report was being written then, and typed page-by-page.

I don't think there was serious deliberation and consideration. I don't think the psychiatrists' reports were seriously taken into account.

And it is for that reason that I am requesting the Court to refer Mr. Zugelder to the Department of Corrections under Penal Code Section 1203.03.

Now I know that the Court feels that such a procedure would be—the Court feels in the present posture that the Court will not grant probation and—

THE COURT: What you asked of me, and I explained to you, the 1203.03 is used as a proceeding and tool where the Court is in doubt whether to impose probation or a State Prison sentence.

And I advised you that if probation is not to be considered, there is no purpose in the 1203.03 study. That is all I stated to you, and that is a matter of procedure.

MR. GEE: I understand that.

THE COURT: That is in every case, not just this case.

MR. GEE: The reason I ask it here is that

I feel the Probation evaluation is not a full and fair one. And I think such an evaluation can be provided by Vacaville, and I understand, and Mr. Zugelder understands, that the Court is in no way committed, regardless of the recommendation of Vacaville.

And I submit there are extraordinary circumstances here, where certainly one will view the letters and reports with a certain amount of skepticism, because the psychiatrists were retained by the Defense.

But nevertheless, they are all positive, and we are asking for an objective evaluation from the Department of Corrections.

And they can look at him and it would—and if, in fact, the Court, as it very probably will, should find that it would be necessary to return him, regardless of the recommendation of the Department, it would aid the Department of Corrections in seeing that Mr. Zugelder is a man that can be rehabilitated, and they will place him accordingly. And I don't think he would be misled by any false hope, or that it would be cruel to send him for a reference to 1203.03.

And I understand the Court's statements, and I don't find fault with them.

But I submit to the Court these are extraordinary circumstances, based on the letters that have been submitted, the representations of Mr. Matthews and the psychiatrists, and I realize the Court is—that the Court in the past has made no promises, and the Court is making no promises by a 1203.03 reference.

I ask nothing from the Court but a fair and responsible decision. Nothing more. I just feel that evaluation here, knowing the overloading of the Probation Department, and the fact that there was no psychiatrist on any other side to evaluate the Defendant, that we put forth what you might call a prima facie case that deserves further looking into. . . . The Defendant will be in custody.

And I cannot say what the Department of Corrections is going to recommend on such evaluation, but I see the People have nothing to lose, and it would be more fair to all parties.

I think, because of lack of manpower, and the press that was involved here, this probation evaluation is not full, thorough, or fair.

And for that reason, I would ask the Court to recognize that these could be extraordinary circumstances, and to make a reference of Mr. Zugelder pursuant to Penal Code Section 1203.03.

But then the district attorney had his chance to make his reasoned, yet impassioned statement:

THE COURT: Mr. Dondero?
MR. DONDERO: Yes, Your Honor.
I think we agree that the crimes involved here are serious. The assault on "Miss X" was

heard by the Court during the trial, the incident that happened to her.

As to the attack on "Miss Y," the Defendant in his statement acknowledges that he was intending to rob a person. He did not even know whether he was attacking a female or male, according to his statement.

The blows she sustained were visible. She suffered a skull fracture. She had some numerous scars to the head. She estimates she was struck 30 times in a period of a minute. Nothing was taken. She was left there.

The Defendant also has pending in Reno, as the Court stated, the robbery, purse snatch incident in a parking lot involving another female.

The crimes are serious. We are not talking about minor violations of the law, nor are we talking about one incident, but rather a series of incidents covering from November until February when he was, in fact, arrested.

The Defendant in his statement represented that he had this problem for a period of ten years, this drinking problem.

It is interesting that he did manage to solve the problem of drugs while in Federal prison. The drinking problem continued.

In June of '73, when he was paroled, he had a parole agent, which to this day has shown what I would only describe as a remarkable faith in the Defendant. I would say it may verge on the question of competency, in view of the total picture.

But she, at least, has shown incredible reluctance to do anything with regards to acting on his Federal parole status.

The Defendant, at the time of June, of 1973, or before, met a female, Mrs. Lazard [Danielle Steel], who showed an interest in him, and has been his companion during the period of time up to and including his remanding into custody.

He had people that appeared to be interested in him. He had people that wrote letters to the Court expressing an interest in him during the period of time since his parole status. He had a job.

Now in November of 1973, the Defendant committed a crime which amounted to robbery. He took a purse from a female, without any cause. And he was chased and apprehended.

His drinking was apparently a motive for the attack. He did nothing after that, except he continued to engage in drinking, this habit apparently he had.

I submit to the Court that the experience which the Defendant had after his arrest of February 4th, 1974, did not come during the period of November, did not come in December or January.

He was supposedly afraid of going back to jail.

And yet we have a parole agent, like I mentioned before, Miss Valentine, who has had a very unusually sincere or positive interest in this particular individual. She did nothing to have his parole status changed in any way.

If the man was interested in reforming his life, something more positive should have been done. He certainly would not have been in this situation if it had been.

We have a man, February 1st, 1974, engaged in, as I stated before, a rather vicious assault on a woman at 11:00 at night.

On the 4th of February, 1974, "Miss X" entered his car, and the Court heard the evidence of what happened after that.

A number of witnesses testified in the trial. . . . They had an opportunity to observe the demeanor and the conduct of the Defendant before the rape, during the rape and after the rape.

None of them made any reference to this degree of intoxication which caused them to suspect his conduct.

Mr. Chong drove with him, and found nothing unusual. Miss Freeman talked to him about the case, and saw nothing unusual. That question was asked of those persons.

"Miss X" was sort of face-to-face with the man. The supposed alcoholic condition did not exist, at least in her observation.

Furthermore, we have the tape of the Defendant, which the Court heard, a tape in which the Defendant had been arrested for

the rape charge. Supposedly he was aware of
the conduct, and was interested in reforming
his life at that time.

But we do know that the night of the rape,
allegedly he called AA, and in that statement
the Defendant does not admit the crime in any
way, but rather discusses the consensual conduct of "Miss X." That everything happening
in her apartment was the product of consent.

And I submit to the Court, that if he was
interested in laying it out, and explaining the
problem that he had, that that particular conversation with the Inspector may have been
the first opportunity, even though it was obviously incriminating, it would be the time to
explain the problems that he had.

In conclusion, Your Honor, the recommendation of the People, in view of the total analysis of the case, and the conduct of the
Defendant over a ten-year period, and the ap-
parent results which the jury reached in this
particular case, is that the Defendant be sentenced to State Prison.

The recommendation of the People would
be as to Count I, the charge of rape, that he
be sent to State Prison.

THE COURT: You are speaking of Action
No. 87814?

MR. DONDERO: That is correct.

The district attorney gave his sentencing requests to the judge, and indicated to the judge that

Count VI, which the jury voted guilty on, "involved the conduct of choking the victim initially in her apartment in the kitchen area and the threats made at that time in the kitchen."

And now, lawyer Gee made yet another desperate attempt to sway the judge, and convince him it would be unnecessarily harsh to send Danny up on anything but the psychiatric 1203.03.

THE COURT: Mr. Gee, do you have any response?

MR. GEE: Yes, Your Honor.

First of all, all of us, as we look back at our lives, we see there are things which we could have done better, and things we should have done at a certain time instead of another.

The fact is, that I am not suggesting that there is a 90-day miracle cure here. I suggest that there has been substantial progress, and it was had up until the time (sic) he entered Walden House, and it was difficult for the Defendant to come to grips with his problems. That is why he gave the statement he did to Sergeant O'Shea that he did the day he was arrested.

But I do suggest that . . . there has been substantial progress, and all the evidence before the Court indicates that.

In arguing against the consecutive sentences that the district attorney had asked for, the lawyer noted the prison could end up keeping Danny in for life. But he felt that would be "attempting to squelch," or "discouraging or frustrating" Danny's own efforts at rehabilitation.

It would give him a feeling of "despair, where he had shown real possibilities and progress for rehabilitation. . . ." He asked that the sentences run concurrently if Danny indeed had to be sentenced to any prison at all.

Finally, probably the most horrible days, weeks, and months, in Danielle Steel's life drew to a close:

THE COURT: I merely wish to state to both you gentlemen, and to the Defendant, and to those that are here in his behalf, that I have considered this matter at great length, and I have carefully examined and considered the letters of recommendations submitted on behalf of the Defendant, the psychiatric reports, and I have carefully considered the report submitted by the Probation Office.

In passing, I might only say that the fact that a probation report, as you say, was only typed yesterday, that does not mean that the Probation Office for the past three weeks have not been conducting a thorough and careful examination and evaluation.

As you well know, perhaps the greatest responsibility of a Trial Judge is sentencing. And perhaps that is a greater responsibility than other parts of judicial work. I take this responsibility very seriously in every case. . . .

This proceeding today is the result of a real tragedy, tragic because of the violence and terror and injury suffered by the Defendant's innocent victims within a short period after having been released on parole for bank robbery.

It is tragic because perhaps, for the first time, within a very short period, the Defendant has gained some insight into his violence and dangerous behavior, and may have a real desire now for rehabilitation.

It is tragic also because of the effect this has on those who have come forward in his behalf, who wish to assist him, and have faith in his state of desire for rehabilitation.

The Probation Report sums up the matter, as far as the Court is concerned.

The Probation Office contains your statement that you feel that the Defendant has serious psychiatric problems, and that you are hopeful for a 1203.03 evaluation.

That is all set forth in the probation report.

The Probation Department states, however, that the Defendant should be sentenced to State Prison, and he is dangerous, and they do not have—the Probation Office could not have the confidence in the possibility that his problems have been attended to to any extent and that he could now be released to the community.

And one last time, Mr. Gee broke in to plead his case for Danny to make it clear that staying at Walden House was not the same as "being released to the community."

The judge brushed him off like a buzzing fly: "The problem that is insurmountable, Mr. Gee," he replied, "is that the defendant was released on parole in the summer of 1973, and between that time and February, he committed three vicious, brutal attacks on unsuspecting and innocent women. I cannot say more than that."

The judge denied probation, and sentenced Danny to prison.

As one gesture toward rehabilitation, the judge ordered that not only the probation report but all the copies of the psychiatric evaluations, along with the letters and recommendations written for Danny, be forwarded to the prison. And he sentenced Danny to concurrent terms.

And when the judge said "The Defendant is remanded to the custody of the Sheriff," the drama was over.

In October 1974, soon after Danny's rape trial, one of Danielle's poems "Tomorrow's Child" was published in *Good Housekeeping*. It spoke about "our tiny precious unborn child."

Danielle Steel, the writer, was still totally unknown. It was not for five more years that *People* magazine would do a story on her, as a best-selling paperback novelist. She was still a struggling writer. But she had certainly lived with an intensity, a sheer will to survive, that gave drive, texture, and gut-wrenching emotion to the novels that came.

Chapter Nine
Now and Forever

". . . Danny was very good at adaptation . . .
with help and coaching."
—A prison friend of Danny Zugelder

Dan Zugelder left his halcyon days with Danielle behind as he trundled onto the San Francisco jail bus, rolled through the beautiful Presidio, and across the glimmering Golden Gate Bridge to San Quentin.

Could Sidney Ehrman have caught sight of this very bus as he savored his beloved view from his Presidio Heights mansion?

Would he have understood Danielle Lazard's passion for this convict while she was still married to his grandson Claude-Eric Lazard? Perhaps. In her book *Crossings*, an ancient uncle encourages Lianne to follow her heart and see a handsome young American officer while her older husband, the former French Ambassador, serves underground in Paris during World War II.

By June 13, 1974, Dan Zugelder had been fingerprinted, photographed, poked and prodded by the prison's "reception center."

He weighed in at a robust 235 pounds. He and Danielle had made quite a couple—the six-foot-five man and the five-foot-one woman, 235 pounds to 100 pounds.

But now he was behind bars. Away from women. And Dan was a model inmate.

San Quentin Penitentiary nestles in a crook of the San Francisco Bay, right under the bridge that spans the water between Marin County and the East Bay. With Alcatraz long closed, San Quentin now wore its mantle as the most fearsome lockup in California.

Other prisoners didn't take kindly to rapists, no matter how many letters were sent to their parole officers about their fine and sterling characters.

There's no telling what sort of savage retribution Danny's fellow prisoners may have taken for the brutality he had practiced on the streets of San Francisco.

But then again, he knew his way around prison, from his experience down at Lompoc.

And he worked on his body in prison, walked in his cell, built up his muscles. Some days, he would walk as much as ten miles a day, all in his cell.

He habitually did two hundred push-ups a day. He could protect himself.

He was contained in San Quentin from about June 1974 to March 1975, and worked there as a counselor and as a clerk, according to the official records later put together in Colorado.

When he got into trouble later, his records indicated ". . . Dan claims to be a professional convict, although indications are in records that he has been viewed as a loving and gentle family person. . . ." The parole officer continued: "Dan states, however, that he is also very physical both in love and in hate which always leads to difficulty whenever he becomes inebriated."

* * *

Dan Zugelder had been drinking alcoholically
when he was living with Danielle in 1974. According to the records, he had withdrawal symptoms
but not D.T.s when he was taken away from her
and put in the Walden House rehab.

But when Danny Zugelder was transferred to Vacaville—the same prison as Harvard's Dr. Timothy
Leary, the LSD prophet—he was not rehabilitated.

The Vacaville transfer buoyed their relationship,
by cutting down on the crushing anxiety Danielle
went through driving across the Golden Gate
Bridge to see her man in Marin. Visiting San
Quentin was like crossing the River Styx and finding one of Dante's rings of Hell.

By comparison, Vacaville was like driving for a
weekend at Stanford.

Bruce S., who saw Danny there, described it as
a prototype for the whole California state prison
system.

"Idyllic as possible," he said, "as many programs
as possible, like landscape architecture . . . horti-
culture."

But rehabilitation? Instead of being put into a
program like AA to get him to stop drinking for
life . . . instead of being put into a program for
violent sexual offenders and monitored on release,
so this would never happen again . . . Danny was
sent to Gestalt therapy. He could have gotten that
during weekends at Esalen.

Danny was also around Transactional Analysis,

another popular therapy of the times in California circles.

Harvard's Dr. Timothy Leary was there, remember, and because of Leary the psychology department built a video lab, videotaped psychiatric sessions and played them back for the prisoners, according to Bruce S.

Left-wing prison reformers instructed the prisoners there in the early seventies, creating the active cell of the Symbionese Liberation Army that mutated into the nucleus of the gang that kidnapped Patricia Hearst.

While Danielle mourned the lockup of Danny behind the walls of San Quentin, she was reading about Vacaville in the newspaper accounts of Patty Hearst's kidnapping.

A tiny, helpless little infant who grows up in a house with a birth father who deserts his family, a winsome little boy of four whose stepfather periodically beats him with his fists: There are deep, deep knots in the psyche that the love of a good woman and a lifetime of daily AA meetings may not solve. It's dangerous to think otherwise, as Danielle was soon to discover. The rapist's tragic flaw is a central damage, interwoven into the character development of the child and adolescent and adult.

The rapist is reenacting his childhood victimization. But this time, he is in the driver's seat. He objectifies his victim . . . the woman he savagely beats, rapes or sodomizes is simply an object in his mind. A wooden packing crate or an inflatable sex doll with a hole in the mouth and holes down below. He has a deep-seated inability to empathize with another human being as a terrified victim. This is not a fellow human being, this is HIS OBJECT. He will often say later "I don't understand why she took it so personally."

The rapist reenacts being abused as a child. Danny acted out the role of the father that once abused him. This time, he was in control. And the cries of Danny's victims were ignored, as his own cries were ignored by his stepfather.

"This is sociopathy," says one therapist. "The [rapists] are tremendous con artists. The challenge for the clinician is to find when you've hit pay dirt. You see sessions with them and they have all the jargon, [they have] good verbal abilities, but . . . they are hard to treat, inaccessible to treatment."

It is a tragedy. The rehabilitation must start with the parents of tiny infants, infants like Danny once was. To stop abuse, you have to wipe out abuse in the preceding generation, and break the cycle. You must provide intervention and support early. A child who has been abused is most likely to grow into a man who abuses his children, or rapes. A child who has not been abused has a good chance of growing into a loving father.

And it is to Danielle Steel's everlasting credit that once reaching her position of wealth and influence, she volunteered time for the National Committee for the Prevention of Child Abuse.

And she tried everything she could over the next months to understand what went wrong. She believed he was totally innocent, despite the jury trial and the guilty verdict. But what about his attack on the woman in the parking lot and the Pacific Heights attack? Wasn't she worried he might attack a friend of hers some night, jumping again from a dark doorway?

She had asked her friends to write letters for Danny, and they had. And it had not kept him out of prison. She and he wrote often, now that he was in Vacaville, still wondering if it was HER fault that Danny had taken that girl home and perhaps "gotten a little too rough."

In October of 1974, Claude-Eric Lazard and Danielle Steel were divorced. A friend blamed it on her defense of Zugelder in court. Claude-Eric Lazard prefers not to discuss his marriage or divorce.

Society wags had always gossiped that Lazard was able to get off with a quick, lump-sum divorce settlement, thanks to Danielle's passionate and public defense of Danny Zugelder. "It was an argument between [Claude-Eric] and her," said someone in the know. "In exchange for alimony, she got a big check. . . ."

Within three or four years, Danielle Lazard bought a house on Green Street in the Russian Hill neighborhood.

Now she was free to marry her prison lover.

* * *

Perhaps it was the comparative briefness of their time together that made Danny seem so dazzling. On September 13, 1975, Danielle Lazard married Danny Zugelder at Vacaville prison.

Their certificate of marriage, filed in Solano County, California, identified Danny as a resident of "California Medical Facility" at Vacaville, the official name of the prison. He indicated that he'd last worked as an "expediter" at an architectural firm (the job Danielle had set up for him) and that he'd completed school through the twelfth grade. (He got his high school equivalency diploma in prison, according to his Colorado prison records.)

His stepfather, Carl Zugelder, was born in Kansas; his mother Joyce Brown, in Oregon.

Danielle-Fernande Dominique Lazard, of 2710 Baker Street in San Francisco, filled in her occupation as "writer," her business "free-lance." She had completed school through grade fifteen—her junior year of college. And her maiden name was spelled out, "Schulein-Steel."

Her father's place of birth, Germany. Her mother's, Massachusetts.

Present to witness the marriage were J. Stephen Peek, of 1245 Fairfield, Reno, Nevada. And for the bride, Joan Patricia Tuttle of 331 Madrone Road, Larkspur, California. (Joan Patricia Tuttle would appear among the list of people she thanked in the dedication for *Now and Forever,* her 1978 novel about an innocent man accused and convicted of rape.)

Performing the ceremony was the Reverend Dale Brown, an American Baptist Minister.

It was September 13, 1975, that they took out their marriage certificate; September 13 that they took their vows.

It was a simple prison ceremony. Danielle wore white, a long-sleeved gown with glowing, transparent arms over her deep summer tan, and a high tight neckline, like a Victorian bride. She carried a simple bouquet of bridal veil and other flowers. Her hair was thick and long down her back, and on her head she wore a beautiful wide summer hat, suited for the races at Longchamps or the enclosure at Ascot. It wasn't the sort of pristine apparition the prisoners often saw floating into their orbit.

Danny beams with joy, and Danielle is laughing happily in the wedding photos, snapped by Danny's sister, Donna Monroe (and later sold by Danny's sister Donna when Danielle became rich and famous).

"Danielle was tremendously supportive," Danny later told a reporter. "We had a parole hearing set for 1976, and she thought they would cut me loose right away."

As a spouse, she could theoretically drive up for weekend conjugal visits with Danny in the married inmate housing there at Vacaville.

The marriage lasted quite long, as prison marriages go. You could see it as a poignant attempt by an innocent young girl to mesh two radically different worlds.

Why did this odd couple decide finally to marry? She still believed him innocent. She has never spoken of it, and one can only speculate. At bottom, it must have made her life in San Francisco easier: she was a young attractive single woman now. Her friends had urged her to get out and meet a suitable man. Now married, she could stay home alone, and stay up until all hours working on her books and establishing her career. There was no man to bother her day and night, no further reason for her friends to prod her. Marrying Danny may have given Danielle the peaceful stretch of time she needed to master her art.

Little more than a year later in January 1977, Danielle's second book, *Passion's Promise*, was finally published.

Publishers Weekly reviewed it on November 22, 1976:

Kezia Saint Martin is not your run-of-the-mill poor little rich girl, for Kezia *writes*. Not only a light-hearted gossip column but socially conscious journalism as well. When she interviews Lucas Johns, a devilishly attractive prison reformer, the inevitable happens and Kezia loses both her cool and her taste for the high life. She follows Lucas everywhere, gives up her own career and, when he is sent to jail on a bum rap, collapses and turns to drink. But good bloodlines always tell and Kezia's are impeccable. Before long she is recuperating at various playgrounds of the rich and thinking of taking up with Lucas's best friend. Noblesse oblige, as they say on Park Avenue.

It wasn't a rave, but Danielle Steel was already holding her own. Once again, the reviewer described a book that strongly resembled Danielle's life.

In 1978, she published *Now and Forever.* Both dedicated to Danny. And in 1979, *Season of Passion.*

Did Danielle, the lonely only child raised by her father, graduate into her fairy-tale Lazard marriage so quickly that she never went through that mushy adolescent-crush stage? Never developed a grounded sense of what was real and what was not real in the world of boys and men?

While the rest of her colleagues at Supergirls were getting engaged to their classmates, Danielle had escaped living with her father into living as a "grown-up" with an older man, Claude-Eric Lazard.

While the other Supergirls were swimming in a sea of available young men, Danielle had a daughter who was cared for by a nanny.

While other girls worried about what to wear to the Harvard-Yale game, Danielle was traveling at eighteen or nineteen from the imposing Lazard family homes in Paris, to her place in New York, and to the big Lazard or Ehrman places in San Francisco.

Danielle may not have had enough experience simply going out on dates, getting crushes, getting over them, and going on. When she fell for Danny Zugelder, maybe she couldn't really distinguish what was real and what was unreal in the intense emotions they were feeling. She could give Danny lessons in the outside things, the arcane messages of the status symbols on his Gucci loafers and her Bruno Magli shoes, the double-ply cashmere and the Cardin jackets . . . just as she'd given her little classmates lessons in Lacoste T-shirts at nine.

Though she had already given birth to a daughter, was she a grown-up yet emotionally? Or was she starving out the emotional part of her development as she isolated herself, year after year, in a self-created closed system, a world of handsome strong men and the women they protected.

Night after night, Danielle sat in her home office, typing out the pages that poured out of her.

Three of the books were built on characters remarkably like Danny, transformed by her author's imagination that sprang out of her with the energy fueled by a tragic romantic separation, Tristan and Isolde, Romeo and Juliet. The reality was that he'd gotten drunk, maybe picked up drugs again, savagely beat a woman, and had been convicted by a jury of rape.

But to read the yearning in the books, it was as if two teenagers had been separated by their strict parents, and the books had supplied a secret way to communicate to her lover, every waking minute. That was the power, the romantic intensity, she put into her novels.

They seemed written as a love offering to him.

DANIELLE STEEL 151

Writing so fast, she's told interviewers, she hopes her reader will sense the emotional urgency.

And the lover in absentia was a more congenial stand-in for the three-dimensional, time-consuming, demanding creature; the bratty little boy, the violent, angry giant that the real Danny Zugelder sometimes became.

Danielle was fighting for her life, intent on surviving as a single mother on an income from her nascent writing career. At bottom, writing to your lover was more cost-effective than living with him, emotionally. It breaks your heart less when you stay up every night banging your real dream lover, the comfy old 1940s Olympia typewriter. Your heart's desire is the treasure of discovering what you love to do, what you were built to do . . . and that's to write. That round-the-clock work created another big published novel on the heels of *Passion's Promise*. She was still driving up to Vacaville most weekends to visit her husband when *Now and Forever* was reviewed by *Publishers Weekly* on January 9, 1978.

A marriage tested to its limits is the subject of this affecting novel. Jessica and Ian Clarke, a San Francisco couple, have life's good things, love, looks, money, a secure future. She runs a boutique, he's a writer. It's a cozy world that is to be shattered when Ian is accused of rape. The slow trial process is endured, until the verdict of guilt, separating them, burdening and challenging their faith, but ultimately proving

to be a maturing experience. Reminiscent of
Helen Van Slyke, Steel, author of *Passion's Promise*, writes with integrity about a difficult subject, about the ways people face inequity, grow
and come through.

Many people are astounded when they read
about Danielle's work schedule, the hours she
keeps round the clock. She must have been taking
drugs, they snicker knowingly, talking about the
Haight-Ashbury scene, speed, disco, the seventies,
all that.

But writing can be a drug in itself: it's neat, it's
clean, it's free, and you don't have a hangover the
next day. The artist in you goes into your right
brain and it's as if you are suspended in an endless, timeless meditation.

And what a prototypical addiction for the eighties: You can step into the dream life of a romantic
heroine, and by sheer persistence and an incredibly supportive metabolism, a need for practically
no sleep, brilliant organizing skills, self-discipline,
and a touch of good timing, become a very rich
woman who is in turn able to create that fantasy
life in the real world.

Danny's story continued to be that his accuser
had picked HIM up but maybe "he got too aggres-
sive for her."

"He was . . . a big lovable teddy bear." That was

the opinion of a friend, Bruce S., who visited him in Vacaville.

"Last time I saw her," said Bruce S., "I had to look twice . . . she was dressed like the Weather Underground . . . it didn't look like her so dressed-down. She's gorgeous, she has an aura about her. . . .

"The two of them gave off a lot of energy.

"In a sense," he continued, "the inmates were able to have intercourse . . . [a woman visitor] could sit on her boyfriend's lap. But Danielle was always the lady.

"Most marriages, after the first year, 60% of the people get divorced . . . In prison, a guy there faces death, day in, day out, you never know from day to day . . . and growing up there created a philosophy like Manson's . . .

"You'd never think he'd committed a felony."

But things weren't easy for him in San Francisco, his friends understood. "Inside [the walls of prison], it's death every minute almost . . . [With Danielle, it's] which fork? When does he open doors? Are people being nice, or are they ignoring you?" said Bruce. He even took him out to the French Consulate once, he claimed.

Bruce S. said that Danielle had gotten Danny the job with the architects to make the relationship look better—"all of a sudden this convict was there."

"But Danny was very good at adaptation . . . with help and coaching."

Bruce compared Danielle to Norman Mailer

writing *In the Belly of the Beast* about Jack Abbott. "Jack Abbott, who ended up stabbing a guy," says the former Vacaville inmate Bruce S.

But after months and months of visiting him at Vacaville, the trips dropped off, and then finally stopped. Danielle had found another man, Bill Toth.

Leaving Danny was a complete about-face from the happy ending of her novel *Now and Forever*. Her fictional tale of an innocent man imprisoned for rape was well-reviewed. The verdict, wrote *Publishers Weekly*, challenged the couple's faith in their love, "but ultimately proved to be a maturing experience." Danny seems to have been devastated by Danielle's request for a divorce.

Dan Zugelder could not contest the divorce. He tried to kill himself.

Chapter Ten
To Love Again

And you *empathic* people with the Great Hearts . . . there ain't no ex-addicts that need your sympathy. Okay? 'Cause they aren't all better yet. They're still suffering from psychiatry and social work, which means they're looking to *use* you—socially, sexually, financially—every way they can.

    —John Maher, head of Delancey Street, speaking to visitors to the rehab, 1974

Danny Zugelder tried to kill himself at Vacaville prison when Danielle said she was divorcing him.

After Danielle's public support at his rape trial in the summer of 1974, she and Claude-Eric Lazard moved forward with their divorce in October 1974.

Claude-Eric and Danielle had been married almost ten years by then. According to someone who knows the Lazard side well she got a big check instead of alimony."

Perhaps that's where she got the money to buy a house on Green Street, because in 1977, she wasn't really making that kind of money at all from her writing.

And when she moved into her own little half-million plus jewel box of a house on Green Street, she fell for her moving man.

His name was Bill Toth, and he was a resident of Delancey Street, a rehabilitation program for hard-core drug users and ex-convicts. The moving company was Delancey Street's.

Bill Toth would soon be husband #3.

And while friends had described Danielle as "struggling" when she was living in the rented apartment, those struggling days were coming to an end.

The day after her divorce from Danny Zugelder in 1978, she married Bill Toth. She gave birth to their child about two weeks later.

And she kept on writing. "She was always more interested in her career, and that destroyed [Danny Zugelder]" said a friend of Danny's.

Toth himself was an only child, just like Danielle.

His father Nicholas was a life-insurance salesman and his mother stayed home to take care of the house at One Diaz Street. He'd been raised in San Francisco, where he went to parochial schools before heading off to Santa Clara University.

But by 1967 he dropped out of Santa Clara and began doing drugs—LSD, hashish, heroin.

By 1971 he was a junkie. He started stealing to support his heroin habit. And after a series of arrests, he was lucky enough to be admitted to Delancey Street in 1975.

"We're just as selective as Berkeley, Stanford and Harvard," says Mimi Silbert, who began the Delancey program with the late John Maher. They only chose the hard-core addict criminals that they believed were salvageable.

When Danielle moved to her new house on Green Street—on the Russian Hill made so famous by Armistead Maupin's book *Tales of the City*—she discovered her own new personal rehabilitation project. It lay closer to home than Vacaville prison. Delancey Street, or more specifically, her favorite rehabilitation resident, Bill Toth, drew her attention.

In fact, this rehab—a halfway house for criminal alcoholic/addicts—had its headquarters in Pacific Heights, right in the middle of San Francisco's upper-class residential neighborhood in the old Mein Mansion, the former Russian Consulate. On a clear day, you could see the Golden Gate Bridge all the way to the Oakland Airport far beyond the Bay Bridge.

Delancey Street was home to ex-cons who desperately needed some structure and family in their lives to break the losing cycle of parole/drugs/robbery/jail, parole/drugs/robbery/jail.

The leader of Delancey Street was a purebred genius from the streets, John Maher. Maher was a charismatic speaker with a Bronx accent and a partner, Mimi Silbert, PhD, who had worked as a prison psychologist and had trained policemen and probation officers. By the mid-seventies Mimi Silbert had become an acknowledged part of the Delancey Street power structure.

CBS's Morley Safer did a piece for *60 Minutes* on this news-making rehab. Steering a course between being too soft on criminals and too antiquated in prison's punishment techniques, John Maher had a third approach, said Morley Safer— "criminals who have decided to heal each other."

Maher, an ex-junkie himself, explained to Safer that "Social victims are generally pretty dangerous, nasty characters because we're pretty twisted, and we gotta untwist ourselves, so we're human beings instead of animals. . . .

"We're caught in this bind between right-wing nuts . . . and . . . vicarious thrill, radical chic creepos who want to kiss your backside, until you're almost a schizo. A lot of our people understand this . . . but at the same time we are taking personal responsibility for our own change."

Delancey Street was tightly interwoven with contemporary politics on a local level: Richard Hongisto, the sheriff, Danielle Steel's friend while she was living with Danny Zugelder, was also a friend of Delancey Street, as was Mayor Moscone.

The judge in Danny Zugelder's rape trial hailed them and Walden House, for the excellent work they did with ex-cons on parole.

One reason Delancey Street swung so much weight politically was because they had a collection of cars. There was an open-topped double-decker bus with polished brass fittings. There was an MG sports car. A glorious old 1935 Bentley. A motor home. Trucks for the moving company. Vehicles and even more vehicles. Delancey Streeters were organized to get out the vote, and deliver it, if need be, in the buses, or even the backseat of the Bentley. Their voluntary Democratic and Republican political clubs had over two hundred canvassers that were ready to fan out into the streets for their candidates.

And their connections reached as high as soon-to-be-President Jimmy Carter—in 1974, a framed photo of Delancey's John Maher with Carter hung in the hallway of the Mein Street mansion. There was other photos of John with Ron Dellums of the Black Political Caucus; with Governor Docking of Kansas; with Dr. Karl Menninger.

Delancey helped establish the Prisoners' Union to give voice to the prison reform movement within the prisons. These were the people to go to when you wanted to find out about prison reform. Despite all the talk about Danny Zugelder being "active in prison reform," research hasn't come up with any iota of evidence of Zugelder's reform involvement.

Delancey Street had terrific political antennae. And they stayed away from any governmental funding, and thus escaped any governmental bureaucracy and red tape.

By 1993, John Maher was dead, but President Clinton called upon his partner, Mimi Silbert, to advise him on how to rehabilitate criminal addicts—a problem that had blossomed and grown wild in the twenty years plus since Delancey first started.

After twenty-three years of resisting any federal involvement, Mimi Silbert was tapped by Lee Brown, Clinton's drug czar, to help model programs on Delancey. After twenty-three years, their method of rebuilding ruined lives in a concentrated, family atmosphere was still paying dividends. Rather than dumping ex-cons on the street, Delancey continued to teach both personal responsibility and accountability.

When Bill Toth got that job moving Danielle's furniture in 1977, Delancey Street was already radical chic—woven into the social fabric of Pacific Heights. The stodgy old socialites were against them, said John Maher.

"Our eviction is pursued by a small group," he explained, "of recent descendents of horse thieves and robber barons who had pretensions to being San Francisco's equivalent of the Hapsburgs."

Add the bright young socialites were for it.

The Radical Chic phenomenon actually angered Delancey Street's chief, when it came to women dating the men he was trying to straighten out in the program.

Listen to a Delancey leader talking to one woman dating a former junkie/jailbird—just like Danielle was—at one of their encounter groups, called Games. Games were open to visitors twice a week. Jo, a divorcée around thirty (just about Danielle's age back then) is dating a Delancey guy who's done five years in San Quentin for armed robbery.

Jo's complaint about her Delancey boyfriend? They had a date to meet at five. She called, and he said he was on his way over. By seven, still no show. So at eight, she called again, then took the Delancey jitney across the bridge to their Sausalito housing complex. Then he said he just wanted to go to sleep.

Bernardo, Jo's boyfriend, blows his cool when she calls him on the way he's been treating her. He slams his fist on the table, which breaks an ashtray and then a coffee cup, and debris flies everywhere. "OK!" he shouts. "We'll call it off. Finished! Forget the whole relationship." Big drama.

The leaders in the Game explain to Jo that it's okay for him to regress, that it's just a Game. Bernardo was like this *all the time*, they explain, just eighteen months ago. They turn to her, and ask her point-blank just what she's doing dating someone in Delancey, and why.

". . . we're wondering if you're not on some save-a-sickie kick. I mean, you're already divorced. You've turned thirty. Your kid, even if she doesn't need a papa, needs a mother who's not anguished all the time. Why are you spending the twilight of your eligible years chasing after losers? You college educated girls—I'm sorry *women*—are always talking admiringly about 'prisoner's consciousness.' Are you sure it's not prisoner's prick? Is there something that *thrills* you about *macho* characters who used to point guns at people and Jimmy Cagney imitations?"

Jo laughs and says she really doesn't think so. The reality is that he can be "tender, considerate, and fun to be with most of the time, and then suddenly I don't know him, like tonight."

Another visitor who's dating a Delancey resident

explains that "they lean on each other, then practice on us to see if they're ready for the wider world."

Then one of the residents gets angry. "I think we're being too soft with this lady," he said. "There's a sweet smell of martyrdom around you, Jo. How come you wait *four hours* for this punk? Next time, give him fifteen minutes or keep him waiting. Don't you know the junkie mentality yet? We *always* want something for nothing! The needle in the arm is so we can get the sensations without the emotional risks!"

Jo's complaint about her Delancey guy was just like the complaints threaded through some of Danielle's books influenced by this period . . . men who become different people, who worry their women sick with anxiety. Men who aren't reliable. And later, men who take drugs, men who are scary. Men who threaten to hit women.

Delancey Street had rules, and moving in with a woman was breaking the rules. And Bill Toth, who calls himself a "middle-class ex-con," still hasn't made it back into straight society—he's been in and out of jail since his run-in with Danielle. On and off heroin and alcohol.

Danielle called Delancey Street to get an estimate for her move to the new house. He was happy to oblige. She seemed interested. There were vibes between them; "a mutual attraction," says Bill.

"I moved her from where she was living at 2710 Baker Street to 1025 Green." It was up Russian

Hill between Leavenworth and Jones. He was still in Delancey, then headquartered in the big mansion on Broadway and Division.

They went out on a few dates, and within several months, Danielle became pregnant.

Then, according to Bill, Delancey Street fired him from his job and transferred him to a much less desirable spot.

He'd been living in the poolside apartments Delancey had set up for residents over in Sausalito, across the Golden Gate. Residents shuttled back and forth on the group's buses.

After Delancey took away his job as head of the moving company, he left. He moved in with Danielle.

His old parish priest was running Eddy Street Boys' Home for the Catholic Social Services, a facility of the City of San Francisco for "Abused, Neglected and Abandoned Boys" from ages seven to seventeen. The priest got him a job as "counselor/warden," continues Bill, and that's why Danielle told *People* magazine in the 1970's that she was "married to drug and alcohol counselor Bill Toth."

"It was all right," he says of his job with the Boys' Home, "it was a job.

"Then she's eight months pregnant. Before we could get married, she had to divorce [Danny Zugelder]. It was probably uncontested. What could he do?

"So we're living together and she's pregnant . . . gets a divorce from him, and two weeks before the

[baby] arrives, we get married." The baby, a boy was named Nicholas for Toth's father.

When they were first dating, says Bill, "we had regular people as friends. Then she started to make it big. The first book [the novelization of the move *The Promise*] started to take off.

"She got $10,000 to do the promo book for a movie [*The Promise*]. If it sells over a million, she gets another $10,000. 'Think I should do it?' she asks me.

"The movie's a flop," Bill continues, "the book sells three million copies. From that point on, Dell was beating down her door.

"She's not big on loyalty," says Bill. "Phyllis Westberg was her agent then." Danielle's agent is now Mort Janklow.

"At this time we had friends who weren't exclusively San Francisco society . . . just people . . . mostly her friends. A private airline pilot. A woman who was black who was a TV reporter. Friends from Beatrix's [private school].

"Her daughter Beatrix was a pretty neat kid. So Danielle was a good mom.

"She goes on these talk shows, a wonderful woman who happens to be a success with nine kids. In reality, that's a bunch of crap. She's got maids, nannies. She had this NEED. . . . I stayed up with the baby all night. When the baby started to cry, the fingers started to SNAP."

While Danielle was coming out to visit with Sidney Ehrman and the Lazard family in the 1960s,

Bill Toth was a hippie. "The closest Danielle ever got to the Haight-Ashbury," he says, "is driving through it in a limousine."

His first real high was surfing down at Pacifica, an ocean beach on the peninsula, or at another spot up north of Bolinas. Bill was proud of having the second of the small boards to come out in northern California—the new short surfboards made by Australian Bob McTavish, with a bottom molded like a "V." He had a strong, wiry body, and he took to the waves like a natural.

Surfers were a society unto themselves in the sixties, living the hippie life before the word hippie even started to gain currency. Surfers could take off for a beach town, rent themselves a garage for something like $20 a month, and move in. Furnishing it wasn't any more expensive: They'd just "find" furniture here and there, on the street, or sometimes, in someone else's house.

If money was needed, it could be scrounged up. The surfing life was surely more fun than living at home with the parents. The sweet dulcet tones of the Beach Boys popularized the surfer life across the United States, but by the time people in Kansas heard about the life, the real surfers were getting mean, listening to Mick Jagger and the Rolling Stones. And their drugs were getting meaner, too.

Bill, like lots of the surfers and hippies before him, got into trouble with drugs and alcohol. He started getting picked up by the police for drugs, and was in and out of jail.

But when he hit into Delancey Street, he became

a star. The moving company was the premier money-maker for the program. Everybody in the Delancey family looked up to the dude that ran the moving company, because he put the food in their mouths, and kept the roof over their heads.

He and Danielle went back to New York to meet her Schulein family. Bill Toth described Danielle's father as "short, maybe 5′6″ and understood him to be German to the core.

Danielle's grandmother Omi, Bill explained, was an early and successful investor in Standard Brands, picking it up at $2 and watching it rise and rise and rise. The story, perhaps apocryphal, was that Danielle's father had neglected to pay income taxes, and the government was after him for lots of money. He borrowed that amount from Omi to pay off the government, but spent it instead. Then he borrowed it again.

But when Omi died, everything went to Danielle's father, John, the only child. John sold off everything, according to Bill. All the things from Munich, the furniture, and the paintings that had been in the brewers' extended family.

Whether these things truly happened, or whether they were the elements of the plot that Danielle was working out in conversations with Bill, is unsure. But her novel *Loving* seems to have many of the same themes as her stories of growing up with her daddy. A reviewer for *Publishers Weekly* summarized it:

Bettina Daniels's four marriages all seem like desperate attempts to fill the void when her demanding and hugely successful father dies, leaving her at 19 to straighten out the family's bankrupt finances.

Her father's best friend, three times her age, is her first spouse, and serves as the thoughtful, understanding father-figure she never had.

But their age difference is too much of an obstacle; next she replaces one bad marriage to an opportunistic British actor with another to a staid, callous doctor.

Bettina changes lifestyles frequently and effortlessly, but finally is able to define herself when her first play is successfully produced on Broadway.

A poor-little-rich-girl story with all the trappings of designer clothes, chic New York restaurants, Soho lofts, Mill Valley housewifery and Broadway glamour, this makes a nice fantasy for those who wish to indulge their imaginations, and who won't be frustrated by the fact that Steel never gets inside Bettina's pretty little head.

He was only sixty-four, Danielle's father, when *The New York Times* noted his death. John Schulein-Steel died in 1978, "husband of Kuniko, father of Danielle, and grandfather of Beatrix and Nicholas." Services were held at Frank E. Campbell on Madison Avenue and 81st, Friday May 19th, near his apartment at 1160 Fifth. Luckily, Danielle and her husband Bill Toth had been able to get together with him before he died.

John Schulein-Steel's last will and testament had been written on March 22, 1976, and witnessed by three men. It asked that no religious service be performed at the interment, at Woodlawn Cemetery, in the Bronx. The executors were his wife, Kuniko Nakamura and his attorney. As for the inheritance, Kuniko Schulein-Steel was award three-fourths of his property, the remaining quarter going to Danielle.

John Schulein-Steel's will also requested, but did not direct, that Danielle allow Kuniko's family to chose any Japanese objects of art that may have been part of his estate.

His grave rests in the Wild Rose Plot under the same tombstone with his parents. Engraved in the granite marker are their names and dates: 12-24-1881 Julius 4-20-1959, 8-16-1893 Minni Laura 11-27-1970, 1-26-1914 John H. Schulein-Steel 5-17-1978.

During her marriage to Bill Toth, and this period of deep grieving after her father's early death, Danielle buried herself in her writing room and turned out novels. Writing was her way to escape the feelings of grief and the fear of having to support the family on a freelance writer's salary.

During the time she was married to Bill Toth, from May 1978 to March 1981, Danielle would publish eight books: *The Promise* (1978), *Summer's End* (1980) *To Love Again* (1980), *Loving* (1980), *The Ring* (1980), *Love Poems* (1981), and *A Perfect Stranger* (1981) Among these would be her first million copy first printing (*To Love Again*), her first collection of poetry (*Love Poems*), and her first hardcover, which was also her first historical, *The Ring*, which was dedicated to Bill Toth.

Bill Toth says Danielle was more "mellow" back then.

Danielle and Bill gave dinner parties at the new house on Green Street and had a circle of friends they enjoyed. "From my point of view, she started to change. San Francisco society became more and more important to her.

"Danielle . . . I'm attracted to strong women, so it was great with me. Run the whole show, fine. But every once in a while, I'd say NO.

"And she'd FLIP OUT!

"She's got to be in control. Wear the pants. Run the whole show," says Bill.

"Fine," he says, "I'm lazy. My manhood wasn't threatened."

One of the books Danielle published during her marriage to Bill was a collection of the poetry she had published in women's magazines. *Love Poems* was reviewed in *Publishers Weekly* in December 1980.

Written in the first person, the poems are emotional, often dramatic.

The initial poems express the rapture of falling in love, of waiting for her lover to call or appear.

Following these are poems telling of love grown cold, of princes turned to toads, of the heartache of lost love.

Steel's closing poems are of a cheerier nature, concerned with finding true love at last and with giving birth to a child. Bearing such titles as "Moonlit Sunshine," "Crying Rainbows," "Champagne in My Shoes," these are sweet snippets that sometime run to sticky. They will undoubtedly hit home with Steel fans.

Bill explained that as Danielle became more successful, the "romance novels" became "contemporary romantic fiction" and "she was bugging them to do hardback—a sign you've made it. . . .

"When the big money started coming in, VAMPIRES descended out of the night. Telling her what they thought she'd want to hear. Kissing her ass. Pumping her ego up.

"We had one maid. She lived there on Green Street in the maid's quarters in the basement. There were three bedrooms upstairs, and one bath up; a big kitchen, dining room and living room downstairs.

"I built a little office for her. I planned it, and other guys did the work. Off the bedroom.

"She goes into this hibernation for three weeks. I'd bring her her meals. Drag her from the typewriter to go to sleep. She'd knock 'em out in three weeks."

But there was a certain problem on and off with Bill's drugs and drinking. "She's a total square," claims Bill. "Doesn't drink. No drugs whatsoever. I started using drugs again."

Chapter Eleven
The Promise: Bill Toth and Danielle Steel

There is a story that goes like this . . . .

The publisher of Delacorte Books, Carole Baron, asked her best-selling writer Danielle Steel what she'd like for her birthday. "A billboard," Danielle is said to have replied. A billboard on Sunset Boulevard, in fact, right across from Spago. Spago, continues the story, is the favorite dining place of Jackie Collins—then another bright and shining star in superagent Mort Janklow's stable— and of her sister, Joan Collins, then a star in *Dynasty*. Almost immediately the huge poster was up, featuring a beautiful portrait of Danielle Steel, and the heading "America Reads Danielle Steel," placed IN THEIR FACE, as they say in Hollywood, exactly where the studio producers, executives, and media stars could see it as they dined at Spago. Danielle Steel had come a long way.

Imagine that something like this happened:

It was the late seventies. The 747 nonstop jetting in from San Francisco was crouching down for a landing, landing gear clumping down. Danielle grabbed Bill's shoulder in both fear of flying terror and sheer excitement at being back—making her successful reentry to Manhattan, that glittering Baghdad-by-the-Hudson city where she grew up, went to school and college, experienced her first marriage, the birth of her first child, and her first job.

It was the 1978 "novelization" of a movie called *The Promise* that gave Danielle the leg up she needed for billboard status in Hollywood. *The Promise* became Danielle's entrée to the high-stakes, high-profile world of New York publishing and promotion. And her husband Bill Toth was the man at her elbow.

Imagine that something like this happened:

Danielle and Bill Toth were coming in for a landing in New York City. Danielle was wearing something like a mink toque, let's imagine—or was it a sable scarf?—wonderful gray gabardine slacks and a luscious cashmere sweater, a double-ply from Scotland, her favorite Gucci shoes perhaps, a good "Kelly" bag from Hermès, and significant, but not outrageous, Real Jewelry.

Bill, the down-home guy that he was, was wearing, let's imagine, his favorite worn loafers, a well-worn brown leather belt with a brass buckle, a pair of chinos, a cowboy-cut shirt and a good Pierre Cardin blazer that Danielle bought him to add a bit of stature to his closet. (Cardin was a favorite of her male characters back then.) The stewardess might have frowned before Bill stubbed out the last cigarette for Danielle and swirled the melting ice cubes in his drinks glass. "Never mind, babe," he reassured both her and himself, "everything's gonna be cool, we'll be on the ground in a couple minutes."

Out the windows, the majestic skyline of Manhattan made its presence felt—the Empire State Building, the glimmer and throb of Broadway, the World Trade Center—and uptown, the darkness that was Central Park.

She already looked the part of the world's bestselling novelist. And she hadn't even had a bestseller yet.

No one young was wearing hats in the late 1970s, no one except Danielle. And she wouldn't even have made it to New York comfortably if it hadn't been for the Fear of Flying school she'd attended back in San Francisco, and that triumphant San Francisco to Los Angeles flight the graduates took to validate their lessons. She was both ecstatic and bubbly after getting her "flying certificate."

But now the ambivalence she'd shown toward doing book promotion no longer had the fear-of-flying as a reason.

And here she was, nearing the heart of Manhattan in the backseat of a quiet black limousine, we'll imagine, sent by the publisher, and heading uptown to the very private Carlyle hotel, where John F. Kennedy once kept a suite. Danielle now had

two published paperback originals under her belt—
1973's *Going Home,* 1976's *Passion's Promise*—but now,
she was finally reentering New York City officially
for a big publicity splash for 1978's novelization,
The Promise.

The Promise wasn't just another romance novel,
paperback original, published and released to the
hinterlands, then forgotten. In fact, *The Promise*
wasn't called a novel at all. Officially, it was that
strange creature called a "novelization." *The Promise* was the key element in a marketing play by Universal MCA to help their movie *The Promise* achieve
blockbuster status.

Universal MCA figured on promoting the movie
as being "based on the best-selling novel by
Danielle Steel." Even though no one had really
heard of Danielle then, the power of the movie
company's publicity and marketing machine, combined with her smooth writing, might possibly,
with a lot of good luck, propel this book to the
best-seller list.

This was an early experiment in the "synergy"
theory so popular in corporate conglomerates today—publishing books promoting motion pictures,
and vice versa.

The tie-in: it was Hollywood's gift to the stodgy
old book business. In Danielle's case it involved
hundreds of thousands of mass-market paperback
originals flooding the market, and heavy-impact

television and newspaper advertising as well as the promos for the motion picture itself.

Universal was the first Hollywood studio to actually set up its own separate division for "novelizations."

Their first big hit was *Jaws II,* published by Bantam in 1978. It sold three million copies.

Writers weren't expected to collect royalties from these down-and-dirty deals.

This novelization was the first time Danielle Steel's writing was promoted so heavily. *The Promise* was an immediate success, and ran through its first printing of two million copies by the end of 1979.

The screenplay on which the novel and the movie was based tells of a young man (played by Stephen Collins) and a woman (Kathleen Quinlan), deeply in love. They plan to marry, until the girl is in a terrible car accident. His evil mother (Beatrice Straight) pays the girl, now horribly disfigured, to go away. She gets a new face from a plastic surgeon (Laurence Luckinbill). Their paths cross again, and he falls in love with the old girl's new face. In spite of the impressive cast and direction by Gil Cates, today dean of the UCLA School of Theater, Film and Television, former head of the Directors Guild (he would go on to produce the Academy Awards), the movie died a quick death.

But Danielle's novelization—based on a screenplay by Garry Michael White—went on to sell over three million copies.

Dell pulled out all the stops: *The Promise* was published with two different covers, one beige, one pink. *The Promise* was very appealing to the wide cross section of women who'd made *Love Story* a runaway hit earlier—with *Love Story* the book, Yale Professor Erich Segal's romantic tale, and *Love Story*, the 1970 movie, a thirties-style tearjerker dressed up with sixties-style words.

How did Danielle Steel manage to snare the job of writing *The Promise*?

Dell knew there would be a lot of muscle and money behind this book, thanks to Universal, and they looked at their lists of up-and-coming romance novelists to pluck just the writer whose career might be made with a promotion budget this big.

Danielle's name came up, and despite certain questions, she made the savvy decision to take the reported $10,000 to write the novelization, in the hopes that her name would be placed before the public. After all, her *first* novel *Going Home*, had only sold for a reported $3,500, and her second hadn't sold for much more than double that. But she had several books under her belt now, published and unpublished. She knew she was addicted to the process of writing.

With her 1978 marriage to Bill Toth, her live-in housekeeper, and her new house on Russian Hill, Danielle could write in spurts of up to eighteen hours a day.

She'd burrow away in the tiny office Toth designed for her, nesting in a flannel nightgown, and just blast on through, eating off little trays left by the door if she remembered to eat at all. She couldn't escape, once she'd started: In the bathroom; she wrote on the walls, on the mirror.

Danielle was probably still ambivalent about doing promotion on the book. But as her car pulled up to the warm lights under the crisp white-and-gold canopy of the Carlyle hotel and the doorman snapped to attention, she was happy she'd decided to return to Manhattan in style.

Aware of her fear of flying, her publishers thought she was very brave to undertake the grueling flight. Dressed the role of the blockbuster-to-be romance novelist, Danielle swept into the Dell offices, and arranged to meet with Bill Grose, the man who put the deal together.

Danielle met with the troops—the front-line people who'd be promoting her and her book. And she brought them all little presents, things like silver bangles and necklaces and little trinkets—none of that silver plate stuff—all as "thank yous" for the work they'd be doing for her.

Everyone just loved it. They thought she was a very generous young woman. And thoughtful.

And even back then, she definitely had The Look—an image about her that said she was somehow older and more sophisticated, certainly more sophisticated in outward appearance, than the other twenty-nine- and thirty-year-olds at Dell. Her hair was always up; wonderful, rich, dark long hair.

Women guessed at a wild streak in her, knotted

up in that great long hair. But then, as now, on the back cover of all her paperbacks, the hair is up, knotted.

The jewels were the real stuff. This was unheard of in the halls of publishing.

Was it Danielle's European background? Working Americans didn't go much for jewels. The people at Dell thought Danielle was French. In reality, she was American, German-Portuguese, and had gone to school in New York City. But hadn't Danielle, they thought, said she was educated in France? Schooled in Europe? Attended something that sounded Continental? The troops figured this Frenchness must have been the explanation for her superb panache. It was all rather unclear, but she drew attention in the—face it—stodgy world of publishing.

All Danielle's publishing parties featured John Mack Carter on the guest list. The editor of *Ladies' Home Journal* was the celebrity she always invited, and the biggest name in publishing she seemed to know back then. Her friendship with Carter went back to her Supergirl days. Her first novel, *Going Home,* had a warm and wonderful male women's magazine editor that seemed modeled on Carter. He's someone she's thanked many times for encouraging her to write, to go to San Francisco, buckle herself down in front of her typewriter, and hit the keys. He was among the fourteen dedicatees in *Going Home.*

A publisher often paid for a quiet black limousine to shuttle writers from spot to spot during the

pressured days of a book promotion. A writer had
to hit nine or ten interviews, radio shows, local
television shows, breakfasts, drinks, interviews,
lunches, cocktail parties, and dinners, all crammed
into one day.

But publishers were never known to pay for the
supreme luxury of a place like The Carlyle for an
unknown writer, where the price of a suite for one
day was about a week's salary for a secretary.

Danielle would invite the people from Dell and
anyone she knew in town to little parties at the
Carlyle suite, and they'd grow and grow each time.
Sometimes her daughter Beatrix—called Bede Lazard—would be there, quiet and well-behaved, very
well-mannered. And somewhere in the background
would be a quiet and well-behaved, very well-mannered nanny of some kind.

Danielle never spoke about Beatrix's father,
Claude-Eric Lazard, to any of the publishing people or journalists. She was "just wild about Bill"
during these years, according to someone who
knew her then.

But wasn't she scrambling for money to keep her
little family together? It's the recurrent theme of
these early books. "I certainly didn't get that impression," said someone who knew her then. "I
think she's just very compulsive about writing."

But publishing people noticed how very different Bill and Danielle seemed: She had all this chic
polish, a European aura, and he was this down-
home guy, perhaps a construction worker . . . and
much more all-American. But that didn't matter a

whit. She could have been married to the King of Siam for all they cared. Their job was to get her as much press as they could.

Unfortunately, *People* magazine and the New York papers weren't much interested at that time. It wasn't until after *The Promise* hit the best-seller list that they'd even bat an eye in her direction. "There was no book," they'd say. (Of course, after *The Promise* hit, *People* ran a nice piece about her, her writing, and Bill and their baby and their life in San Francisco.)

For Valentine's Day, Dell hosted a fabulous romantic party for Danielle Steel in the Crystal Room at the Tavern on the Green in Central Park.

Danielle gave them a guest list, but there weren't that many people there. "The room was sort of empty," said a guest.

The publishing people sent Danielle off to a book autographing event, but since she hadn't built a following for her romance novels yet, it was quite painful. Only three or four people showed up. But she was charming to each of them, totally professional, in this, one of the hardest rituals publishing has to offer.

The book people never heard a thing about her two previous husbands.

With Dell, in the beginning, it was always just BILL, and how wonderful BILL was, and how terribly in love with BILL she was. And she was!

Those working with Danielle saw she was always

wonderfully affectionate and loving with him in the midst of all the publicity pressures in New York City.

Danielle was very gracious, very accommodating once she'd convinced herself that the strain of doing promotion would help her career.

On the one hand, she had a conflict: saying things along the lines of "oh, no, don't promote me, nobody knows who I am and it will be embarrassing." But when she finally agreed to promote, she did it with a great flourish. *Season of Passion,* probably written during this period of promo for *The Promise,* tells it all:

Kate, the heroine, has just sent off a novel to her publisher. Clearing the decks, Kate tells her good friend Felicia that she's finished it, now it's the publisher's job to sell it. Kate doesn't really want to do any promotion that makes her "uncomfortable."

Fooey, says her friend, this is your shot to capitalize on a hit so your next book will sell even *more,* and you'll become a recognized name on the bestseller lists. You've seen the ads for the book, but now how about sticking your neck out and doing some publicity appearances?

And just a few pages later, Kate's checked into the Beverly Hills Hotel and is about to do something like the Johnny Carson show. No sooner has Kate's book hit then her little boy Tyge wants to run away from home; the perfect time for her New York agent to call, telling her she's got to do another publicity tour, to spend a week in Manhattan to keep the novel riding high on the best-seller lists.

Don't go, says her man. But I know you will, he continues, "because you've always been suckered into that whole horseshit game of success." (This is just the way Bill Toth would put it.) In the book, she goes off to New York and checks into the Regency. Something any self-supporting woman with a single child and a serious career would have to do. Not a "horseshit" game of success at all.

And in New York, *Publishers Weekly* reviewed that title in December 1978:

Beautiful, naive Kate is in her first year at Stanford when she meets and falls in love with pro-football star Tom Harper. Her parents disown her when she drops out of college and marries Tom.

He turns 30 and can't accept the fact that his career is on the wane.

He becomes a heavy drinker and eventually shoots himself, causing severe brain damage that leaves him with the mentality of a six-year-old. Kate places him in a sanitarium and poses as a widow as she has Tom's baby and leads a hermetic existence.

She begins to write: After six years she publishes a best-selling novel about football that changes her life.

She agrees to promote the book on TV and falls in love with the show's producer, a flawless character. Although Kate is reluctant to tell him about Tom, the truth finally comes out. Love prevails, making for a predictably happy ending to this warm if occasionally slow-moving tale by the author of *The Promise*.

In real life, she wasn't the Danielle Steel that she is now. It was very early in her career, and Dell was trying to build her into a name writer. Dell hoped that by making *The Promise* a best-seller she would be catapulted into stardom. And she was.

It wasn't that her publishers felt that she needed the money. They didn't care about that. It was just that she was so compulsive about writing. The women who worked with her marveled at the hours she put in. "You just can't hold that woman down!" they'd joke among themselves at the publishers, as they struggled to keep up with her.

Back then she was still writing at night, alone in the dark, from something like ten P.M. straight through to three or four A.M.

The books were just pouring out of her. She wrote poetry. *Cosmopolitan, Ladies' Home Journal, Good Housekeeping, McCall's* published it. Dell published it in a paperback book, first reviewed in 1980, *Love Poems*. They saw her as sort of a romantic flower—a frail, romantic blossom who loved to read poems. And these romantic novels were just a natural outgrowth of her essential being.

Today, except for John Grisham, whom everybody's talking about, she and Stephen King are the best-known novelists in the world. All Danielle

Steel's paperbacks today are wrapped with a gold band, declaring "America's #1 Bestseller." It's mind-boggling, say those who knew her then. But of all her earlier novels, *The Promise* was the most popular, it garnered the most fan mail—and strangely enough, the romantic plot was concocted by a *man*.

The Promise introduced the American public to something entirely new: "The Danielle Steel novel." It was a little like the Jacqueline Susann phenomenon. Susann had died in 1974 as the most successful mass-market writer of the 1960s and 1970s. Danielle Steel told *Good Housekeeping* in 1974 that Susann was the writer she most admired when growing up. Later, she rescinded that comment, explaining she merely admired her *success:* Susann's book *Valley of the Dolls* had sold more than twenty-two million copies in paperback.

In the late seventies, there really were no books out in the market that were like Danielle's. There was something called "category" romances—they were 192-page paperbacks from places like Harlequin or Silhouette, books that were numbered and came out in a series. There were the so-called "mainstream romances," a single-title book, either hardcover or soft, that wasn't part of a brand-name series.

But Danielle was writing "contemporary" love stories that no one else was doing. Totally unique.

People in the book business started seeing that her books always had a heroine that you could identify with—maybe she'd made mistakes, but she was very sweet inside. Maybe she'd suffered, but in the end she always got her man. They took place in a lovely setting like San Francisco. And her writing didn't have the hard edge of Harold Robbins or Jackie Susann, the monarchs of the 1970s, nor any of the trashy sex or the vengeful motives.

Everything was a question of timing for Danielle Steel. And hers was perfect. She was the ideal woman for the upcoming 1980s.

Prices were going up in publishing.

"You won't find a lot of these writers sitting in attics these days. You'll find them sitting in their big houses on their big estates. Or in their Rolls-Royces," said Oscar Dystel, former chief of Bantam Books.

Because of the huge profits to be made with brand-name writers (whose books could be almost guaranteed best-sellers) publishers started to focus on potential producers of best-selling novels, and with *The Promise,* the eyes of Dell fell upon Danielle Steel.

It was also a time when the power of the old-line hardcover houses was giving way to the marketing clout of the mass-market paperback publishers.

Phyllis Westberg, her first agent, was a member of the very old and highly esteemed Harold Ober literary agency in New York.

But another new power was also emerging in the literary world, and that was the Superagent. Witness the $3 million-plus sale of the paperback rights for Judith Krantz's *Princess Daisy*. Behind it, superagent Mort Janklow.

Often trained as lawyers, the superagents used their adversarial skills to negotiate the best deals for author-clients.

Before such agents came on the scene, Janklow explained to a reporter, ". . . writers were being treated like children by publishers. Nobody told them anything. . . ." And, Janklow added, the publishers didn't even really know or appreciate it when they had a best-selling author like Danielle Steel under contract. "They feel they *need* someone to tell them they've got great judgement. They *need* to have the *Ladies' Home Journal* say they'll buy the serial rights."

The confluence of media, the movies, television, mass-market paperbacks, the superagent, and the eighties was about to make Danielle Steel a very rich woman.

But first, she had some private business to straighten out on the home front, fears of kidnapping to deal with.

Chapter Twelve
Remembrance

"I want you to know that I'm so goddamn scared that if you breathe heavily I'm going to blow your brains all over this car."
—Female arresting officer's first words to Danny Zugelder

Danny Zugelder got out on parole from Vacaville prison about ten months after Danielle married Bill Toth. He had been in prison five years since his rape conviction.

The word is that he came after her.

A. Savedra, his parole officer in San Francisco, wrote in his evaluation that "he was a large man" who "impressed me in numerous ways."

Danny had "much interest in developing initial relationships with women," continued Savedra.

"He impressed me both physically," and he was "intellectually alert . . ." could do well in a "college course." Danny told Savedra he'd like to be "wealthy."

That was a month before he went on his May 1979 rape and robbery rampage.

Danny Zugelder got out of prison and drove by Danielle's new house. He hadn't been drinking or doing drugs at all since his release from Vacaville. But he later told law enforcement officials that when he saw Danielle in front of a "mansion" on Green Street and holding her baby, he blew off all those years of good behavior and model prisonerhood. He couldn't handle the evidence of what his life had become, compared to hers.

Danny didn't take his rage out on Danielle, as far as we know. But his rage set him off on a drinking and drug jag that twisted him up into Methedrine (speed) and out onto a violent crime spree which took him from San Francisco to Colorado. 1979 was a reprisal of 1974. He attacked one woman. He kidnapped, raped, and sodomized another, with a deadly weapon. He also forced her to give him a blow job. She was a nurse.

He went back to work after the May 9 attack, but perhaps not after his May 13 attack. Somehow he learned the police were looking for him. He was working at the architectural firm where Danielle had set a job up for him six years earlier. And as soon as inquiries were made, he disappeared. He was living with a woman then, and when the police questioned her, she said he'd gotten up, left for work, and that was all she said she knew.

The San Francisco police guessed, by that time, that the rapist was possibly Zugelder, mainly from the description of a huge, muscular 6'5" or 6'6" guy. And now he's a repeater, back in San Francisco on parole.

He'd been charged with statutory rape before he met Danielle, according to his records, a problem he ran into with a minor.

The police came to visit Danielle and Danny's former neighbor, Dan Talbott.

But did Danny get in touch with Danielle?

Since she told a friend in New York she'd had
to have a twenty-four-hour round-the-clock security
detail, and another friend said she'd gotten crazy
threats and had every reason to have tight security,
it seems as if Danny did get through to Danielle,
because she was terribly relieved when he was
caught in Colorado.

After Danny took off from the job Danielle had
set up, he went over to Marin County, across the
Golden Gate Bridge.

First there was a drug deal or a drug argument
which involved a shoot-out—they were probably
high on heroin or speed, according to one police
officer, and they were raided by Marin officers.
Danny escaped.

Danny was involved in some other things in Marin County. But the next incident that stands out—
the thing that got him caught—was the bank
robbery in Santa Rosa.

The bank robbery drew the attention of the
F.B.I., who already knew that the S.F.P.D. were
looking for him for the rape, kidnapping, and
forced oral copulation with the nurse and the felony assault on "Miss Z" in San Francisco.

That's when the F.B.I. connected his name with
the shoot-outs, the bank robbery, and the kidnapping, rape, and assaults. By then he was headed
for Colorado.

Danny Zugelder's size alone was enough to intimi-
date anyone. He didn't need any knives and guns.

The F.B.I. put him out on a country-wide bul-
letin, and he was picked up in Colorado by a pa-

trolwoman who walked up from behind the car, drew her gun, and said, according to the district attorney on the case, "I want you to know that I'm so goddamn scared that if you breathe heavily I'm going to blow your brains all over this car."

"She scared the shit out of him," according to the lawyer. This is why the Highwaypatrolman was so scared:

It was nearing sundown in the small Colorado town. The victim, who we'll call Donna Smith, had walked over to the high school to play a game of tennis. No one was there to play, so she got her exercise by jogging down the road and back. When she got back to the high school, she stopped to talk for a while with the custodian.

She'd noticed that a green car had passed her a few times, a nice-looking car that caught her eye, not a car she'd seen around this small town. It was a green Mercury Cougar.

The car passed again, going in the other direction, while she was talking to the custodian. But she really didn't think much about it. When she got home, her mother told her that her little sister Rebecca and her friend Sally were swimming down at the gravel pits, and they wanted her to meet them down there.

She walked out to the gravel pits, about a half-mile from town, and while she was sitting talking to her little sister and her friend, the same car came down to the pits and turned around.

The man driving the car parked, got out, got a fishing pole from his trunk, and started fishing.

He was tall and had on boots and white corduroy pants. Donna stayed there about a half-hour, and then had to get back home.

When she'd walked up to the main highway back into town, the man in the green car pulled up and asked her what highway he'd take to head into the state capital. She told him to go straight and then right onto the freeway. He asked her to repeat the directions, and she did.

Donna started walking on toward home when the man opened the driver's door. A short gun with a piece of wood on it and one big barrel was trained on her. It was a twelve-gauge sawed-off Remington shotgun Model 11-R, with the barrel and the butt sawed off, and tape wrapped around the butt and the stock of the gun.

"If you move one muscle or say one word, I'll blow your fucking brains out."

Danny stepped out of the car and told her to get in, and do it fast. He kept the sawed-off shotgun on her.

She was afraid he was going to shoot her. She got in on the driver's side and slid over to the passenger side. He told her to roll up her window.

Danny got in behind the wheel, pressed the gun to her neck and said: "This is a sawed-off shotgun, do you know what this will do to you?"

"Yes, it will kill me."

"As long as you cooperate, you won't have nay problems."

Danny took out a roll of thin black tape and told her to put her wrists together. He taped first her left wrist. Then her right. He bound her wrists together, and cut the tape with a knife.

He taped together her ankles. Then he taped together her knees.

He asked her once again if she knew what a sawed-off shotgun could do to her. "Yes," she replied.

"Kiss the barrel of the shotgun so you remember it."

Danny wasn't pleased with the way she kissed the gun.

"That's not good enough. Scoot down in the seat. I want you to put your whole mouth over the barrel of the shotgun."

She did as she was told. Danny asked once again for directions to the capital. Again, with the sawed-off shotgun in her mouth, she gave him directions.

"Do you know what I am going to do to you?"

"No."

"I'm going to fuck you." She did not reply. He asked her if she understood, she nodded yes.

"When I speak to you, you answer, if you don't want to die." He asked if she knew of a place where they could turn off the highway, a place with few people. She replied she didn't know of any. You're lying, he said, you live here. They came upon an old road cutting across the highway. Where does that lead? Back into town, she said.

They continued driving, with the sawed-off shotgun in her mouth.

Danny asked her her name, her age, and questioned her about the girls at the gravel pit, her little sister and her friend.

He told her to start thinking of a place to turn off.

Danny turned off the highway onto a road to some farms and asked if there were many farms in the area.

He went about one mile, stopped, turned around, came back to the highway, and continued going on.

"If I decide to go through the next town, if you as much as smile, I'll blow your brains out." The gun was still in her mouth, and he now put the gun under her arm and said, "It will kill you just as fast there."

Danny then took a left off the road onto a side road into the hills and drove a half-mile until he came to a small tin building, a gun range.

He parked the car behind the tin building and got out, taking the gun with him. "Stay there, I'll be right back."

He went to the trunk, got out an orange sleeping bag, came back to the door, and told her to get out on the driver's side. When she got out of the car, she dropped a pink comb out of the waistband of her shorts onto the ground.

Danny got out a knife about six or eight inches long and severed the tape on her knees and legs so she could walk. He told her to walk in front of him. He put the shotgun at the back of her head. "Next time you flinch when I do that your head will be gone," he warned.

They started walking around a little hill near the tin building. When they got on the other side of the hill, Danny told her to stop and put the sleeping bag on the ground. He took out the knife again, put it to her throat, and said, "This will kill you just as fast." He put the gun down on the ground.

He told her she was shaking and wondered if she was frightened.

"Yes," she replied.

He asked her if she had ever done anything like this before with a guy.

"No," she replied.

He told her he could not have picked a better one. "You'd better make it worth my time . . . you better be the best I've ever had, or you won't live to see tomorrow."

Danny then took the knife and sliced away the front of her T-shirt, cut the sleeves, and the shirt fell to the ground. He then cut off her bra, all the while her hands were still bound with the tape. He then took off her shorts and underwear and told her to sit down on the sleeping bag.

Danny loosened his belt buckle, unzipped his pants, took his penis out, and asked her if she had ever seen one before. He told her to lie down, got on top of her, and started kissing her. He told her she wasn't cooperating, and she'd better start.

He then inserted his penis into her vagina and told her again that she wasn't cooperating.

He asked if he was hurting her, and she said, "yes." He told her to repeat that a couple of times.

"You're hurting me," she cried.

"You're hurting me," she cried again.

He then got up, told her to turn over on her stomach, and put her hands beneath her.

She started to do that when he said "Just a minute, I've got to have a smoke and a rest." Just to compound the terror, he said again, "I don't know what I'm going to do with you."

She bargained for her life, telling him she wouldn't tell anyone. He was sure anyone who saw her torn shirt would know something happened. She promised she'd stay there until he left.

He told her to turn over on her stomach and put her hands underneath her. He put out his cigarette, and told her he would try it a little differently this time. He told her to get up on her hands and knees, with her head on the ground. He proceeded to have anal intercourse with her, and told her to tell him if it hurt. "It hurts," she said. He told her she would have to put up with this pain, or else a bigger pain.

After he had completed anal intercourse, he got up, and took the time to smoke another cigarette. He then told her to turn over and sit up. He asked her if she had ever given head before. She said "no."

"You are going to learn. Get on your hands and knees."

She did that, and the man told her to put his penis in her mouth. When she hesitated, he put the knife to her neck and said whether or not the knife went into her neck depended on the job she did giving him head.

He told her to swallow his penis, and warned her it would be the biggest mistake she ever made in her life if she threw up or gagged.

After he finished, he pulled out, picked up the sawed-off shotgun, and pointed it at her again.

Once again she bargained for her life, asking if he were going to shoot her, promising him she wouldn't tell anyone if he didn't kill her.

"I won't kill you," he said, "but if the cops stop me I have a friend around here who will come and kill you."

He zipped his pants, fastened his belt, rolled up the orange sleeping bag, and told her to sit on a rock for thirty minutes and not move.

He walked to the car, the door slammed, and she heard the car drive off.

Using her teeth, she tore the black tape from her wrists, freed her hands, then grabbed up her torn clothes and started running in the opposite direction.

She ran down a small gully and up a hill when suddenly there he was, standing outside the car. He fired the shotgun at her once, perhaps twice.

Dust flew up beside her from the shots. She kept running, over the top of a hill, running until she got to the highway.

She tried to flag down a couple of cars, but they drove by. She ran all the way into town and reported the assault.

The trunk of the car driven by Danny Zugelder contained a set of California license plates, later determined to have been stolen from San Francisco. The orange sleeping bag. And two boxes of shotgun shells in a brown paper bag.

The arresting officer, Beth Bascom, later told the court she sensed if she hadn't been backed up by two other police cars, that Zugelder would have shot it out with her.

The Federal Bureau of Investigation helped with the identification. And the FBI told the officers of at least two other outstanding warrants for his arrest. One for rape, a kidnapping, and a stolen vehicle.

He went to trial in Colorado in 1979.

And he's now serving a forty-fifty year sentence in Colorado prison. He'll be eligible for parole in four years.

Two years after his Colorado bench trial, the SFPD brought him back for bench trial in San Francisco on charges of kidnapping, rape, forced oral copulation, robbery and assault with a deadly weapon. There he pled guilty to get a sentence concurrent with his Colorado prison term. He was wearing leg irons on the plane except for take off and landing.

Zugelder was sitting in the very last seat of the plane, and there were several officers with him. He was smart enough to realize that he was going to get more time than if he just pled guilty . . . he was facing those years in Colorado already.

In *To Love Again*, Danielle writes of a woman whose husband is kidnapped and killed, and who fears her small son will be next. Danielle Steel could take these nightmarish, threatening circumstances in her real life and use them to strengthen her resolve to succeed, strengthen the depth of her writing, and start writing even faster. Her publisher scheduled a one-million-copy first printing. And no matter what—despite her second husband being on a threatening crime rampage, and her current husband Bill Toth beginning to behave erratically, beginning to be there some nights, and gone others—she would prevail.

Here's the *Publishers Weekly* take on the novel:

Isabelle has everything she could want: a loving husband and child, a flourishing designer clothing business and an extravagant Roman villa. Soon, after a close friend warns Isabella not to flaunt her new 10-carat diamond in public, her husband is whisked away by kidnappers. They demand $10-million in ransom, yet kill him before Isabella can present them with the money.

Fearful that her son will be the kidnappers' next victim, Isabella flees with him to New York City, where they live with her old roommate, Natasha. Isabella devotes all of her time and energy to running her design business via telephone, and seldom ventures outside Natasha's apartment.

After initially resisting his advances, Isabella allows herself to fall in love with Corbett, a friend of Natasha. The relationship seems to be permanently severed when Isabella learns that his company has been unsuccessfully trying to buy out hers, and she accuses him of using her heart to acquire her business. But

Steel, author of "The Promise" and "Summer's End" is a pro at devising the plausible happy ending, a skill she demonstrates again in this pleasant, tightly constructed tale.

Once Danny Zugelder was safely tucked away in the Colorado prison, Danielle had to put out some fires on the home front.

Danielle was having horrible conflicts with Bill Toth inside her own house. Bill, who'd been clean when she first met him, had started going back and forth to his old love, heroin. "Danielle's a total square," Bill said later. "She doesn't drink. No drugs whatsoever. I started using drugs again. And then I straightened up and stopped. I assumed we'd be back together again.

"Danielle went to New York," he continues. Then she went to Stinson [Beach] for vacation. I don't know if the lawyers were involved yet.

"One day, she comes back, and she stops sleeping with me.

"SHE cries on my shoulder," says Bill, "and asks me for a divorce. SHE was the one who wanted the divorce, why was she crying?

"Then the lawyers started getting involved."

Danielle's first hardcover novel was dedicated to Bill Toth, "who said I could." And she also gave special thanks to Eva McCorkendale of the German Consulate in San Francisco and Nancy Eisenbarth, who'd both helped with the research.

The Ring was Danielle's first historical novel, dealing with a period that fascinates her: the time between World War I and World War II. The book was promoted as being based on a real incident in Danielle's own family in Germany. Her publisher announced a 65,000-copy printing and it was selected by both the Doubleday Book Club and The Literary Guild, a major, step in her quest to move into the publishing mainstream.

Publishers Weekly reviewed it on September 19, 1980:

> Although it marks her debut into hardcover, Danielle Steel's new novel sticks close to the style and tone of her bestselling Dell paperback romance. . . .
>
> Supposedly based on an actual incident in Steel's own family, the plot has all the accoutrements of soap opera, including a love affair between two youngsters whose parents were once disastrously married to each other (à la "The Forsyte Saga," which did it better), and a coincidence that unites a brother and sister after 27 years of separation.
>
> We begin in prewar Berlin. Kassandra von Gotthard, a breathtaking beauty whose affair with a Jewish writer ends brutally when the Nazis kill him, commits suicide, leaving a noble husband; a daughter, Ariana, who rivals her mother in beauty; a son, Gerhardt; and two enormous rings that will figure throughout the narrative.

A very early publicity photograph of Danielle Steel, the author.   (*AP/Wide World*)

Danielle and Danny Zugelder, husband No. 2, in 1972. (*Star Magazine*)

The Lompoc Motel where, Danny Zugelder claims, he and Danielle made love for the first time, minutes after he was paroled from Lompoc Prison in 1972.   (*Star Magazine*)

Danielle and Bill Toth, husband No. 3, on their wedding day in 1978—the day her divorce from Danny Zugelder became final. (*National Enquirer*)

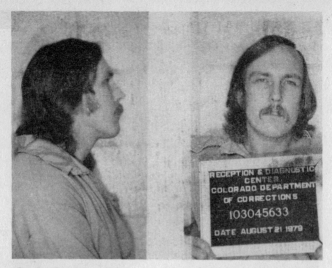

Danny Zugelder, 1978. *(Colorado Department of Corrections)*

Danny Zugelder's current home: Colorado's Shadow
Mountain Prison. *(Star Magazine)*

Bill Toth today.   (*National Enquirer*)

Danny Zugelder
today.
(*Star Magazine*)

Danielle Steel, 1982. She had published 14 novels and had more than 15 million books in print. And about to start truly enjoying it! (*AP/Wide World*)

The Spreckels mansion was already a San Francisco landmark before Danielle restored it to showplace stature
(*Michael Llewellyn*)

Danielle's current home, facing south where it has a magnificent view of San Francisco Bay and beyond. The small
building to the left houses a pool.　(*Michael Llewellyn*)

Another view of the Beaux Artes mansion.   (*Kent MacDonald*)

The Traina family pet stands guard. *(Kent MacDonald)*

Danielle and her handsome husband No. 4, John Traina,
out for a glamorous evening in San Francisco.
(*Ed Kashi/Liason*)

Danielle still puts in 10 hour days in her office at home.
(*P.F. Bentley/Black Star*)

Tombstone for the enigmatic John Schulein-
Steel, buried with his parents in Woodlawn
Cemetery in 1978. Note that his parents,
Julius and Minni, kept the original spelling:
Schuelein.

Danielle Steel with her Prince Charming, happy at last.
(*P.F. Bentley/Black Star*)

Separated from her family by a cruel irony of fate, Ariana endures all kinds of indignities at the hands of the Nazis until she is rescued and married by an idealistic German officer who dies in the last days of the war.

Ariana begins a painful odyssey that eventually brings her to the U.S., where further traumatic experiences await her. Many trials later, she ensures happiness for her son and herself through her mother's rings, symbolizing a family made whole again through love.

Danielle's novel *Loving* was reviewed the previous month in *Publishers Weekly*, and was being sold in one coordinated push with her first hardcover, *The Ring*. She was still an unknown: the reviewer even spelled her name wrong.

Loving, of course, was the novel which she may have written just after her own father died in 1978. It dealt with the struggles of a young woman desperately trying to sort out her late father's tangled and bankrupt affairs. This may have been how Danielle felt after her father's death, since he seemed to have been working only as a consultant to his late father's food company, Presco-Vegex.

After her marriage to Bill Toth disintegrated, Danielle started dating a tall, handsome fireman/actor/model, Thaddeus Golas. He was what San Franciscans in the 1970s called "a Brebner face" after Ann Brebner's star stable of commercial actors and models.

"He's a wonderful person," said Ann Brebner. "Kind and clear. I liked him a lot as a person. I remember, he did go out with Danielle Steel."

Thaddeus Golas got into the acting business by being chosen as what they called "real people" for a commercial for a sinus headache medication. Thaddeus A. Golas appeared for over a year in a commercial with his name emblazoned across it— leading to much confusion with another San Francisco resident, Thaddeus S. Golas, the author of a classic volume titled *The Lazy Man's Guide to Enlightenment.* ("The extent of his metaphysical interest," says Thaddeus S. Golas about Thaddeus A. Golas, "was attendance at 'est' weekends, a folly I would never engage in.")

Thaddeus A. was on the disaster fire squad at San Francisco Airport. He'd come on television and say, "I use it, and I'm a fireman," in the commercials, explained Ann Brebner. "He was very good-looking, very attractive."

The commercials got him a SAG card, membership in the Screen Actors Guild. He did some minor roles in movies, got a screen credit in the Star Trek movie with the whales, and did some *Streets of San Francisco* episodes.

Danielle dedicated her book *Palomino* to Thaddeus. Her publishers continued to experiment with marketing Danielle. Now they published *Palomino* in a "trade paperback" edition, larger than most paperback originals, but at $6.95, cheaper than a hardcover book. It was the story of a cowboy handsome enough to be a Marlboro man.

"This novel will reinforce the illusions of those who persist in believing that women—even ambitious career women—are stirred by the animal appeal of macho men," groused the reviewer in *Publishers Weekly*.

Samantha Taylor is a blonde, brainy, up-and-coming professional. As the creative director of New York's second largest advertising agency, she's a threat to husband John, who soon abandons her for a mousier mate. To ride out the crisis, Samantha's boss suggests she spend six months with an old friend who owns a dude ranch in California.

As soon as she arrives, this fast-track career woman falls in love with one of the cowboys—taciturn Tate Jorden. But bliss is short-lived. Proud Tate suddenly disappears when he sees no solution to their conflicting lifestyles. It takes a climactic riding accident, that leaves Samantha paralyzed from the waist down, to reunite the lovers.

That Steel writes with convincing polish comes as no news; nor is her conventional plot line any surprise.

But when Danielle's real-life cowboy Thaddeus Golas went out with Danielle Steel, he was written up in the San Francisco society columns. They didn't call him an actor, not even a model, but the very working-class "fireman."

Danielle was starting to hit the San Francisco society columns. The press reported that she was a fine catch, worth $7 million from earned royalties, according to Thaddeus S. He warned Thaddeus A. to remember that "if you don't have any money in that milieu, you're considered a plaything."

Danielle's Thaddeus Golas has built a financially secure life for himself.

His job as a rescue fireman at the San Francisco Airport was on the city payroll: he worked nine days straight then had the rest of the month off. The City also gave their workers a comfortable, secure pension.

And Thaddeus was creative: He didn't write like Danielle, but he once created a videotape of firehouse cooking, and the ladies adored him.

"But Thaddeus discovered Danielle wanted to marry him and have babies," according to Thaddeus S.

While married to Bill Toth, Danielle's following had gone international. Her books had been translated into sixteen languages and sold, according to Danielle, "maybe 30 million" copies.

Bill Toth says he'd straightened up and stopped using drugs again, and assumed he and Danielle would start living in the same house once more. He'd been living at the El Driscol hotel, the only hotel (and a rather run-down one at that) in Pacific Heights. Danielle lived there sometimes as well, according to Bill.

But their on-again, off-again romance was soon to grind to a complete halt.

Danielle's initial attraction to Bill Toth seems to have been transmuted into the fictional relationship with the magnetic, tragic figure of Vasili in *Remembrance*, who was in the bathroom with matches, a spoon, and a hypodermic needle. He was self-indulgent when it came to his battles with drugs eventually, yet gentle and tender.

Bill Toth and Danielle Steel were divorced in 1981. Her divorce came through on March 6, 1981.

"After that I just blew it," says Bill Toth. "I went to jail after that." Arrested for shoplifting, he was sent to Folsom Prison for ten months.

"She tried to have me arrested," Bill complains. "Set me up . . . with the police . . .

"She finally got me declared unfit. I'm unable to see the kid ever again . . .

Then the custody hearings started. It took until May of 1985, but Danielle convinced a court to withdraw the father's visitation rights. Bill Toth says he hasn't seen Nicholas since 1984. Nicholas is now sixteen.

"I was in love, see, I was in love with her," he says.

"I got a divorce settlement of about $50,000. It was the biggest check I've ever had. Now I think back on it, I should have gotten more money. Half of her earnings. At that time, it was a great insult to me."

And in the midst of all this productivity, she hit the newspapers with her third divorce, from Bill Toth. As Danielle's friend Pat Montandon, the former *San Francisco Examiner* society columnist, wrote, Danielle's court appearance was a romance novel spectacular. She went to court in designer suits and heavy-duty jewelry "with two bodyguards, three lawyers, and a Christian Science practitioner."

"I always wondered," Bill Toth told another reporter, "what was a woman like this doing with me?"

One of the reasons the doctor didn't see Bill Toth during the divorce and custody rights dust-up is that he was becoming increasingly unreliable, flirting again with heroin, drinking, and drugs.

The former surfer has a long and involved tale of why he didn't show up for the meeting with the psychiatrist, how Danielle set him up, and why missed the court date. Throughout, one hears the plaintive notes of an addict who has not yet taken responsibility for his actions, a man who blames his problems on his ex-wife, the system, the lawyers, the private investigators, the police . . . everyone but the man who keeps having the problems.

The promise Bill Toth showed as a star resident of Delancey Street, running the moving company, has washed away with the years. Sometimes he drives a delivery truck. He says he's taken deliveries for Saks Fifth Avenue to Danielle's old mansion.

He'd drive past the Trainas' house, hoping for a glimpse of his son.

And at other times, he is unemployed and unemployable, living with a girlfriend, and blaming Danielle for the tragedy he's made of his once promising life as a "middle-class convict" on the mend at Delancey Street.

But once Danielle had left Bill, her time was open to live the life she'd been writing about all these years. She now had a lifetime's worth of experience to draw on. She could share with her readers the lessons learned from the "man problems" she walked through and survived.

She moved on, into the San Francisco high society crowd that John Traina ran with. And into what people in San Francisco were calling a merry-go-round of marriages and divorces that included Danielle's friend, *San Francisco Examiner* society columnist Pat Montandon, her multimillionaire husband Al Wilsey and John Traina and his soon-to-be ex-wife Dede Buchanan.

Chapter Thirteen
A Perfect Stranger

". . . it's a modern-day fairy tale, complete with a princess cloistered in an ivory tower and a prince who comes to rescue her."
—excerpt from *Publishers Weekly* review of *A Perfect Stranger*

How did Danielle Steel meet John Traina? According to someone who talked with her back then, "Danielle said they were at a masked ball. They were both married to other people when they'd first met in these historical costumes. And they danced together, and one thing led to another, she told me.

"John Traina was the only thing she wanted to talk about—he was off-limits when she first met him."

The San Francisco Chronicle soon ran a story about the very confusing new marriage arrangements among high society:

> The San Francisco social set being as close-knit as it is, a divorce can sometimes set off a chain reaction. Take Pat Montandon . . . who married developer Al Wilsey (worth $125 million) in 1969, three years after her short-lived marriage to lawyer Melvin Belli.
> One of Montandon's best friends was the well-born Dede Traina, Dow Chemical heiress, daughter of former US Chief of Protocol

Wiley Buchanan, and wife of handsome shipping consultant John Traina. In 1980, Dede and Wilsey took a shine to each other.

The same happened with Traina and Danielle Steel, author of romantic blockbusters.

Wilsey left Montandon for Dede, who divorced Traina. Once free, Traina tied the knot with Steel, who had been married three times before.

At the Traina-Steel wedding, guests were shuttled up a Napa hillside, where they drank $66 bottles of champagne and danced to an eighteen-piece orchestra. Two French chefs fixed dinner.

Montandon, the odd woman out, was forced to settle for $3 million in community property and $20,000 a month in alimony. Dede Wilsey sold her house in Pacific Heights to Steel for seven figures. And all lived happily ever after.

Danielle was about to stop dallying with inappropriate men, and move into San Francisco society, thanks to the fallout of the Wilsey-Traina breakups.

And Bill Toth was left with a divorce settlement that he blew on drugs and alcohol. Within months of Danielle's marriage, he found himself in Folsom Prison, while she was marrying into the lap of the San Francisco jet set and buying into the house that had belonged to John Traina and Dede Buchanan Traina before her.

* * *

Pat Montandon blossoms in the sun and in society—she's a sunny blonde critter who charmed
her way out of Waurika, Oklahoma, where she was
the preacher's daughter, and into the heart of San
Francisco society and an apartment on Russian
Hill, near Danielle and Bill's house on Green
Street. Her brother, Dr. Carlos Montandon, carried his doctor's bag to Hillsborough, the city's
elite suburb and the Hearst's hometown. Pat Montandon's Japanese wedding to lawyer Melvin Belli,
no slouch in the celebrity department himself, was
declared null and void in April of 1967. And there
was quite a buzz around town.

Perhaps to cheer herself up, Pat Montandon
wrote a classic 1968 self-help book for the blues:
How to Be a Party Girl, [McGraw-Hill]. "Entertaining . . . is the most feminine thing you can do,"
said Pat. "It's resourceful, and you put yourself
forward—give of yourself. A lot of potential host-
esses are just afraid to put themselves forward and
have a party. After all, if you're not doing anything, you can't be criticized for anything."

Then the shining blonde advised "Don't be
afraid of failure." She was a fresh voice in the
stodgy San Francisco society of the sixties. "Create
something different," she advised in her 181-page
book.

She'd moved to San Francisco in 1962, according
to *The San Francisco Chronicle*, and found herself a
job on KGO-TV as host of the morning movie.

By late 1967, after the height of the Summer of Love in San Francisco, *Esquire* listed her as one of the country's top party givers.

By 1969, the host of *Pat Montandon's Prize Movies* was propped up in a bed at her 1000 Lombard apartment, sick as a dog from the flu and pneumonia. After Alfred Wilsey telephoned the police to fetch an ambulance for her, she was feeling better. "I've lived so much and have so much to live for," she said. "I have an abiding faith in God—I am, after all, a preacher's daughter." That was the year she married Al Wilsey.

In 1973, Pat started hosting splendid Round Table women's lunches mixing society and activism in the two-story Russian Hill penthouse she shared with her husband.

Every first Thursday of the month, a three-course formal lunch with a shifting guest list of twelve was a splendid example of the principles in her party-giving book.

Guests left their cars with a uniformed doorman downstairs, and took the elevator to the top of the building. There at the foyer, they were met by one of the maids and brought into the living room for cocktails. A Round Table she held in 1974 with columnist Merla Zellerbach, included guests Jessica Mitford, whose book on prisons was about to be released, Delia Fleischhaker Erlich, supporter of Delancey Street; Dianne Feinstein; Dr. Lorel Bergeron, a plastic surgeon; and Aileen Hernandez, past president of N.O.W. Servants in black uniform, individual soufflés, and white wine in crystal, surrounded by twenty-foot floor-to-ceiling views of San Francisco on all four sides were intercut with Pat's insistent efforts to encourage her guests to state their case and comment on political issues of the day. Dianne Feinstein, now a senator from California, for instance, said back then that she found Gloria Steinem cold. (She'd never met the lady, however.)

Pat Montandon told a reporter she felt "sisterhood" was a very powerful idea. "I think it's terribly important for women to learn to be friends and not be threatened by one another. . . . Women have had to derive any identity they have through a man. If some other woman comes along and seems more attractive to that man, a woman is threatened immediately."

These words would come back to haunt Pat when her husband Al Wilsey became taken with another woman, Dede Buchanan Traina.

Al Wilsey is a very rich San Franciscan whose fortune flows from the family firm founded in 1919, just after World War I.

Wilsey-Bennett Company is a food and floral products manufacturer, also in transportation. In 1988, the Wilsey-Bennett company ranked number twenty in the *San Francisco Business Times* review of the Top 100 Privately Held Companies in the Bay Area, companies like Levi Strauss, Esprit de Corp, Safeway, and Bechtel. With an annual estimated revenue of $300 million, Wilsey spun off plenty of profits to start Wilsey's development fortune and his high-flying lifestyle.

In 1979, during Danielle's marriage to Bill Toth, Pat Montandon and Al Wilsey hosted a "Gone With the Wind" party at their Napa estate in little Rutherford. River Meadow Farm, their country estate, was transformed into a mini-circus, with a thirty-piece orchestra and booths for fun. The women were wearing tight-waisted hourglass silhouette dresses with wired hoop skirts, and the men came in tails and top hats—the more authentic chose knee-length frock coats of the Civil War era. One guest made three trips to L.A. for fittings by the original costumer on *Gone with the Wind*. Lunch, served outdoors, was somewhat awkward since none of the women knew how to sit in the skirts.

If Danielle indeed met John Traina at a masked ball, this lavish hoopla thrown by Pat Montandon and Al Wilsey was just the sort of high-society bash they met at.

Pat, by this time, had taken Danielle under her wing. But did Pat ever guess how sadly the party would end for her?

Dede Buchanan is the daughter of Wiley T. Buchanan, former United States chief of protocol and former Ambassador to Luxembourg, and Ruth Dow, heiress to the Dow Chemical fortune.

The Buchanans had a grand house, Underoak, in Washington, and an even grander place in Newport, where they bought and polished up the mansion of the late Mrs. Cornelius Vanderbilt.

Dede had a fun job as the receptionist in the office of late right-wing Texas Republican Senator John Tower. Around the summer of 1964, she moved out of her parents' place and in with a couple of girlfriends. She was soon to move in with John Traina.

By the summer of 1965, *The San Francisco Chronicle* wrote that "John Traina, Jr., the San Francisco bachelor . . . has pursued her for more than two years." But Dede's Washington friends said it was an on-again, off-again romance of a year.

When news of the heiress's upcoming marriage to John Traina was made public, her father issued the following statement:

"My daughter has told us of her intention to get married," Wiley Buchanan told the United Press in June of 1965. "It has come as a shocking surprise," continued his statement to UPI. "We do not know when or where the wedding will take place. We are terribly upset." Her mother added, "We are not happy about it."

Buchanan refused to discuss his objections to John Traina, then an employee of the American President line being transferred to San Francisco, his hometown.

The wedding was performed on a Friday night in a Methodist church.

In the San Francisco paper, John Traina's mother Lea disputed the age Mr. Buchanan had given for her son, saying he was thirty-two not thirty-five, not really that much older than Dede, twenty-one.

But perhaps *The Chronicle*'s headline of the time, "Those Star-Crossed Lovers," had it right.

In 1980, a friend of both the Wilseys and the Trainas ran across Dede Buchanan Traina and Al Wilsey shopping together in Napa. She wouldn't have thought a thing of it, she said, if they hadn't both started blushing.

"Dede was the first real blue-blooded Social Register person Al had ever met," said the friend.

In the years that followed, John Traina moved from the American President line, which became American Hawaii Cruises. When China opened to Americans, he established himself as an expert in luxury cruises there as CEO of Pearl Cruises.

He and Dede had bought a beautiful 1895 Episcopal Bishop's house in Pacific Heights, and Dede had decorated in big-money style. Their life was picture-perfect, they had two healthy sons, and all looked to be happily ever after.

But then Al Wilsey took a shine to Dede, and set San Francisco on its ear.

John Traina's great-grandfather had originally come to San Francisco from Italy in 1850, joining the same Gold Rush that drew the Lazard brothers.

Rather than going into banking like the Lazards, the Trainas went into the confectionery business, making candies and becoming well-known in the city for Traina Chocolates.

The Trainas' money also came from the rich land of California. The Traina family's real estate developments included two areas in San Francisco. There was residential development of the dunes in what is today known as the Sunset District. And there was housing developed in another section of San Francisco, the Richmond District, near Golden Gate Park and the old Haight-Ashbury neighborhood.

John's father died in 1984 at ninety-one, and the newspapers recalled him as "a lifetime socially prominent San Franciscan."

His wife had a hand in that. Lea Castellini and John Traina first met in 1925 in Italy and married the following year in San Francisco at St. Mary's Cathedral.

About nine years later, the local paper ran a three-column photograph of Lea Traina, an "attractive member" of the Auxiliary of the Chamber Symphony Society meeting on Jackson Street, the street where Danielle and John would soon live.

And in 1948, young John Traina's red jalopy was the central focus of a gang of teenagers posing with a newspaper columnist seeking the inside scoop on teenage folkways. They took her for a drive to see "how well a jalopy can take the San Francisco hills."

And by 1965, John, Jr., was still collecting those old cars, and had a new bride to bring home to San Francisco.

* * *

Finally, the San Francisco couples started to get sorted out.

Dede Traina divorced John Traina, and married Al Wilsey, who divorced Pat Montandon.

Pat Montandon encouraged her friend Danielle Steel to grab John Traina while he was still available, and she did.

Danielle Steel and John Traina were married in a lovely outdoor wedding held at a business associate's of John Traina's Palladian mansion in Napa. Danielle wore white and said it was her first real marriage.

Pat Montandon and Bill Toth did not marry.

And then the fun began.

In the first six months after their marriage, Danielle's book *A Perfect Stranger,* dedicated to her son Nicholas, was published and reviewed in *Publishers Weekly*.

The book concerned an ambitious woman who put her career before her marriage, and was divorced by the male lead—something Danielle may have been worried about—and a manipulative career woman who is threatened by her brother with a child abuse trial—something Danielle may have been mulling over as she considered taking Bill Toth to court for sole custody of their son.

"Alex, a successful San Francisco attorney, is still licking the wounds caused by a painful divorce from his overly ambitious wife, who put her career

before their marriage," reported the reviewer for
Publishers Weekly.

Catching a glimpse of beautiful Rafaella,
Alex is immediately enchanted and falls
deeply in love. Rafaella is a young European
woman who's been protected all her life; she's
married to very wealthy John Henry Phillips,
many years her senior and incapacitated by a
stroke. Alex and Rafaella find happiness in
each other's arms, but their love is clouded by
Rafaella's guilt over deceiving John Henry.

Unbeknownst to Rafaella, however, her husband has discovered the affair and given Alex
his blessings. When John Henry commits sui-
cide, Alex's conniving sister threatens Rafaella's family with scandal and nearly succeeds
in destroying Alex's and Rafaella's love.

Steel's latest romance is bound to please her
legion of fans—it's a modern-day fairy tale,
complete with a princess cloistered in an ivory
tower and a prince who comes to rescue her.

Danielle's publisher set her first printing at 1.2
million copies, her largest yet.

Chapter Fourteen

Once in a Lifetime

Sweet are the uses of adversity,
Which, like the toad, ugly and venomous,
Wears yet a precious jewel in his head.
                    —William Shakespeare

With Danielle moving into John Traina's mansion in Pacific Heights, her marriage to the handsome older man seemed an invention in one of her books. This marriage was yet another reworking of the Cinderella stories she'd developed in *Passion's Promise* and *Now and Forever* and *Remembrance*. But it worked.

It was her "first real marriage," that marriage in white, and though Danielle insists her plots aren't autobiographical, her life continues to develop along the lines of her plots.

In 1982, the first year of her new life as Mrs. John Traina, Danielle submitted to an in-depth interview with Cyra McFadden, author of *The Serial*, the late seventies tale of life in Marin County.

At thirty-five, and after three failed marriages, Danielle finally seemed to have it all: a forty-two-room mansion in Pacific Heights; a rich, handsome husband; two children she adored; and fourteen books in print. It had been a little over a year since her divorce from Bill Toth.

Danielle told McFadden that she and her new husband enjoyed collecting antique cars: She had two 1940 Fords, he had a 1930 and 1931 Ford and

1938 fire engine, and together they owned three station wagons, two of them Mercedes.

While other writers were celebrating a printing of ten thousand copies, the first printing of Danielle's latest hardcover book, *Crossings*, was 150,000. Her paperbacks now hit the racks with a 1.5-million first printing.

While other writers had no staff problems—because they had no staff—Danielle had to count on her fingers for McFadden to determine the number of people she had "in help." A secretary who handles her mail and "international stuff." A baby nurse for her six-month-old daughter Samantha and a mother's helper for her four-year-old son Nicholas. Someone who comes around to take care of her garden, two full-time cleaning people, and a driver "for state occasions, or if I have a particularly terrible day and don't want to worry about driving myself," says Danielle.

Money can't buy happiness, you might say. Danielle assured McFadden that she was blissfully happy in this, her fourth marriage.

She and John were combining families, just like the couple in Danielle's book, *Changes*—her two children, Bede and Nicholas, and John's two sons, Trevor and Todd, who live with the Trainas half-time. Danielle moved into the house in which John had lived with Dede—reluctantly, because she felt they should live somewhere new after their marriage.

It took eight months to remodel it so it was really

theirs, and in the same year they moved four times, twice in the city, and twice in the country.

And Danielle was pregnant with their first of five children together, and they had to decide whether to buy or rent in the Napa Valley, which John loves, and in the meantime, Steel was under contract for two new novels. . . . All in all, it was an epic year, but now they have a storybook marriage, the kind people end up with in Danielle Steel novels.

She calls him Popeye. He calls her Olive Oyl. *Remembrance*, the first book she dedicated to him, introduced these pet names. The dedication ran along the lines of "a different one this time, one that's never been done before, for the rest of my life, me to you. . . ."

Crossings is also dedicated to John, she writes, beyond love, words, or anything. John "inspired" the book and read it in manuscript aboard one of his Delta line ships on the way to Acapulco, so moved by it that, as he tossed the pages overboard one by one because *Crossings* was not yet copyrighted, he cried.

Here's what *Publishers Weekly* said about the novel when they reviewed it that July:

Steel is in the habit of writing bestsellers, but her fans may be disappointed by her latest effort, a novel quiet to the point of dullness and conventionally romantic to the point of sentimentality.

The story features two married couples: Armand, who at the start is French Ambassador to the United States, and his American wife Liane; and steel magnate Nick, who only stays married to his selfish but tantalizingly beautiful wife Hillary so as not to lose custody of his small son.

Armand causes trouble for his wife, children and friends in the U.S. by joining the government of Petain (though he is *really* working for the Resistance).

Liane and Nick fall deeply in love as they cross the Atlantic but are unable to stabilize their relationship until Hillary has found a lover as "rotten" as herself, and Armand, who conveniently loves his country even more than his family, has died a hero's death.

Liane is so passionate, intelligent, wise and brave as to be less than interesting, and the whole pale narrative is premised on the noble but vague idea that "Strong people cannot be defeated."

"I write stuff that touches people," Danielle explained to McFadden, without self-consciousness, adding that she herself sometimes cries over her novels while writing them. In fact, she says, her work is so powerful that she wouldn't want to read it if she were at a low point in her life. "If I were feeling fragile, I'd be nervous about reading a book that's going to grab my gut, which mine do."

The Danielle Steel appearing on the jacket photos on these books of the late seventies and early eighties is a misty-eyed, backlit vision, dark hair floating around a flawlessly made-up face. The woman who turned up for her interview with McFadden was in designer jeans and a black T-shirt, looking like a private-school girl.

"All that glamorous crap on the back of the book jackets," she told McFadden, "I showed my mother a copy of *Publishers Weekly* with my picture on the cover—it's a beautiful picture, the one from *Remembrance*—and she said, 'She's gorgeous. Who is she?' "

McFadden sensed that Danielle was on full alert, wary.

Her writing is secondary to her domestic life, she said earnestly and often. "If I could have a magic wand, I'd probably give up working. I'd be happy staying home and only taking care of my children." Yet she also wants to write two books a year "until I'm an old lady, holed up in the attic, and still thinking I'm writing a novel, with the kids saying, 'You know she's crazy, there hadn't been a typewriter in that room for 12 years.' " Homebody aspirations notwithstanding America's most prolific writer isn't choosing early retirement.

No one, except perhaps Ronald Reagan, believes more devoutly in the work ethic: "I admire women who are accomplishing something. There are so many dead-ass people out there, boring each other to death."

On the phone with McFadden, arranging for an interview, months before the actual date, Danielle was simultaneously having a massage; giving marching orders to her secretary, Paige Healy; and fending off other phone callers. To McFadden, her end of the conversation sounded like a one-woman band.

McFadden made an appointment to meet at Danielle's country house in the Napa Valley. Her secretary broke it. Her daughter Bede was coming back early from France, Healy apologized.

They scheduled another interview. Steel's press representative in New York phoned to cancel that one, explaining that the firm's most profitable client was up to her ears promoting *Crossings*.

After thirteen phone calls to and from New York, Danielle managed to find a free afternoon. At the last minute, they agreed to meet at McFadden's house rather than hers. She was having staff problems, Danielle explained.

When Danielle briefed the writer on her schedule for the rest of the day, McFadden learned why it's easier to get an audience with the Pope. Determined to be "the perfect wife and the perfect mother" and still write two books a year, Danielle explained that she blocks out each day, the night before, in fifteen minute segments.

Danielle rummaged in her purse and pulled out a crumpled page, in tiny meticulous handwriting, from what she calls her "sacred book."

Then she launched into "A Day in the Life of Danielle Steel."

"At 6:30, I woke up with John," said Danielle.

"At 7:00, he changed our plans for part of the publicity tour for *Crossings*. I'm doing the *Today* show and a buncha [sic] stuff, and he's coming with me for part of the trip. So I had to make some calls and change the arrangements. *Then* I called my agent. *Then* I'm giving John a birthday party in Washington, while we're there, so I called a whole buncha people for that. Then my daughter was sick, so I had to deal with that. At 8:20, I took her to school. I also brief her on some things about when I'm gone.

"Let's see . . . came home, had a meeting with the bodyguard about some things I need him to do." McFadden noted that the unenviable thing about Danielle's celebrity, and perhaps a backwash from her marriages to Bill Toth and Danny Zugelder, was that she worried about the safety of her children. Hence the bodyguards.

"At 9:00, I took the next youngest to nursery school. Then I came home and called three churches about a christening for the baby, Samantha. *Then* I had to track down a doctor at Stanford Medical Center." *Changes,* one of the books she was working on, was about a heart surgeon; the doctor was checking it for accuracy.

"Then I tried to track down a potential godmother for the baby, and then I had to talk to the nurse about some stuff, and then I nursed the baby.

"Then I had to talk to my agent again."

She was now at 11:00 A.M. and about an inch down her schedule. Get dressed, buy groceries, interview, a fitting for the clothes she will be wearing in New York. Home to preside over a cocktail party John was giving for a few friends. Return the twenty-five to fifty phone calls she averages each day.

At 10:00 P.M. she could begin editing her manuscript. McFadden wondered if the last notation of the page read "2:30 A.M.—go to bed with John."

But, McFadden acknowledged, these draconian measures with her time seem to pay off. Once, presumably due to the second marriage to Danny Zugelder which was then grist for the San Francisco rumor mill, she suffered writer's block for over a year.

In the weeks preceding and following her interview with McFadden, she made a half-dozen television appearances. In each, she talked about her twenty-hour working days, when the muse descends on her shoulder and she closets herself with her typewriter, caught up in the creative process, forgetting to eat. Her health was delicate, she told McFadden, but the awed reporter noted that "this fragile-looking woman is a high-speed writing machine." In late 1982, McFadden reported she was working on three novels in progress and her first nonfiction, the book about conception, pregnancy, and childbirth, written with six friends and called *Having a Baby*. "We're going to treat the subject with reality, sensitivity, and humor," Danielle promised. "It will be somebody finally telling you the truth."

By now, Danielle was chafing at the "romance writer" label and wanted the respect due an important, mainstream writer.

Speaking about *Once in a Lifetime*, Danielle acknowledged, "Sure, it's got romance in it, but it's really about the problems of raising a deaf child."

As for *Crossings*, romantic trappings notwithstanding, it was about World War II, its theme the ringing affirmation that "Strong people cannot be defeated."

Taking a narrower view, *The New York Times Book Review* dismissed *Crossings* with the comment, "There is no writing to speak of." But the book was already number seven on the *Times*'s own bestseller list, and climbing. Danielle was hoping this would be the one that put her on top. She'd been number three for weeks at a time. Just once, she told McFadden, she'd like to be number ONE.

It was this longing for greater recognition that led her to press for hardcover publication, despite her publishers' objections:

"They told me, you're not that kind of a writer."

Next, over similar objections, she courted a male

readership with *Palomino,* the cowboy book that isn't a cowboy book. Men soon began to sidle up to her at parties "and whisper, 'I've read all your novels, but don't tell anyone.' "

Now she's fighting for the right to approve her book covers: "They wanted to put *flowers* on *Crossings.* I had to make an absolute stink."

Afraid of losing their romance audience, Delacorte Press (Dell's hardcover affiliate) "made a last-ditch stand with the jacket copy, which makes it sound like a ghastly, sappy, book." Actually, she told McFadden, "There's a lot of historical stuff in it."

Not that Danielle and her publishers have an adversarial relationship. She nails down book contracts on the basis of her signature alone—no outline, no sample chapters, only a commitment for two more of the same—and champagne corks pop on the East Coast. All that remains? Do the usual detailed outlines, write the first drafts, write the second drafts, edit the proofs, and, according to San Francisco's Cyra McFadden, "run the Trainas' version of the Medici Palace."

Listening to Steel describe her life (the unremitting hard work, the promotional tours, the chunks of time she carves out for her children), McFadden found herself wondering whether the writer had a clone.

Danielle assured McFadden that she *hated* the social ramble and is "painfully shy." It's John who loves the limelight, while Danielle, as a good wife, merely goes along with it. "Anyone who knows me also knows I'm intensely private."

Despite this self-image, McFadden reported that Danielle and John once found themselves in black tie twenty nights running.

Danielle assured McFadden that her five-week tour for *Crossings* was only "because I believe in the book."

This was her second understatement of the interview, McFadden noted, the first being "I'm pretty scheduled."

In a "Dear Friends" letter Danielle wrote for the Waldenbooks chain, she described *Crossings* as "the most powerful book I have written, powerful in the strength of its characters, and the insights they have into themselves and each other. The relationships which bind them are intense and loyal and demanding, sometimes difficult—bonds that you will undoubtedly identify with, and which will make the characters as real to you as they became to me."

Her heroines aren't ALL rich, Danielle pointed out, insisting that she was not an elitist.

Besides, Danielle pointed out to McFadden, "I think people would rather read about somebody well-heeled than someone in a housedress." They like knowing, she added, that difficult things can happen to rich people, too.

Danielle gets between one hundred and two

hundred letters a week, she told McFadden, mostly
from admirers thanking her for lighting up their
lives. And she believes passionately in her work—its
power, its compassion, and its redeeming social importance.

Her book *Once in a Lifetime* was reviewed March
5, 1982, in *Publishers Weekly,* and here's what they
said:

Bestselling author Steel's 12th novel offers
a heartrending, dramatic and increasingly absorbing story. Internationally acclaimed
author Daphne Fields, whose wonderful novels have changed people's lives, lies in an intensive care unit after being struck by a car
on Christmas Eve.

As she fights for her life, we return to the
tragedies which have contributed to her compassion and wisdom: the death of her beloved
husband and daughter in a fire, the birth of
her deaf son and the accidental death of the
lover who helped put her life together again.

Fresh from a year in Hollywood, where she
wrote a screenplay and had her heart broken
by a gorgeous matinee idol, Daphne needs the
calm, supportive love of Matt Dane, her son's
teacher, if she is to pull through.

But Daphne thinks he loves someone else,
and she cannot bring herself to tell him of
her love. Daphne is a strong and poignant
character who will charm fans of romance,
right up to the tearful and satisfying ending.

Chapter Fifteen
Changes

". . . Steel is a masterful plotter who knows exactly how to please her crowd—with breathless cathartic drama, soppy romance, historical ambience, a host of strongly defined minor characters, numerous well-integrated subplots, and, yes, a happy and satisfying ending"

excerpt from *Publishers Weekly* review
of *Thurston House*

When Danielle moved in with John Traina, she was moving into the house that Dede built, so to speak.

It was the living room Dede, the ex-wife, had decorated, the bedrooms that Dede had arranged. Everywhere, Trevor and Todd's mother's fingerprints were upon the house. John Traina had lived here on Jackson Street for over fifteen years with his wife and their two sons. And now Dede had moved out, but only up the street, with her new husband Al Wilsey.

San Francisco property records showed that toward the end of 1981, Danielle Steel was also an owner of their house on Jackson Street, with a transfer on November 16, 1981, in to the name of John A. Traina, Jr., and Danielle Steel.

This dilemma of the eighties—the successful woman making sense of her second marriage to the successful man, and blending their respective children—was a situation made-to-order for a Danielle Steel novel, and it probably inspired *Changes,* which was published in 1983, a year and a half after her marriage.

Changes dramatized the move: (Melanie) Adams, a New York successful network newswoman with a cozy town house on East 79th; the successful man, L.A. heart surgeon Peter Hallam, with a house in Bel-Air.

Could the New York town house have reflected the love she felt for the first real house she'd ever owned, the one she sold for over a half a million after marrying John Traina?

The fictional Dr. Hallam's Bel-Air mansion on the other side of the continent feels more like an impersonal hotel suite than the warm home Mel wants for herself and her two daughters.

Mel's worries about not being able to work as hard as she wants and as much as she wants, once she's married, are solved more easily than the presence of Peter's old German housekeeper. Mel eventually wins; the housekeeper is out.

It's amusing to read in an interview with Danielle that her housekeeper won out over his—this is what's called their real life—and that truth sometimes is remarkably similar to fiction.

The reviewer for *Publishers Weekly* summarized:

At 35, lithe, copper-haired Melanie Adams seems to have everything: a townhouse on New York's Upper East Side (and a summer cottage on the Vineyard); a coveted spot as a newswoman and for a major TV network: and—most important—the love and respect of her 16-year-old twin daughters, serious-minded Jess and sexy, boy-crazy Val.

The entrance on the scene of Peter Hallam, Los Angeles thoracic surgeon with three motherless kids and a heart as big as the swimming pool in his backyard, is fraught with more complications than the continental distance that separates his life from Mel's.

Isn't there something untoward in the forbiddingly formal Bel-Air house still dominated by a wife-and-mother dead for two years? And perhaps a touch of "male chauvinism" in a man who insists—when their friendship has burgeoned into passionate love—that Mel, not he, transplant home and career when they marry?

Will the grafting of her family onto his create insuperable problems and inordinate strains?

In a style and manner undeviatingly direct and uncluttered by complexities, this steadfastly contemporary fiction addresses these central questions squarely, embellishing the tale with details as timely as the lead stories on the six o'clock news: teenage pot smoking, pregnancy and abortion; heart transplants and triple-bypass surgery; the attempts of madmen on the lives of TV stars and presidents. Steel's faithful audience will find itself well-served by *Changes*, her 16th novel.

The month *Changes* was being published to that strong review in *Publishers Weekly*, Danny Zugelder was returning to San Francisco—in leg irons—to face charges for the 1979 San Francisco kidnapping and rape of the nurse and felony assault on another woman.

He came back after putting through a request for a speedy trial within ninety days, his Constitutional right, then cut a deal with the D.A. (Otherwise California would have simply kept a "detainer" attached to him in Colorado, and at his 1998 release date he'd be returned to San Francisco to face the charges for raping the nurse, and attacking the other woman, "Miss Z," four days later, as well as any charges from the bank robbery and possible shoot-out in Marin County.)

Danny Zugelder was held in the Hall of Justice, on the sixth floor, the place Danielle had described so carefully in *Passion's Promise*.

Jeff Brown was the Public Defender at that time, and Gregory Pagan, his Deputy, was assigned to the case.

Looking back on it, Pagan remembers Zugelder as "a real big guy, real scary-looking." Pagan has worked on a lot of rape cases, but says the rapists who abduct their victims in their car and take them to another location are generally the more serious criminals.

The grand jury indictment was dated August 12, 1981, against Danny Zugelder, after hearing the officer on the case, the kidnapping victim, and the felony assault victim.

The D.A.'s office negotiated a settlement basically to "clear the case" on the following counts: kidnapping, robbery, oral copulation with force, and rape on May 9, 1979, and assault with a deadly weapon on May 13, 1979. They added something called an "enhancement" for another year, and then added another year for his prior prison terms, bringing the total term imposed to fifteen years.

Then Judge Claude D. Perasso and the public defender made a deal: If Danny didn't take up the San Francisco's court's time pleading innocent and going to trial, California would let him serve the entire sentence at the same time as his Colorado sentence.

There was no trial, simply a change of plea and a judgement and sentencing, with James Goodman on the D.A.'s side. Goodman and Pagan got together and cut a deal that Danny could in actuality serve no time on the California charges. They dropped counts 1 and 4, for 209B Kidnapping and Felony Assault, and they struck the remaining priors.

The D.A. did point out, however, that Danny's conviction on the felony charges of rape and forcible oral copulation required him to register as a Sex Offender if he should ever come back to the state of California.

As Judge Perasso said at the end of the sentencing, "The bottom line is that this was a negotiated disposition."

No probation report was ordered, according to notes attached to the sentence.

Danny wanted the judge to hurry things along and save time for him. He told the judge it would be convenient to not get a California probation report on him (the presentence report). "Mr.

Zugelder is not trying to be difficult," explained his lawyer. "There are priority cells and he has a top priority cell in Colorado, and if he loses any more time . . . when he goes back, he has to start all over again and work his way up. . . ."

Danny told the judge, "I've done five and a half years in the State of Colorado."

Either the court stenographer heard Dan Zugelder wrong, or he got away with lying to a San Francisco judge, D.A., and public defender that he'd been in jail in Colorado for five and a half years, when he'd only been away from San Francisco for two.

While Danny was worrying about being on a waiting list for a good cell in Canon City, Danielle was worrying about redecorating the mansion that had belonged to Dede Buchanan Traina before her.

In a visual reprise of that old song "I'm Going to Wash that Man Right Out of My Hair," Danielle decided to get every stick of furniture out of the house. Meanwhile, she and John and Beatrix and Nicky lived elsewhere.

She had moved reluctantly into this house, because she felt that as a new wife in a new marriage, they should have their own new family place. But it was not to be. So they remodeled for eight months.

In one year, Danielle moved two times in the

city, and two times in the country. And she got pregnant.

The visual evidence of Dede was gone with the furniture, and the couple had a blank canvas on which to paint their new life. They got to know each other better while picking out bits and pieces that made them both happy.

But the few little changes she wanted to make, she wrote, soon "rivalled the building of the Boulder Dam."

She wrote in *Architectural Digest* in April 1985 about this period of moving out and moving into the mansion where John had lived with Dede, Trevor, and Todd for fifteen years.

The 1895 Neo-Classical Victorian mansion in Pacific Heights had been the residence of the Episcopal Bishop in the 1950s. There had been lots of changes made to the house over the years, and portions of it were going unused, especially the basement.

At first, Danielle outlined relatively simple changes: a marble floor for the entry, several crystal chandeliers, gilding for the plaster detailing on the Victorian ceilings, and a truly fine paint job, the sort that picks out columns and pilasters in three- or four-toned and creamy shades that define the room.

Danielle Steel is a very busy woman. So she writes that she decided to hire a decorator. But she and John apparently talked to a variety of decorators in San Francisco and finally came to the decision that they'd rather do the work themselves.

The woman famed for her energy level even managed to do a complete makeover of the disused basement. They got all the junk up and out that had been stored there for twenty years or longer. Then they built a big gymnasium with Nautilus-type equipment, a sauna and whirlpool, and deck chairs to lounge on after a hard workout. They had a private trainer come in to make the workouts more efficient.

The teenaged boys, who went to private school in San Francisco before heading off to the East Coast, had a chance to really impress their friends with the new gymnasium. Even the town's mothers heard about it, mothers who had to make do with the Nob Hill Club, not too shabby in itself.

When Danielle worked on her nonfiction book *Having a Baby,* she was able to invite all the pregnant women over to her house for a workout together in the gym. She heard firsthand reports of various birth experiences, gathered material for her book, and had a chance to get together with friends during the day, something she'd never allowed herself.

Glamour magazine's Nancy Evans reviewed the book in April of 1984, and explained how the seven pregnant women were united by Danielle for the exercise class, and "they also compared notes on Lamaze vs. Bradley, breast-feeding vs. bottle, returning to work vs. staying at home, and were soon as much a support as a fitness group." The women ranged in age from twenty-seven to their late thirties, and in the book, each woman takes her turn in telling about her experiences in the various stages of pregnancy and the first few months after birth. "It's when the women don't agree on the subjects of nursing, postpartum depression and getting back in shape, for instance—that this book becomes even more valuable." But, notes the review, for them the issues of child care are easily resolved by hiring the right nannies or au pair girls. But the book is a warm, sharing gesture on the part of all these women to let other women know what they may have ahead of them in a pregnancy.

Also down in the basement, they added a game room for the older boys, Trevor and Todd, then Nicky. For their many dinner parties, they set up wine cellars. And for the ongoing construction in the house, a workroom for the carpenters, as well as storage rooms.

The younger kids had their own rooms on their own floor, the third. Nicky's room, before he was ten, had a ceiling painted with sheep going over clouds. He slept in a bunk bed painted as a double-decker bus, on a blue rug. Nearby, a nice red picnic table. And, of course, the requisite books and toys.

One of the girls got the old solarium. Her ceiling was painted with both flowers and lively cherubs blowing trumpets. The wallpaper was pink, and the view sublime.

The other daughter's room was garlanded with flowers on the ceiling with wonderful trompe l'oeil paintings on the furnishings, and lovely blues throughout the room.

Each child got a very individual room to express himself in, and to retreat to when needed.

Danielle's novel *Thurston House*, one of her very last paperback originals, could have been written during the time she was studying the history of the old house. She was introduced to the generational saga of John Traina's family, with the old San Francisco roots, and in her own history, having the Lazard and Ehrman families with their long California history. *Publishers Weekly* reviewed it on May 27, 1983.

Crises and celebrations crowd the pages as dozens of births, marriages and deaths follow hugger-mugger in this generational saga, Steel's latest bid for bestsellerdom.

Jeremiah Thurston is so busy building his fortune that he is well into middle age before he falls for a social-climbing southern belle young enough to be his daughter, one Camille Beauchamp.

For Camille, Jeremiah builds the splendid, palatial Thurston House in turn-of-the-century San Francisco.

Since Camille is afraid of losing her figure, Jeremiah is obliged to rape her in order to get his daughter. Once Camille runs off with her paramour, Jeremiah raises feisty Sabrina to fill his shoes running the family mines and vineyards. Sabrina also falls for an older man and has a son who eventually plots with his grandmother Camille to take Thurston House away from his mother.

Do they succeed? Don't be silly. Steel is a masterful plotter who knows exactly how to please her crowd—with breathless cathartic drama, soppy romance, historical ambience, a host of strongly defined minor characters, numerous well-integrated subplots, and, yes, a happy and satisfying ending. This is the top of the genre and Steel fans will love every minute of it.

On the second floor of the old mansion, construction enabled Danielle to totally reshape the working and sleeping arrangements that had been in effect before her arrival.

Basically, she and John divided the second floor into two separate houses almost, so the teenagers would feel as if they had some privacy. (And the parents as well, one guesses.)

A totally separate stairway was carved out to lead up to one end of the second floor. This end now housed the older children, Beatrix, Todd, and Trevor (Todd and Trevor lived sometimes here, sometimes up the street at Dede and Al Wilsey's house).

The boys' rooms were done up in masculine colors with an English flavor. And Bede's room was all lilac and white—with lilacs floating about on her ceiling as well.

The main stairway from the downstairs reception rooms led to John and Danielle's wing.

Where John and Dede had once found their master bedroom, the construction workers knocked down walls and built a wonderful new upstairs sitting room. Danielle and John did it all in white.

John's at-home office came next. Looking up at the house from below, Danielle explains, they noticed a terrace outside a wall that was bricked up. The construction workers took out the wall, and put in French double doors. John's office now has a lovely view of San Francisco. They found an Empire day bed for him, and slathered the wall with a dark green moiré fabric wall covering . . . all presided over by a very amusing monkey portrait by Carlos Marchiori. The bed looks very cozy for reading, with what looks like a mink or sable fur throw and pillows, accented with silk.

Danielle's office is next to John's. Here, the ceiling has been painted with tiny red hearts amidst clouds. She's again kept her writing corner cozy and small.

On the main floor, John and Danielle brought a welcoming gleam to the public face of the house. Here they have given the fabulous parties they are now famous for in San Francisco: the annual birthday party for John, christenings for the five new babies they have brought into the world, black-tie

Christmas balls, New Year's Eve festivities, birthday parties for friends, and cocktail receptions for business associates as they travel through town.

There is a lot of money in the Traina household.

But the children here are not spoiled, according to all accounts.

John Traina has always been very careful with the allowances he gives the children. They are paid for useful jobs around the house—their paychecks used to top out at $20 for a complete car wax.

There have been graduation parties here for Bede and Trevor after they came home from Princeton, and even a jazz party. The glass half-dome on the landing of the stairwell shapes a perfect stage for musicians. And at Christmas, the stairwell is the site for Danielle's thirty-foot Christmas tree.

The main-floor rooms are lovely. There is now marble on the floors of the entryway, just as Danielle had envisioned, the ceiling has had its arch transformed into a light blue summer sky with gentle clouds drifting in a light breeze. The living room is quietly comfortable in cream and gilt—the details on the ceiling have been picked out in gilt, echoed by the brass of the chandelier. High windows draped with quiet silk polish the elegance of the room. And a lovely painting by San Francisco artist Babs Cole hangs in the hall; another by William Malherbe is above the fireplace.

The "chapel," formerly the Bishop's chapel and now a sitting room, has a wonderful eighteenth century portrait by Jean-Marc Nattier and antique satin hangings for the windows, said to be from a château in France. Underfoot, a beautifully detailed needlepoint rug.

Other rooms along the first floor are the main hall, off the entryway, with the leaded half-dome on its axis.

The library, with a beautifully hand-carved ceiling, framed by columns twelve feet high, has one entire wall of books and a roaring fireplace. This contemplative room opens up to a little garden at the side of the house.

The dining room, where dinner is served, features dark rosewood paneling, with pilasters and columns, arches and artwork, all serving as a warm environment for the Biedermeyer dining table that can seat twenty-four guests. The lighting comes from both silver candelabras and a wonderful old Tiffany chandelier converted from gas—it was there since the time the house was built in 1895.

Out past the dining room is the kitchen, and the pantries through which the servants pass with the food.

Off the kitchen is another smaller dining room. Danielle's former cook talks about routines and life with Danielle Steel in the next chapter. . . .

Chapter Sixteen
Accident

"Everybody used to say that she was moody or difficult and I never saw that side of her at all. She just never gave me a hard time"
—Danielle Steel's former cook

Danielle had good instincts in hiring the servants—but she slipped up when she hired a Brazilian couple to cook their meals. They didn't know about American refrigeration and hygiene in the kitchen, and the entire family got deathly ill one night from eating meat that had been left out overnight, and then served at dinner. Shortly after that incident, Danielle hired Lois Korotkin to shape up the kitchen: to teach their cook how to cook. Here's an insider's view about just what it was like to work for Danielle, John, and their children inside the mansion soon after they moved in.

Q: How did you hear about the job?
A: I used to go dancing Monday night with their nanny—who's from England—and a couple that were friends of mine. I was in cooking school then at Tante Marie's in North Beach [San Francisco].

Q: Was Danielle Steel a good boss?
A: I had heard from my cooking teacher—who'd heard through the grapevine—that "you are going to have a very difficult woman to work with."

And I didn't find her difficult to work with at all.

I thought she was just a stunning woman, especially the way she dressed.

Q: What was your first interview like?
A: Well, first she talked to me on the phone, and asked me about myself. She met me in person a few times . . . and she checked me out. Then her husband met me in person . . . and they told me what happened with the meat. Everybody got sick. John and Danielle too.

Everybody used to say that she was moody or difficult and I never saw that side of her at all. She just never gave me a hard time.

All these people who worked there came through all the time, but I just did my job. The social secretary, and the guy and the girl from Brazil who lived in the back house [the converted carriage house with an ivy-covered roof that could be seen from the dining room], the nursemaid, the nanny.

Q: So it was teaching the cook to cook that brought you into Danielle's house?
A: Danielle didn't cook. What she did was to hire a Brazilian couple, a young couple that had just come up from Brazil. And he didn't know how to cook food American-style. He left the meat out, served it to the entire family the next day and everybody got very sick.

So she wanted me to teach these people

how to cook American food, American-style. Things like using refrigeration for meat. . . .

I was getting $15 an hour, and I was in school. That was what a teacher suggested to charge. Everyone always overcharges them, but I thought that was fair. I had no budget for the food; I bought whatever I needed.

Q: What were Danielle's diet secrets for staying so thin—did you keep the calories to a certain level and cut out the fat?
A: No. She didn't give me any rules at all. The only complaint she had was asking me not to use a lot of lemon.

And when she had a cold, she wasn't eating—she'd get chicken soup in that looked homemade. When she had the cold, then she got to call me on the phone from upstairs . . . her bedroom. And the doctor came by with a jar of chicken soup.

Nobody told me what she ate, or what the kids ate or anything. I asked the kids to tell me what they ate. I talked Nicholas into eating shrimp . . . prawns, in lemon and butter . . . and he ate them.

They had chicken, lamb quite a few times, baby vegetables, artichokes. I'd call up and order food a day ahead to be delivered from the store.

Q: What was your first impression of her?
A: One afternoon, I was chopping garlic, and

I looked up and she was standing in the kitchen. I turned and said, "You are beautiful." She had been at a luncheon, and she had on a designer outfit and her hair was just perfect . . . this outfit must have been a $30,000 designer outfit, I mean I just looked at her and went "wow. . . ."

I mean, that woman could really dress. I thought she was just a stunning woman.

And I thought she was a very classy lady, very well educated, very well spoken, and she looked just great, dressed beautifully, I was like "wow"!

Q: And what was your first impression of the house?
A: Oh, it's gigantic. I really liked it. There are all back passageways through the house. You don't have to go walk through the middle of the room.

It is a formally decorated house.

And the kids . . . I've never seen so many stuffed animals, all sizes and kinds, an entire wall. The hallway wall on the third floor. There was just Nicholas then, and the little baby. The ceilings were painted with sky and things, the whole third floor.

I never knew where she was in the house, because the house is so big. All I know is that I'd get a phone call and know when she'd be down.

One day, the nanny took me on a tour of

the house, and she [Danielle] had a really big
room.

Q: And what was John Traina like?
A: He was out of town a lot, but she was always there. He was a really nice guy. I found
him very attractive.

John Traina has kids from another marriage [Todd and Trevor from his marriage to
Dede Buchanan Wilsey]. And she had a
daughter in junior high [Beatrix Lazard].
Beatrix and her girlfriends were always in the
kitchen talking to me. Beatrix was just a regular person, not snobby or stuck up. And then
there was Nicholas and the little baby.

But John's kids Trevor and Todd were
away at school. They would only come home
for the holidays.

They [Trevor and Todd] were in the house
once when I was there.

But John Traina is tall and thin. She did
pretty good!

Q: When did they eat? (She described their cozy
family dining room off the kitchen, and their
more formal dining room.)
A: The kids ate at 5 P.M.. And the grown-ups
at 7 P.M.

The kids don't eat [dinner] with Danielle.
It is a very formal household. She had a separate dining room off the kitchen for the
nanny and the nursemaid and the kids.

But once a week, Danielle eats with the kids.

When I came in, she had two sets of silver from Tiffany and dishes. And the silver wasn't ever polished. I asked the couple, "Do they eat on this every night?" and they said "yes," and I told them that somebody had to polish it. It really bothered me that no one had noticed . . . I think it was just lack of knowledge by them [the Brazilians]. The dishes, the silver from Tiffany, and none of it polished and it drove me crazy. But then, I grew up in a house where my mother had me constantly polishing the silver!

Q: And Danielle is friends with Mitterand, the President of France?
A: This is a really funny story. I almost had to cook for the president of France, and serve him tacos made with hamburger meat! Mitterand was in town, and Danielle's good friends with him. . . .

I knew the president of France was in the house, and I knew he was supposed to leave for Washington, D.C., that night. Meanwhile, Nicky had asked me for tacos for dinner. And I just panicked . . . I'm a cook, I can't serve the president of France tacos for dinner. But, whew, he didn't end up staying for dinner.

Q: So was Danielle very social?
A: There was always something going on in the house. I think she is pretty social.

Q: Was this the time she was working on the baby book with the other women in San Francisco?
A: She had a lot of baby showers for friends, [probably because she had been working on *Having a Baby* with them]. I came in only to cook the two dinners, one for 5 P.M. and one for 7 P.M., but I'd see the chocolate from the caterer. They said she had another baby shower every week. But I didn't cook for them. They were catered.

Q: So she didn't eat with the children. What did the children do?
A: Well, the limo driver would be called, by the social secretary I guess. I never talked to her.

The nanny would go everywhere with the kids in the limo. The nanny would take the kids to dinner all the time at Trader Vic's, or to concerts.

And I just loved Nicky. He liked chocolate a lot. It was his favorite dessert. And he have me a little ring from a gum ball machine that I still have.

Nicky really liked this Michael Jackson video "Thriller," with Vincent Price, and he watched it on MTV all the time. He actually memorized the whole Michael Jackson routine to "Thriller." And then when he started doing that, Danielle cut off MTV to everybody in the house.

But the nanny got really upset, because she

was at the age where she was stuck with all
these kids, and the television and MTV was
her only way of being in touch with that
world.

But Nicholas was always looking very
good, his hair was always combed . . . he was
this charming boy, he just charmed me to
death. I love him. He was great. He gave me
that darling little ring.

And basically, I found that Danielle, his
mother, was just a really charming lady too.
Q: And who did the security in the house?
A: They were kind of paranoid.

Her husband, John Traina, was very, very
concerned, very conscious of what went on.
The grocery store delivers their bags of groceries, and one day, another package was
thrown over the gate after the delivery. It was
a package of meat, wrapped in butcher paper,
thrown over the fence. Their security is really
tight, and John heard about it in the house.
He was afraid the meat was poisoned.

He came into the kitchen right away, asking, "Where's the package? Where's the package?" There to protect her.

And the limo driver is security. And I
don't even know where they kept all the cars.
They'd just say, call for the limo, and it would
show up. I never even saw it.

*Q: And why did you leave Danielle Steel's house-
hold staff?*

A: I was just hired to train the Brazilian couple about the food, so there wouldn't be any more food poisoning. And I gave them a *Joy of Cooking* cookbook, so they would understand about the American way of preparing food.

Chapter Seventeen
Fine Things

"Danielle Steel, whether she be a person, a computer, or a combine . . . is no more to be underestimated than President Reagan is. Each is sincere, and each knows his or her audience."

—excerpt from *Vogue* review of *Family Album*

There is really no shortage of money in Danielle Steel's household to pay for exotic trips to faraway places. But Danielle prefers to say close at home: close by the children, and close by that million-dollar machine of hers, her 1940s metal-body Olympia typewriter.

By the 1990s, what would it cost to convince Danielle Steel to consider leaving her publisher?

Twenty million dollars a year—that's the number bruited about the back rooms of New York publishers plotting to lure Steel away from her home of the past eighteen years, Delacorte Press. Delacorte's president, Carol Baron, is also Steel's personal editor.

The big money in the book business, and especially the literary romance genre, staggers the uninitiated.

When Danielle Steel first started typing on that old Olympia of hers, it was for $3,500, from Pocket Books, a division of Simon & Schuster which is now part of Paramount, part of Viacom, an international media conglomerate. The executives are probably kicking themselves that they lost Danielle

Steel right before she became a world-famous California goldmine.

Going Home was a paperback original first selling for $1.25. By the nineties, Pocket had cranked out forty-plus printings, and it was selling for $5.95. So in 1991 Pocket Star Books made the wise publishing decision to bring out a "special keepsake edition," which has already raced through about a dozen printings as of this writing.

That's just one little book.

A Yale Professor of Humanities reviewed Danielle's *Family Album* in *Vogue*, 1985, under the headline of "Venus Envy" and said he felt her novel genuinely sprang from real emotions. He also noted that Danielle Steel was by then the author of eighteen novels translated into eighteen languages and selling, all told, over fifty million copies.

These highly successful eighteen novels had all been negotiated by Phyllis Westberg, the agent who'd been with Danielle since Steel was in her early twenties, stuck by her through the five novels that were rejected by publishers, and continued to build her career.

Phyllis Westberg started working with Danielle Steel as her client back around 1971. A friend of Danielle's introduced them, and they seemed to work well together. Phyllis was with Harold Ober's prestigious old-line agency in New York.

Danielle actually wrote her first novel *Going Home* around 1971, and Phyllis sold it in 1972. But Pocket didn't actually publish it until 1973.

Phyllis simply couldn't sell Danielle's next five books—no publisher would have them—but she never once discouraged Danielle from keeping at her work. She finally hooked Danielle up with Dell. Dell's offer in 1978 to Danielle to write the novelization of Universal's *The Promise* was the push that lifted her sales and made her career take off.

By the early eighties, Phyllis Westberg was negotiating successive three-book contracts for Danielle with her publisher Dell.

One such contract ended with *The Ring,* her first hardcover book, dedicated to Bill Toth.

On her next-to-last three-book contract negotiated by Phyllis, two of the three books were published in hardcover: *Thurston House,* published in paperback, the hardcover *Full Circle,* published in 1984, and hardcover *Family Album,* published in 1985.

The last three-book contract negotiated by Phyllis for Danielle was all for hardcover books: *Once in a Lifetime, Crossings,* and *Changes.* Phyllis also negotiated the contract for the simultaneous hard/softcover publication of the April 1984 baby book written by Danielle and her friends in San Francisco, called *Having a Baby.*

Back then it was unheard of for a writer who'd been working on paperback romance originals to start publishing in hardcover. Danielle Steel was the first. But it drove Danielle crazy that Dell took so long to start publishing her in hardcover—where the potential profits for the author are so much higher.

But leaving her original agent in the spring of 1983 to find a newer, tougher agent seems to have given Danielle a stronger hand in the market.

In 1984 Mort Janklow's name started appearing as her agent in *Publishers Weekly*, at first selling the foreign rights for *Family Album* and the repackaging of her 1980 poetry collection *Love: Poems* in November of 1984.

Publishers Weekly reviewed the repackaged book on October 5, 1984:

> The theme, as expected, is love, upper case. Steel describes the ending of one relationship, the beginning of another and the loneliness in between. The bestselling novelist, however, is out of her metier here.
>
> These are not poems, they are adolescent scribblings, filled with simplistic emotions and cliches. . . . Many of these verses appeared originally in a paperback of the same title; others are reprinted from *McCall's* and *Cosmopolitan*. Literary Guild and Doubleday Book Club alternates. Foreign rights: Mort Janklow.

Mort Janklow's very strong hand is visible here: a flimsy paperback volume, several years old, is now repackaged, and despite a grisly review becomes both a Literary Guild and Doubleday Book Club alternate and a perennial favorite.

Another twist to her career came with the creation of Benitreto Productions, Ltd., with her businessman-manager-husband, John Traina, a legal entity set up, in part, to ease the tax burden on the author. In a few years, with a change in the tax laws, Benitreto was replaced with the Danielle Steel copyrights on her books.

"Danielle Steel," concluded the *Vogue* review of *Family Album*, "whether she be a person, a computer or a combine (the book is copyrighted by Benitreto Productions, Ltd.), is no more to be underestimated than President Reagan is. Each is sincere, and each knows his or her audience."

Today, her superagent Mort Janklow has molded Danielle Steel into the word's BIGGEST selling author in terms of gross sales in over thirty countries.

But how did Mort Janklow snag America's top novelist?

It was because of John Traina.

"I couldn't do anything without him," said Danielle, talking about her fourth husband. "He made it all happen."

Before she married John Traina in the summer of 1981, her books were doing very well indeed, but there was no big organized corporate push behind her. John Traina, who was surprised by

Danielle's lack of rock-solid business experience, set in motion the review process to select a new agent.

Mort Janklow's multimillion-dollar secret for Danielle: getting her OUT of the romantic fiction list, and into the mainstream commercial fiction category.

Janklow got involved with cover design and typography and advertising. It's a big responsibility keeping track of all this when the books are being published in something like twenty or thirty countries.

Lou Blau, Danielle's Century City lawyer, called Mort Janklow while he was on vacation at St. Martin in the Caribbean.

Danielle's left her former agent, he told Mort, and you're one of the three people we're considering to be her new agent. Would you be willing to come out to San Francisco to talk with her about it?

Sure, said Janklow, but only when my vacation's finished.

The superagent soon boarded a plane to California and he and Danielle had a nice long meeting in her house. The two found that they made a terrific team. Mort was eager to work with her because he felt he could "maximize" the work the publisher was putting into marketing her books.

In other words, they could figure out ways to sell even more hardcover and paperback copies, expand her readership nationally and internationally, and make more money. Her backlist of books started working for her like money in the bank, an ongoing source of income, selling and reselling to readers just discovering her.

Danielle already had built up her loyal audience, and she was already well-respected in the industry as an incredibly disciplined and hardworking writer. Mort now made sure people paid attention to her—that her books came out properly in hardcover, in paperback, and that they looked handsome, and didn't have blurb copy that embarrassed her, or cover illustrations she thought were silly, or other things that kept her reading audience at levels less than it could be.

As she'd done with Phyllis Westberg, she writes so many books that she always seems to have two or three "in the pipeline"—books that are totally finished but not published for one or two or three years, whenever the marketing team feels would be a good time to bring them into the bookstores. Since Janklow represents so many best-selling authors, they can even coordinate the timing of their own clients' best-sellers, to give their writers a clear shot at hitting *The New York Times Best Seller List*, which every bookstore in the country uses for ordering books.

Janklow's agency soon discovered that Danielle was an extremely generous and gracious woman.

And they discovered that Danielle was also a very strong-minded woman. She knows what she wants. And she's prepared to sacrifice to get what she wants. Which means her organization and her schedule comes first. And the books come second only to her schedule and the children.

But she's NEVER missed one of her own self-imposed deadlines: she knows the value of sacrificing shortsighted fun for her long-term goals.

"Because of the romance thing," Steel said the following year, "people wanted not to take my writing seriously. I put an enormous amount of work into the books and an awful lot of time and effort goes into them and they should be treated with some amount of seriousness. They're a going concern."

And Steel has a massive audience. The Steel books rachet to the top of the best-seller lists, sit there in the bright sunshine and luxuriate, while the golden coins rain down upon her trademark products.

In fact, Danielle Steel's publisher was trying to sell her books with a 900 number, the kind that the caller pays by the minute to use. [Infotrac]

Although Danielle changed agents, she so far shows no inclination to change publishers.

Delacorte/Dell does its best to keep her happy. "She's supporting this house," her editor told a reporter. "I think this is a case where everyone is making money—including [agent] Mort Janklow."

Delacorte and Danielle have developed a superb working relationship over the years, and they do a brilliant job with her books. It was obvious in her 1982 interview that Danielle was chafing with the romantic covers, mushy cover copy, and lack of respect paid her work, but that was something Mort Janklow straightened out.

Occasional glimmers of the sort of back room negotiations that keep Steel so loyal to Delacorte/Dell have surfaced in the press. In 1990, *Publishers Weekly* ran a brief item noting that Mort Janklow had gotten his client $60 million for her next five books. Janklow himself would neither confirm nor deny the $60-million contract.

Since Steel sometimes writes a book every nine months, she may have raced through those five books in forty-five months, in somewhere between three or four years. Figuring this further, that's more than $15 million a year for her new books if she doesn't falter in her almost inhuman writing schedule.

That $15 million may be on top of her current income stream, reported in *Woman's Day,* 1990, of $25 million. (And then later denied, quite strenuously, by her public relations firm, Rogers & Cowan.) Whatever it is, it's definitely over a million a year, and something under $40 million annually.

But if we read in *The New York Times* that Barbara Taylor Bradford, runner-up to Danielle Steel, is zipping up $36 million for her next three books, Steel's $60 million makes sense.

Bradford, at number two, is getting $12 million

per book. Steel, number one, is signed for precisely the same, $12 million per book. Steel just writes shorter books, twice as fast.

Danielle won't disclose her income. She told a reporter that people in cattle country considered it quite rude to ask how many head of cattle you own. "I always feel like saying, 'Would you like a piece of paper and a pen?' "

Danielle's first novel fully agented by Mort Janklow may have been *Secrets,* in 1985. Her blockbuster career was thrusting forward, full throttle. But Janklow came along to fine-tune the contracts, fine-tune the international sales, and make sure the publisher was doing as much for Danielle as they could.

Secrets was reviewed, for instance, in both *The New York Times* and *Time* magazine. Publication of her books was perceived as an "event" now in the book world, a publishing phenomenon, though the reviewers still had a hard time making sense of their precise appeal to the nation's women.

Publishers Weekly reviewed *Secrets* on March 6, 1985, and admitted that Danielle's fans just keep coming back for more:

> Midas touch producer Mel Wechsler casts five actors for his prime-time TV series "Manhattan," but the price of soaring opportunity for its stars forces hidden lives into the limelight.

Bill Warwick's secret marriage to a drug addict threatens both his contract and his sanity, while Zach Taylor's ambivalent homosexuality imprisons him in an accidental history.

Gabrielle Smith hides her family heritage, while Jane Adams faces another family secret: a violent and abusive husband.

The glamorous and clandestine details, in a New York-Beverly Hills setting, add the usual glitter. If "Secrets" sometimes plunges into the implausible (could Jane Adams actually pull off a decade as a soap star, while hubby thinks she is doing volunteer work?), dreams, power, and searing family loyalties are more to the point.

The center of power (no shortage here) is the duo of ageless star Sabina Quarles—whose secret is withheld to the end—and producer Wechsler, who exemplifies a quality that keeps Steel fans coming back for more: the art of adoring the woman who meets his match.

The New York Times Book Review guessed that Danielle modeled her fictional show *Manhattan* on *Dynasty*, which makes sense, knowing that her television producer-to-be, Doug Cramer, also produced the prime-time soap. The reviewer, who now reviews for National Public Radio, found the plot "painfully predictable." But then David Bianculli isn't one of Danielle Steel's fans. He just doesn't understand.

Time, in their review, noted "In the continuing saga of How the Book World Turns, Danielle Steel is queen of the immaculately coiffed romance." The characters in *Secrets* are both "busy professionals and powerful love goddesses. The most impressive of the trio converts a homosexual into her lover and the father of her child."

But with Danielle's concern with the external beauty of her handsome characters, notes *Time*, "The effect is to raise physical perfection to a spiritual value."

Chapter Eighteen
Mixed Blessings

All you need to succeed is a yellow pad and a pencil.
> —André Meyer, Lazard Frères, New York

Visions of $60-million dollar book deals inspire thousands of writers to try their hand at writing romance, and many of these first novels do make it to publication.

But it's a very crowded field, and the personal price is increasingly steep on the top rungs. Danielle Steel has paid a high price in personal and physical uneasiness both for herself and her children.

Some observers wonder if she's writing what may be called thinly veiled domestic dramas with true-crime heroes—blending her own personal experience and imagination to create dramatic stories of love and revenge.

Unfortunately, the people who really seem to make Steel nervous aren't the unknown fans. They are well-known former residents of San Quentin and Vacaville, Lompoc and Folsom Prison. They are her second and third ex-husbands.

"Zugelder is the final chapter," says Bill Toth, legally her husband at the time.

"He gets out [of prison on parole], contacts her.

"She gets uptight.

"Nicky is [Danielle's son with Bill Toth] about a year old, Beatrix is about nine . . ."

* * *

In 1979, she told a friend in New York she had just been going through a period of terrifying threats on her family.

An ex-con had read one of her novels in prison and now, out on parole, accused her of basing the novel on his life. Danielle denies this.

Danielle didn't mention to the friend that the ex-con had until recently also been her husband, Danny Zugelder.

Danielle, terrified, hired a twenty-four-hour bodyguard, but "luckily," said the friend, "because the ex-con [Danny] raped the daughter of a law-man in another state, he had been put back in prison."

Mort Janklow later said he didn't blame Danielle for being security conscious. She's had "crazy threats" he told a reporter, and she's got all those kids.

Danielle Steel tries to keep her address a secret. But she is a stellar resident of one of the most beautiful cities in the world, the town columnist Herb Caen calls Baghdad-by-the-Bay. Herb Caen serves as San Francisco's, perhaps the nation's, longest-running hardest-working daily columnist, and Steel's comings and goings have been fondly observed.

But Steel has asked mass-market women's maga-zines for years not to reveal where she lives. But Herb Caen's column, and of course photos of her new house, the landmarked Spreckels Mansion, in the national magazine *W,* and in *People,* and the old mansion in *Architectural Digest,* make it obvious she lives in San Francisco.

But sociopaths, criminals, and just plain fans have their ways of finding people, unfortunately.

Plots featuring criminals have often drawn the attention of criminals. So one would guess Steel takes the same precautions as those taken by true-crime writers themselves. And almost all true-crime writers seem to have been threatened, according to *The Wall Street Journal.*

"If a guy's a vicious rapist, then you've got to describe him that way," says Seattle-based writer Jack Olsen. "And if that makes his friends want to hurt you, then that's part of the cost of doing business."

Stories abound of criminals plotting revenge in prison cells and hiring freed inmates to carry out hits for him. Remember that when Danny Zugelder was brought in by the Colorado Highway Patrol in 1979, the town marshal wrote, "This is one mean man." The Marshal added "he makes Bundy look like a church boy."

When Danny wrote to Danielle, his ex-wife of little more than a year, asking for money for a defense lawyer on one of his rape charges, he was stunned by the result. Since she'd put up about $17,500 for his last rape trial defense five years earlier, he had assumed she would be equally generous.

The money from her books had started rolling in after *The Promise* hit, and she was becoming increasingly involved in San Francisco high society. She wanted nothing to do with Zugelder.

According to Zugelder, she turned his letter over to the warden of his Colorado prison. The warden, again according to Zugelder, determined that he was blackmailing Danielle by promising not to reveal he'd ever been married to her in exchange for her monetary help. He was forbidden to ever write her.

He will be up for parole in 1998. Again, as in his California prison career, he shows signs of being a model prisoner.

Danielle Steel's dramas are now increasingly domestic, but there is always the threat of sudden, tragic violence that disrupts her characters' lives.

In *Vanished* (1993), dedicated to Nicholas, Danielle returns to the mysterious abduction of a child, a theme she also used in *Fine Things*.

In *No Greater Love* (1981), also dedicated to Nicholas, a girl is beaten and raped in Central Park.

Fine Things was reviewed in *Publishers Weekly* on June 2, 1987. (By this time, Mort Janklow and Delacorte were saying she had 70 million books in print.) *PW* wondered if even the staunchest fans could believe the plot line of the book, and yet the elements of the woman dying of cancer are true (a friend of Danielle's had died around 1983 or so when she was writing the book), and the custody battle for her child with the father, who was a threatening ex-con, drug addict . . . and black-mailer . . . could have precedents in Danielle's real life.

"Working on this book was an intensely draining experience," she says. She wrote it "to honor a dear friend who had recently died of breast cancer, and the memories of her struggle were sometimes very painful. She fought the cancer for five years, and in the end, it was devastating to watch. My friend was a woman who was not much older than I am, who also had a large family. Seeing someone so much like me with a fatal illness was terrifying. I love everything about my life, and it scares me to think of it all coming to an end."

Reviews were mixed. *Publishers Weekly* was visibly harsh.

Bestselling novelist Steel has put yet another pot on to boil, but even her staunchest fans are bound to find the book's extremes hard to swallow. Bernie Fine has no luck with romance until, as the manager of a glitzy department store, he accidentally meets Liz and her young daughter, Jane. A saccharine courtship is followed by a perfect marriage, but their idyll ends abruptly when Liz develops cancer.

Bernie's palpable anguish as she dies is increased when Jane is kidnapped and held for ransom by her ne'er-do-well father.

Despite the crime, an indifferent court of law awards custody to the kidnapper, who is conveniently killed while robbing a bank on the very day he's scheduled to take his frightened daughter away from the only home she knows.

Then a lovely pediatrician steals Bernie's heart, causing him to believe he's utterly betrayed the love he shared with Liz. Credibility is ebbing fast when the book is salvaged by passages depicting Bernie and Jane's convincing, true-to-life feelings about the death of a loved one.

And now, even when Danielle steers away from domestic violence and writes stories about Europe that may be based on her family myths, she gets into trouble with reviewers for political naivete.

Her first hardcover hero, Walmar von Gotthard of *The Ring*, is a German banker who works with the Nazis, while helping a few others flee on the side.

A 1981 visitor to her San Francisco house recalls that among countless old family photographs, there are photos of her German father, the Schuelein who became Schulein-Steel, in white tie and tails, looking very dashing; pictures of the family castle in Munich (looking much like the von Gotthard *schloss* in *The Ring*); and photographs of her family's stables and several family members riding to hounds.

In a 1992 look at *Jewels,* with Danielle's "extraordinary" heroine Sarah Whitfield, the *Wall Street Journal* reviewer wonders how "you can call flirting with the Nazis and postwar profiteering extraordinary."

"After the war," continues the reviewer, "[her heroine] finds a new hobby buying up fabulous pieces of jewelry from refugees, impoverished Jews and Nazi collaborators. As her husband the duke puts it: 'It's actually a very nice, clean way of helping people, and lending them money.' "

But perhaps some of the stories Danielle Steel has told various interviewers about her past, and the fabulous German side of her family, are just that—stories. As we know from her relative in New York, the grandparents kept a few cows at their country place, not horses.

In *Jewels* Danielle seems to be writing about her personal family myth, untarnished by the horrors. After all, she told Bill Toth that a great-aunt had left Germany and after World War II sold old oil paintings in Manhattan, paintings from the same milieu.

Remembrance, written while she was still married to Bill Toth and constructing those fantasy romances to make up for what she missed in real life, was reviewed August 28, 1981, in *Publishers Weekly,* a couple of months after her marriage to John Traina.

Those readers who love to lose themselves in long romance will not be disappointed by Danielle Steel's new novel, although they will have to be patient, for it is slow to gain momentum.

Dealing with two generations of beautiful

women, it first focuses on Serena, the impoverished green-eyed Italian princess who moves like a grown-up Barbie doll through one elegant setting after another in her fairy tale romance with wealthy American Brad Fullerton.

After her death the novel finally gets rolling and soon the reader is gripped by more realistic characters and a compelling narrative involving an orphaned child and wrenching custody fight. Recounting the struggle of Serena's daughter to deal with her tragic past, Steel may keep some readers up long after they should have turned out the light.

A moving ending in which emotional wounds are healed and long-broken relationships are restored will leave lovers of romance weepy and well satisfied.

The other book Danielle published in 1987 with *Fine Things* was called *Kaleidoscope*. As with *Fine Things,* reviewers couldn't imagine anyone believing in the plot, yet elements of the plot (the young girl married to the French aristocrat, the woman doctor, and the cold, ambitious New York executive) were from worlds Danielle knew well. Here's the *Publishers Weekly* review of September 25, 1987:

The pages of Steel's newest novel are packed with an assortment of one-dimensional characters, each one more broadly sketched than the last. Sam Walker and Arthur Patterson, American soldiers in war-torn Paris, fall in love with Solange, a proud young French-woman. Having won her, Sam brings his beautiful war bride to New York, where he instantly sets Broadway agog at his acting talent, mercurial temper, and restless love affairs. Tragedy strikes when he kills Solange during an argument, and later himself, orphaning their three pampered daughters.

Arthur cravenly arranges adoptions for the youngest two, but nine-year-old Hillary is dealt a life of utter misery. Determined to reunite her little family, she grimly survives only to find that the man responsible for her torment has lost all traces of her sisters.

Years later, John Chapman is hired by a dying, penitent Arthur to find the sisters and bring them together. As he follows their trails, Chapman becomes obsessed by his quarry—one the wife of a French baron, one a doctor in Appalachia, and the third a cold, ambitious network executive—and his search for a happy ending that will wipe away the awful past. The book gets off to a slow, overly sweet start, but by the midway mark Steel has given these tired characters a fresh look and vibrant momentum all their own.

Had Danielle willed herself into a life of great wealth by her insistence on writing books set in this luxe world? And by her obsessive push to get the books finished and published on an almost inhuman work schedule? Perhaps that's the secret of her belief in Christian Science—that the mind can actually create the reality you live in, if you wish it hard enough.

She now lives in the most fabulous mansion in the Bay Area—rivaling those in any American city—high atop the Pacific Heights.

But such a fast, rapid climb extracts a price in personal privacy.

Chapter Nineteen
Having a Baby

"The lively plot and fast romp over the past three decades make the book a good read."
—from *N.Y. Times* review for *Full Circle*

Lois Korotkin, Danielle's cook, was just one of many assistants helping her life as a working mother to function smoothly.

Danielle had her own live-in housekeeper by 1978—it was the only way she could be a working mother.

By the time she moved into her new mansion with John Traina, her staffing problems were multiplying exponentially, as were her responsibilities.

Soon, in addition to Beatrix and Nicholas, she had one, two, three, four, then five babies with John Traina, all in a row. Five babies in about six years. Maxx, their son, came next to last.

She employed a "social secretary" in 1983, following the style of the Pacific Heights society she'd moved into. There was a Ms. Moorehead for Ann Getty, Ms. Gotcher for Dodie Rosekrans (who used to live in the Spreckels mansion), Ms. Fulton for Lita Vietor, and Ms. Wheeler for Danielle Steel.

Stand-in organizer for the kids, arranging play dates for the children, and calling the limo for transportation for the children to school, social events, etc.—these are the social secretary's duties.

Her other job back then was riding herd on the construction of the new nursery in the mansion. This nursery was designed by the Trainas for their second baby, due in the fall. She also handled all of Danielle's correspondence, according to a newspaper article. The Trainas were then making frequent trips to New York, where the publishing business is, and to Beverly Hills, where the television and movie businesses are located. John Traina himself was making frequent trips abroad in his role as travel consultant.

A world-famous author with a full-time job writing contemporary novels for her millions of readers, Danielle was the quintessential career woman. Danielle realized that she had to be totally organized and self-disciplined to be able to handle the new responsibilities of babies.

In mid-1984, Danielle's novel *Full Circle* was published. The novel is a handbook for the woman who wants to have it all. Tana Roberts is born poor, raised by her mother, and at eighteen raped by her mother's lover's spoiled rich son. She's a Berkeley radical in the sixties, and by the seventies, a successful San Francisco prosecutor, addicted to her work, living in a tiny jewel of a house, but starting to want a man to share her life with, maybe even have children. Tana Roberts, a strong woman on her own, discovers she can have two children late in life, and create a happy family team with the older, sexy man that she loves and marries. *The New York Times* reviewer noted that Danielle Steel wrote "none of this women's lib . . .

for her." And that her husband, a judge, advised, "But there's no reason why you can't have a career and a family."

Danielle had just been working the kinks out for herself with John Traina, and it is becoming increasingly obvious that any woman *can* have a career and a family, if she's as well-organized and as well-heeled as Danielle Steel. Besides, adds *The New York Times*, ". . . the lively plot and fast romp over the past three decades make the book a good read."

Just the way Danielle sets about shopping for Christmas gives some indication of what kind of organization her life with five new babies will take: shopping for nine children, her beloved husband, her staff, all her friends, and perhaps a few things for her publisher and editor and support staff back in New York.

In January, she orders what she calls "the Biggie," a fresh tree that's over thirty feet tall. (In the old mansion, it rose up the central staircase like the towering tree the City of Paris once had in downtown San Francisco.)

She starts making lists for the family's gifts, one would suspect, as soon as the current Christmas has been celebrated. They have the photo taken for the Christmas card—one year it was at the Napa ranch with some of the colorful antique cars in the background. The photo has to be chosen, the cards printed and addressed.

By October, she has finished most of her shopping.

She's now mainly finished with her shopping, and then she has to try to figure out which gifts were for which child, which color was for whom. (Her father, she's written, asked in December what she'd like for Christmas. When he asked, he didn't mean for this Christmas, but the NEXT!)

So Danielle, true to her father's example, starts looking around for the Christmas lights in September, and lining up the Christmas stockings for all the kids.

She and the children bake brownies for their friends each year.

The children help to decorate the house.

And mid-December, they buy more trees to add to "the Biggie." There's a big Christmas tree for where the family gathers, and then each child gets to pick their very own tree for their own room. They decorate them with their homemade ornaments.

And spend Christmas day lounging around.

Lounging is not something Danielle often finds the time to do. Just running her domestic staff, which in 1988 consisted of a full-time nanny, housekeeper, cook, secretary, and baby nurse (plus probably two full-time cleaning people), would be more than some people could handle. But, according to both Danielle and others around San Francisco who have seen her in action, she certainly doesn't just hand over the kids to them and delegate all responsibility to her staff.

She's a compulsive organizer, a gift she'd have

to possess in order to keep track of this household: her husband John Traina and the children: Beatrix Lazard, twenty-six, Trevor, twenty-five, Todd, twenty-four, Nicholas, sixteen, and the younger ones, all under sixteen—Samantha, Victoria, Vanessa, Maxx, and Zara.

She plans her work years in advance with her editor and agent in New York. She also plans her life with her children up to six months in advance.

She and her assistant keep that set of very complex books that tell her exactly when she needs to take a child into the dentist for something like braces, or probably even when the children's pets need their shots and visits to their veterinarians.

These schedules mesh with her work schedules—her times for trips to New York.

In the eighties, she usually went to New York with the children in June, which made for quite an undertaking.

Luckily, by the early nineties, she'd had her nanny with her for twelve years, so there were no surprises on that front.

And within the day, she organizes to shave off every bit of wasted time.

She groups things together for different parts of the house, and schedules only one trip to save time.

When she goes out to run errands or goes shopping for presents, she also organizes her time. Instead of going where the spirit brings her, she has an organized itinerary, like a company president taking off for a one-day business trip to another town.

And, of course, she uses the telephone wherever possible, in these times when it's so easy to shop from catalogues all over the country and the world.

She does use the phone, especially with the children's clothes. Since she's now had so many children, she probably has a favorite saleswoman she can touch base with to order fashionable togs, and have these delivered to the house.

Again, time saved.

On Monday, she publishes her schedule for the week, including details of where she'll be at all times.

She goes everyplace with a beeper. (No, it's not trimmed with diamonds!)

That way, if there's an emergency with a child, she can be found at any time, any place, and rush back.

But the most important schedule, she says, is the one that centers around the family which she publishes on Friday (something anyone with a computer—or for that matter a typewriter and a xerox machine or even carbon paper—can do to organize their own household). With children working in town (Beatrix, the oldest), another at one time in Europe at grad school (Trevor, in England), another at Connecticut College and all those who still haven't taken off for school, it's a loaded schedule.

Gym classes, ballet classes, self-defense classes, dancing school.

And then, of course, the visiting between the children, the parties and their play groups.

When Maxx was two years old, on a prearranged schedule between Danielle and the other mothers, he would have his friends over to visit with him. She has always organized a play group like this for her children before they went off to nursery school.

In 1988, she would take Victoria and Vanessa to a gym class in the afternoon.

And send the children off to a music class on Mondays.

On Tuesdays, Maxx went to a play group at the church for three hours.

On Wednesdays, Maxx went to his gym class.

Two of the girls went to gym class as well, at another time.

And one went off to karate class, because she was being bullied by a classmate.

Another daughter was off to a cooking class. And there was probably soccer for Nicholas, the older son.

Three of the girls also went to an hour-long ballet class during the week.

On top of this wildly scheduled life, Danielle herself schedules her own time for writing books, keeping up with her agent, sometimes daily, talking with her editor, writing out the detailed outline of her next book, and writing and finishing a book that can be published usually every nine months.

But she does make a commitment, she said several years ago, to pick up each child from school two times a week, at the minimum. That's hard, with six school-age kids.

And to eat lunch with the kids every single day when they're home.

To take them off to all their doctors' appointments.

But when all else fails, and there's a crisis afoot, she'll dispatch her secretary to pick up one kid, and perhaps call in John to pinch-hit with another.

While Zara, the last child, was a baby, she nursed her. They had a half hour alone that way, without the other children bustling about. Yet she's written in *Having a Baby* that she doesn't feel breast-feeding is crucial for establishing a bond with the infant.

She's made her child-raising secret obvious: organization. And a lot of love. And why all the organization? She says it's so that she can manage to spend some time ALONE with each one of the children so they don't feel like a nameless face in the crowd.

This commitment to giving love and attention to her children means she has had to give up on some pleasures. A reader, looking at that glamorous picture on the back of the book jacket, would imagine that Danielle lunches constantly with her high-society friends, or flies down for the day to lunch with celebrities in Hollywood.

So while they were little, she says she didn't do

anything during the day that didn't involve the physical presence of one of the children.

In other words, no time given to the PTA, no time spent having coffee with the other mothers, and no lunch with girlfriends, except for a certain time around Christmas.

So despite the glamourous image, she's very isolated with the husband, children, and the typewriter in that big house of hers during the day.

The children take up so much time, that she has had to schedule one lunch with John, her husband, every week. That romantic lunch they have together, out of the house, come hell or high water.

Now, of course, that the children are growing older and she's taken over the Spreckels Mansion, she'll be going out more.

But the kids still adore her.

At Easter break, she may fly the whole family, along with one friend for each child, to Hawaii for vacation. According to a reporter, she's booked as many as twenty people into a first-class compartment.

And when she goes to get her Easter eggs, she doesn't just buy food-coloring kits. A reporter wrote that she was buying up $90 decorated enamel easter eggs at I. Magnin in San Francisco— THIRTY of them!

Chapter Twenty
Jewels

"[Danielle] doesn't like getting away without the children. . . . for her, the children come first."

—John Traina

"We had a beautiful wedding up in the Napa Valley," John told a reporter, "a lovely sunny day at a friend's house.

"I had a little house that wasn't big enough for all of us," explained John Traina.

"And now that we've settled into an old farm with lots of buildings, we have different buildings for different sets of kids . . . we have a compound, very informal, very natural . . . and we've kept it all farmlike."

Several times a year, Danielle may leave San Francisco to closet herself away up at the charming little country place she and John created in the Napa Valley.

According to one report, she'll stay up there at the ranch for days at a stretch, typing through the day and night to complete work on a book, stopping only to sleep her minimal four hours a night. She wrote one novel up there.

Other times, she may use the country hideaway for concentrated creative time, working through the bare bones of a new book idea, filling it in with the wonderful characters and scenes that she imagines so endlessly.

* * *

Her husband John Traina's inspiration got her out of the city and into this new vacation spot. As her husband John told a reporter, "when we married, Danielle liked going to the beach, and I of course have business in the [Napa] Valley, and I lured her away to the Valley. That's our getaway." But isn't it hard getting Danielle and all the children on the road and out to the country?

"I think we're both used to the business world and a busy life," says John Traina.

"Danielle has her career, I have my career, and we probably approach things well because of that," explains John.

"She's far more organized than I am, however. . . . It is hard for her to get away. And also, she doesn't like getting away without the children . . . for her, the children come first."

It takes great organization to get the family off to Napa. Once everyone is organized and out of the house with their clothes and bags and pets and tapes and books and friends, John Traina has two specially made vans that seat eighteen people, and John usually drives Danielle and the children. Another van comes up with the dogs, the pig, and the groceries.

The beach itself—its moods, its beauty, its drama—is a prominent character in her books, beginning from the very first, 1973's *Going Home*, with a sexy, seductive scene on horseback at Stinson Beach near Sausalito.

For three summers, the family rented houses in the blast-furnace heat, while she and John made a serious business of searching for their own corner of Eden. As John Traina explained in an interview, his place in Napa was definitely too small for Danielle's family plans.

But no matter, John was determined to find them a house in the Napa Valley . . . and he seemed to be a man of the land, happy to be outside in the sun, motoring around on the back of the tractor Danielle found for him, digging up the rich earth of the country's prime wine-growing valley.

Besides, their wonderful old antique car collection was getting bigger and bigger, and it would be nice to have a home away from home to garage them. Hadn't Herb Caen, in *The San Francisco Chronicle*, joked that neighbors of the Trainas were happy to see them finally moving to the Spreckels Mansion—that they didn't think of it as losing neighbors in 1991 but "gaining twenty-two parking spaces"?

San Francisco, like New York, is one of those places where land values are so very high in neighborhoods like Pacific Heights that people just don't have garages eating up their precious square footage. (*W* once reported that the Gettys were having so many hassles with their on-the-street parking that they bought the house next door, which came with its own garage.)

* * *

Before his death in 1984 John's father, John Traina, Sr., and his wife, Lea, had been part of the beloved extended family for the Christmas festivities Danielle planned and carried out each year. The elder Trainas themselves carried on a vary meaningful Italian Christmas tradition. There was baking, special Christmas wine, trees, and special Italian decorations, traditions about how, when, and where stockings were filled.

The only time John's father hadn't had a house in San Francisco was during the 1906 earthquake, when the family had gone across the bay to Sausalito for a year until things were rebuilt.

John, Jr., like his father, had graduated from the Lincoln School. His father and his mother had supported the charities and cultural life of San Francisco. They were early and strong backers of the San Francisco Opera, and entertained at delightful opera parties during the 1930s, 1940s, and 1950s.

One of John's sisters, Marissa, married the man who became head of Volkswagen, and went off to live in Germany after her marriage; and among them they had nine grandchildren at the time of his father's death in 1984.

John and Danielle were looking for the perfect country place so they could have a country compound for their own family.

They'd been renting for several summers, according to Danielle, but none of the properties they'd been shown by real estate agents in Napa particularly enchanted them. They wanted to establish a place in the country that would become a gathering spot not only for them and their six young children and the older siblings, but for family and friends through several generations—imagine the brood in twenty years, when everyone starts having children.

Danielle's reconstruction of both the Pacific Heights house and the Napa place to make room for more new family may have inspired her next novel, *Family Album*. She quoted the Bible in the preface to the book: "God places the solitary in families."

Here's what *Publishers Weekly* said about the book on March 8, 1984, when it was first reviewed:

Fame, fate and enduring marital love loom large in Steel's latest saga, tracing the 40-year union of astonishingly beautiful and talented movie star Fay Price and playboy/shipping heir Ward Thayer.

The novel begins with Fay's interment at Forest Lawn, a major media event, and then flashes back to the duo's first encounter in, of all places, the sweaty jungles of Guadalcanal in 1943. Their love was meant to be.

After V-J day, Fay and Ward meet again in Hollywood and the rest is history, breathlessly recounted, Steel-style, and featuring nearly every kind of good and bad event that happens to people in life. It's the stuff of melodrama over the decades, what with the vicissitudes of Hollywood life and the growing pains of the Thayers' five children, but Fay hangs tough.

Indomitable, she becomes "the most important female [film] director in the world" and dies quietly in her sleep in a villa at Cap Ferrat.

The *Los Angeles Times Book Review* ran a review of *Family Album* by Jacqueline Briskin that explained much of the "publishing phenomenon" Danielle had become by the mid-eighties. Her character "cares about her children as she cares about her husband. And here, it seems to me," writes Briskin, "is the key to Steel's success. *She* cares about that family too . . . through all these travails, love rules them. Critics might not consider sympathy an ingredient of literature, but the rest of us want our friends to be warm and caring."

By now, Danielle has written eighteen novels, according to her publisher's press kit, with fifty-five million copies in print. Even *The New York Times* is coming around to seeing that Danielle's entertainments have a place in women's hearts. *The Times Book Review* said "*Family Album* . . . manages to be absorbing. Throughout, the reader turns pages without pain, and sometimes with much satisfaction. Miss Steel certainly knows her craft, and knows how to how to project a sense of caring about her protagonists."

* * *

Think how uncomfortable it must have been taking their lively household and spending hot summer days in Napa squeezed into a rented fifties-modern house.

But then one day, they hit pay dirt. A practically untouched old house, a tiny little three-bedroom Victorian cottage, that was still full of the things that had been there when the owner had put it on the market.

It was the tradition, in the last century, to plant a stand of palm trees on ranch land to indicate the location of the owner's house, and after they'd followed a road lined with walnut trees and oleanders, they came upon what was to become their own stand of grand old palm trees.

The house had been built in 1856, and outside it, there was a formal front door and a small porch, a small screened porch on the back, and lots of Victorian gingerbread. Inside they found all sorts of Victorian treasures. There was faded wallpaper from the period. There were the original gaslight fixtures. There was Victorian furniture upholstered in horsehair. And even little hooked rugs, according to Danielle's description of the place in *Architectural Digest*.

How could they possibly shoehorn their kids and their menagerie into this tiny little three-bedroom Victorian jewel they had finally discovered?

On the first floor, there was a living room, a

small study with a fireplace, a small dining room, and a small kitchen.

Upstairs, there was one old bathroom and the three bedrooms.

As Danielle tells it, they had to have it. So they made it work.

Walking around the place, they found a water tower. A small caretaker's cottage. A horse stall. A milk shed. Pens for animals. Lean-tos. And a beat-up old barn.

They figured perhaps they could expand out into the surrounding buildings.

John and Danielle may have been inspired by the success of their friends the Charles de Limurs. Charles, like John Traina, is a car collector and wine enthusiast. He is the grandson of San Francisco banker W. H. Crocker and the son of a French count. His wife Nonnie also has deep roots in San Francisco society.

In 1959, after moving back from Paris with their three children, the de Limurs looked for a place in the country and found an ancient three-room cottage in the wine country.

Within two years their place had grown to four cottages, a large orchard, and a vineyard.

So this strange little old house that Danielle and John Traina finally found did have possibilities. And, besides, this countrified spot would give them an untrafficked country lane on which John might practice skateboarding in the turquoise suede high-tops that Danielle bought him one Christmas.

The caretaker's cottage, it turned out, had only

two small bedrooms. Along with the kitchen, it also had a living room, a dining room, and a little storage porch.

Figuring they could make the porch and dining room into two more bedrooms, they would have four.

If they built a fairy-tale three bedrooms in the water tower, they would give them seven bedrooms now.

And if they managed to get one bedroom into the horse stall, and three into the guest house, they would now have eleven bedrooms, instead of the three bedrooms they first thought they were stuck with.

Danielle writes that she and her husband decided to serve as both the decorators and architects on their country place, as they had earlier on the San Francisco project.

And it was the perfect timing—a pristine little farm coming on the market at a time when Danielle and John had both the experience, from the San Francisco project, and the checkbook to really get it done right and on time.

The project took them six months from the day they began construction—the day after Christmas. One can only imagine the extraordinary lists that kept Danielle moving through this project, and her books, and her children, at the same time.

The older children would be in one outbuilding,

with three bedrooms, with a bath and sauna on the main floor.

The little cottage was turned into four bedrooms and room for a wonderful little kitchen. And the horse stall was yet another place for guests (and no horses, thank you).

Danielle and John had discovered more treasures about their old farmland—a deserted overgrown garden in a stand of pine trees, many mysterious little outbuildings. And the children discovered more—an old Indian mound where they could find arrowheads, a river with a swimming hole.

And John Traina would soon set to work with the vineyards on the land. And designing a porch for the main house, setting the tone for further construction on the buildings.

The main house itself was expanded out, by the addition of a two-story balustraded porch encircling the entire house and picked out with more gingerbread detailing. It's now decorated with wicker furniture and such treats as a huge old popcorn cart. It was designed to be a great outdoor meeting place, with its comfortable furniture and views of the vineyards, sky, and hills.

As they had in the city, Danielle and John decided to move walls inside the house. This way, they enlarged the dining room and squeezed in space for an extra bath. They got rid of the walls around the kitchen and combined it with the back porch, creating a family-sized kitchen space. Here they could have meals with the kids, or be alone, since this was no longer the only cozy kitchen on the property.

By June, they'd carved out eleven bedrooms and five baths.

And they'd added a very romantic and cozy fireplace in the living room, the last touch needed on this warm and welcoming family getaway.

Perhaps the best room is the guest bedroom. Danielle found wonderful Victorian furniture, and dressed the room in a blue moiré fabric to match the Victorian-flavored wallpaper. Then she added a pink moiré trim. (Her decorating is much like the rooms she puts together in her fictional rooms, like *Changes*.)

The guest bed is canopied and romantic, with swagged double draperies. She has dressed the room with the perfect little touches: next to the room's washbasin are two pairs of antique lace bloomers, an old tin trunk, a Victorian hatbox. And into this special room go the Victorian-era clothes that she has begun collecting, inspired by this special little house. A white wool walking coat, handbag, and fan. A nightgown lavished with lace.

The master bedroom is decorated with white wicker furniture, like the cozy wraparound porch downstairs. Underfoot, rich blue carpeting, and funny old paintings of unicorns and monkeys, as well as portraits of children, dominate the space.

In the big old country kitchen Danielle and John carved out on the first floor, she moved in a big, serious restaurant stove, the kind that professional cooks swear by. The counters are yellow, and the room is lit by a couple of wooden chandeliers from Italy, hand-carved with charming little fruit and bird designs. And underfoot, the couple chose well-waxed hardwood floors. They found a player piano for this room, and Danielle writes in *Architectural Digest* that they often dance to its music at breakfast.

The dining room of the main house is only large enough for a sit-down dinner for twelve, but more serious entertaining is done in the city. They had a charming, hand-painted round table made to their order for the room, decorated with Danielle's trademark clouds and sky, along with birds, squirrels and rabbits . . . and a portrait of their well-loved dachshund, Swee' Pea, Danielle's gift to John the day after they were married.

A painted corner screen by the artist who did the dining table shows his interpretation of the four seasons. In another corner they put a friendly old suit of armor the children call "George." And also in this room they installed the framed Victorian murals which had come from John's grandfather's house.

The living room itself has that handsome new fireplace, with a perfect French sandstone mantel. Danielle writes that a nineteenth-century English gilt-framed mirror is her favorite piece, since it's hung with grapes, perfectly themed with the vineyard country outside. Their furniture here is Victorian, and they found a wonderful old French armoire to grace the ensemble. On the floor, a big old Persian rug they already owned gives a glow to the room.

Danielle writes that they also had fun with the other little living room, which they decided to do up as a black Victorian study. For the fireplace, they found black marble with pink veins. They painted the walls a high-gloss black, up to the moldings. Above that, a black wallpaper with a small pattern. And into this room they sent the favorites from years of sifting through antique shops for the perfect Victorian pieces: Danielle has an old sewing machine that's been converted to table use. An old gramophone. An old barber's chair. And two hard-to-find and very expensive horn chairs.

But where do Danielle and John keep perhaps the most engaging accessory of all, their pet pig?

The couple has a Vietnamese potbellied pig, which has also been seen strolling the halls of the house in San Francisco. It's a tiny little thing, for a pig, and only weighs in at eighty-five pounds. They're bred in California by Kayla Mull, and there are about six thousand of them in the United States now, with a male going for $1,500 and a breeding female a bit higher, at $5,000. *Elle* magazine reported in 1990 that there were potbellied pig shows with conformation prizes; potbellied pig newsletters, and a line of products including "No More Squeals" shampoo, a hoof and body moisturizer, an astringent called "Oinkment."

The pig rates just under the porpoise in its IQ—which ranks it much smarter than a dog. The pig is a pet that charmed Danielle. They are endlessly curious, just like a small child. And they are rumored to be extremely clean, and can be litter-trained, although, Danielle once told a reporter, "I've seen more pig shit in the last six months than I'd like to see for the rest of my life."

But, she added, "He's the sweetest animal, completely without malice, never cranky, and wonderful with the kids." Does he sleep in her bedroom? After all, Vietnamese potbellied pigs are known to curl up in their owner's bed like a dog. "Who'd want to sleep with a 90-pound animal with hooves and bristle hair?" she asked.

John once told a reporter that if he had to choose just ONE thing to grab in a crisis, it would be the tractor that Danielle gave him one year. And one can imagine he's put it to good use at the country place. A happy smiling-sun tavern sign reading "THE FINEST WINES, ALES, SPIRITS" hangs outside their wine cellar, which used to be the carriage house. It's here that John Traina and friends have fun with tastings . . . serious business for owners in the Napa-Sonoma-Mendocino area, the country's premier wine-growing area.

Nearby at Inglenook, Château Petrus's Christian Moueix and John Daniels's daughters at Inglenook got together to create the wine called Dominus.

Francis Ford Coppola, another neighbor in Napa and an enthusiastic presence at opera opening nights in San Francisco, had been encouraged by

Robert Mondavi to concentrate on producing only the very best wine at his property. His output eventually was called Rubicon, which critics called exceptional. It will be interesting to see what John Traina creates with his little corner of Eden.

Since John is a former executive with Pearl cruise line, he has travel in his blood. While married to Bill Toth, Danielle had taken her fear-of-flying classes, and overcome that difficulty. But she still wasn't ready to fly off to Bali.

It sounds as if prying Danielle away from her family and her house to actually wing away on vacations may be a hard thing to do.

But John, with his vast experience in travel, was able to get Danielle tripping off to one of California's most luscious vacation destinations: Hawaii.

Sometimes they head to the "Big Island" and the Kohala Coast, where they might have a romantic dinner alone at the Mauna Lani Bay Hotel.

The hotel's restaurant, Canoe House, is just a few sandy footsteps from the moonlit beach and melodious surf. And their other restaurant, Le Soleil, opens onto a garden, with mysterious pools and outdoor lighting. Danielle and John's new San Francisco cook would approve of the wonderful Pacific Rim food: for an entrée, the chef fine-slices and deep-fries tortillas, sets them beside a grilled Hawaiian fish with a papaya relish, and garnishes the plate with Scotch bonnet pepper. Desserts are equally reflective of the Hawaiian atmosphere: a *lilikoi* cheesecake of passion fruit, or a lemon-grass *créme brûlèe* nestled in a crisp cashew cookie.

Other times, they may dine at the Mauna Kea Hotel, or order room service.

If they want to venture out with all the kids and their gang of friends, they might just head to the industrial part of the island and Sam Choy's Restaurant. It's the insider's place to eat for both locals and visitors, just opened in the nineties. The tables are made of formica, and the lines are long.

The owner, Sam Choy, once helped his father prepare traditional Island luaus on weekends when he was growing up. Now, he cooks up a traditional *laulau*—delicious to see and smell—filled with fresh fish like ono and sprinkled with fresh vegetables. Sam Choy seasons the *laulau* with soy sauce and steams each order in the Island's ti leaves before it arrives, wafting Island fragrances, at your table.

But for longer trips to faraway places, John Traina may have to travel solo. Especially during the years when she was having one child after another, it would have been difficult to imagine Danielle taking off for Tahiti with John. But he's been able to go to exotic places like Tahiti and Chile with his older sons, Todd and Trevor, from his marriage to Dede. And he takes off for Europe or Asia at times when Danielle is with the children and the nine-month book schedule.

A former CEO of Pearl Cruises, a company he left about a year after marrying Danielle, he continues his interest in the Far East as a consultant to travel companies and the government of China itself.

John Traina was one of the first Americans to get cruises into China when they opened their borders. And he did the same with Indonesia. He's continued to keep an eye on China's tourist industry development, going back occasionally to help them with cruising interests.

In fact, one of his most exciting trips was at the beginning of his marriage to Danielle. Doug Cramer chartered a ship for *Love Boat*, and did an episode called "Love Boat Goes to China."

"It was the most fun trip I've ever had to China," John Traina told a reporter, being up on the Great Wall with Ursula Andress and Susan Anton and Linda Evans. "It was a great way to see China."

Staterooms on the luxury cruise once run by John Traina now come with multichannel music systems, individually controlled air-conditioning, phones, and a private bath or shower with thick terry cloth bathrobes and scented toiletries.

The Pearl Cruise suites are wonderfully spacious compared to those on the newer passenger liners. These have all the amenities of a first-class hotel. But it seems Danielle has never taken the time from her busy schedule for a leisurely, romantic cruise through exotic Asia with John Traina.

Pearl Cruise's one ship is now owned by a French company, Paquet. Paquet also owns the *Mermoz*, France's only luxury cruise liner.

The *Pearl* is the only luxury liner specifically designed for cruising in the Far East, with well-designed interiors of Asia's natural woods and brilliant textiles. The *Pearl* mixes European officers and Filipino crew, with guest hosts—chosen from among former diplomats and experts from universities and museums—leading seminars and land tours.

Pearl has more than one crew member for every two guests, with one of the highest ratios of crew to guests in the cruise industry. John Traina, with this luxury background, possesses the training to keep a luxury household running smoothly, and to sit at the head of the "Captain's Table" at their own mansion in San Francisco.

An ad on the cover of *Publishers Weekly* at the beginning of 1988 claimed there were already sixty million copies of her books in print. Her eighteenth novel, *Wanderlust*, had already been optioned for a miniseries by Aaron Spelling, producer of *Dynasty*. Still sitting in the pipeline, *Wanderlust* wouldn't actually be published for half a year.

It was no surprise when Danielle came out with a book in 1988 that was dedicated to both her late father and her husband, both named John and both bewitched travelers. *Wanderlust* was reviewed in *Publishers Weekly* on June 6, 1986:

Romance fans can expect to pick their way blindfolded along the familiar, rocky path to love in Steel's 18th novel, which begins in the 1930s. Audrey Driscoll often thinks that she might like to journey to exotic lands, but dutifully remains in San Francisco, keeping her wealthy grandfather's household running smoothly.

But when her spoiled younger sister marries, Audrey indulges her whim by setting off for Europe. In Antibes, she falls hard for Charlie Parker-Scott, a well-known travel writer. Though torn by responsibility for her lonely grandfather, she throws caution to the winds and follows Charlie all the way to China. Despite his loving entreaties, she stubbornly remains there, trying to save a group of abandoned orphans.

Finally returning to England, she finds that Charlie has married, angered by her defection. The lovers are later reunited only to be separated by World War II, until Audrey finds a way to combine their talents for the war effort.

The book is largely unsatisfying, especially in its repetitious language. It seems that Steel has lost the spark that fueled *Changes* and *Crossings*.

Chapter Twenty-one
No Greater Love

"Real isn't how you are made," said the Skin Horse. "It's a thing that happens to you. When a child loves you for a long, long time, not just to play with, but REALLY loves you, then you become Real."

"Does it hurt?" asked the Rabbit.

"Sometimes," said the Skin Horse, for he was always truthful. "When you are Real you don't mind being hurt."

"Does it happen all at once, like being wound up," he asked, "or bit by bit?"

"It doesn't happen all at once," said the Skin Horse. "You become. It takes a long time. That's why it doesn't often happen to people who break easily, or have sharp edges, or who have to be carefully kept. Generally, by the time you are Real, most of your hair has been loved off, and your eyes drop out and you get loose in the joints and very shabby. But these things don't matter at all, because once you are Real you can't be ugly, except to people who don't understand . . . but once you are Real you can't become unreal again. It lasts for always."

—Margery Williams, *The Velveteen Rabbit*

"But no matter how tired or crabby I get," she's said, "I have a total sense that I love my life."

But the simple physical act of writing these books, staying up for days and weeks at a time, is starting to take a physical toll on Danielle.

She only writes on that good-luck old manual 1948 typewriter she adores. "Someone broke it," she explained to a reporter in 1990, "probably irreparably . . . and tried to fix it, and it's terribly tight, it's like hammering concrete. I've been trying to play with it and get them to loosen it.

"Finally," said Danielle, "they got to a point where they said 'it's all in your head' . . . well, the second morning of typing, I popped a tendon in my left hand, so I typed the whole rest of the book, another 600-pages from there, with the hand the size of a baseball mitt.

"I felt," she said, "like one of those football players with the injuries who are out there getting kicked in the shin. When I finished work every night and I'd sleep for two or three hours, [my husband John] would keep my hand in an ice pack."

"She wouldn't switch to an easier typewriter," explained husband John Traina, "because she just felt at home with her typewriter."

Wasn't John afraid she'd end up in the hospital? "No," he said, "because actually, when she was moving [her hand], it was better for her than when she had stopped. And when she stopped, a few ice packs got it down again.

"But that's because," John explains, "her typewriter got sticky on her . . . when someone feels comfortable with one way of doing things, it's hard encouraging them to change that, especially when they've been as successful at it as Danielle has. It's her good luck."

She's said she's never lonely when sitting at her typewriter creating a dream life for her readers. She wrote men into her life.

Over the run of five rejected books, she kept telling herself, "I'll do just one more, and then I'll quit!" She didn't make a penny off her writing in six years, she says. And, of course, she never quit. The books are now sitting somewhere in a closet, gathering dust. It must have been "foolishness," she admitted. But she discovered that writing was addictive and that she wasn't only a workaholic, but a "write-aholic."

Someone who knew her as Danielle Lazard back in the early seventies said that most of the time "she was living an easy life in San Francisco." Danielle was obviously quite adept at shielding her private decision to become a successful novelist from her social friends. Those friends would have been shocked to discover she'd been up all night, every night, banging away on that lucky charm typewriter of hers. But her neighbors certainly were aware of the constant typing, typing, typing.

Around 1971 she found her old, cast-off "magic typewriter," probably the metal-body typewriter pictured on the back cover of the *Message from Nam* hardcover. The author photo is a lovely shot by Roger Ressmeyer. It's a 1948 metal body Olympia manual typewriter with a carriage, typewriter ribbon, roller, and platen.

This "ancient typewriter," she told a reporter, "is an old friend by now and I love it." She doesn't type terribly neatly, but her editor can certainly make it out.

"I have an absolutely brilliant editor," she said years ago. "It's been a long time coming, but she is rare and extraordinary."

Danielle Steel says that her religious faith has sustained and energized her.

"I'm a religious person. I grew up as a serious Roman Catholic and, when I was 20, became a serious Christian Scientist.

"I now believe," she says, "that there is no physical, financial, mental or personal problem that can't be worked out. That is a wonderful thing to teach your children—*never to be a defeatist.*"

* * *

Danielle was always waiting for Prince Charming to come up and knock on her door.

She didn't set out to write romances in particular. The way she explains it, "I just wrote what was in my head. I don't think anybody sets out deliberately to do a certain kind of writing—unless they do porno. I think most people just do what's in them and are sometimes startled to realize what's there. But the books did get much bigger, because I wanted to appeal to men and I wanted the hardcover market too."

After her move to the Pacific Heights mansion with her fourth husband and first true love, John Traina, she often spent eighteen hours a day writing.

In the late seventies, she told a friend she had completed a novel in nine days. "I have been known to hand in a completed full-length novel in six weeks!" she told a reporter in 1982.

Actually, a week before she and John Traina got married, "the moving men were taking my house apart while I was trying to meet a deadline . . . So I had the typewriter on the toilet and was sitting on the floor trying to finish the book. And that's exactly where I did it. In my bathroom."

In the Traina mansion, while the living and dining areas were more formal, her office and private bedroom in the early eighties were awash in color, with a very modern mood: posters, photographs, hearts, old dolls, and her trademark clouds painted on the ceiling.

After she had given birth to another few children, she still found herself in a small office, with beige walls and clouds painted on a blue sky on the ceiling.

"The conclusion," she told a reporter, "I am happiest writing in small rooms. They make me feel comfortable and secure.

"And it took me years to figure out that I needed to write in a corner," she explained to a reporter. "Like a small animal burrowing its hole, I shift furniture around, get myself into a cozy corner with my back to the wall . . . and then I can write.

"I'm not happy in big, airy spaces," she continued, "with elegant views, and my back in thin air. I like to lean against the wall in my chair as I struggle with the words. A good light on my left, a small table to my right . . . my trusty old Olympia typewriter under my fingers—and away I go!

"I've been known to transform hotel rooms and furnished houses to create the corner space I need."

When she and Traina's family started growing from the four they came with to the eventual gaggle of five new babies, her work habits changed a bit.

She learned to write in blocks of time, rather than working through the day as she could when she was married to Toth and Zugelder, when she had the luxury of time for herself.

But she still liked to write in a flannel nightgown, with hair in a braid down her back, and absolutely no makeup.

But when she's full tilt into writing a draft, the muse perches on her shoulder, and the pages just flow from her, through her fingers, and onto the pages flying through the Olympia.

"It kind of comes through me," she says. "You write what's in you and you have very little control over it. I sit there writing and the story comes to me and I say, 'Gee, that's really neat. Where'd that come from?' "

She doesn't necessarily write every day. When she's outlining, she can schedule the time around her other commitments and not write daily. But when working on a first draft, it's almost round the clock. The second draft, editing and galleys do not demand her daily writing attention.

So she has been able to break up her time in between intensive blocks of work to take care of the five little children with their occasional sniffles and her big daddy-husband with his skateboarding sons.

The Promise was the book that first started getting her a lot of fan mail, and she's been flooded with mail since her books have been on the best-seller lists. In the mid-eighties, she answered it all herself, sometimes two hundred letters a week. "I'm deeply grateful to all my readers for all the nice things they've done for me."

Because of the romance label, critics didn't want to take her writing seriously.

She was upset by that. "I put an enormous amount of work into the books and an awful lot of time and effort goes into them and they should be treated with some amount of seriousness," she said in 1986. But, her husband adds, when Danielle gets together with another writer like Sidney Sheldon . . . the one thing they seem to agree on is that once you're successful, you have bad critics.

"I have a great old retro gold Cartier watch," Danielle told a reporter. "It has a big gold disc with a little tiny watch. And on the disc is carved the word P-U-N-C-T-U-A-L-I-T-Y—and it's SO great! . . . Sounds like it was made for me."

The only way Danielle can run a household of eleven, while writing all those best-sellers is engraved on her Cartier watch: punctuality and The Danielle Steel Organization.

Using a detailed one-hundred-page outline, she isolates herself in what she calls a 6 x 6 office next to her bedroom.

She begins at eight A.M. and works obsessively until she finishes, in her cozy burrow, a room she's described as filled with family pictures, her children's artwork, tricycles, and framed dust jackets.

She works straight through then goes to sleep for three or four hours.

"I become totally crazed, I'm in a trance . . . and will go for a month without leaving the room," says Danielle. "It's like carving a big piece of marble out of a mountain," she told an interviewer.

"I can't leave it or I'll lose it. I'm terrified," she admits, "that block of marble will go back to the mountain." What she does is instinctive, working until she finds a "click" of recognition with the characters in her book. "I can't do it in real life, but I have that knack in books."

She then had five completed books in the pipeline, to be released in nine-month cycles from 1990 through 1992.

"Danielle hates long faxes," says Doug Cramer, her television producer for the miniseries. "You must condense things for Danielle. But she's got it all covered. I was married to a [woman with kids who wrote] and I ran her life—she wasn't organized.

"The ones who are organized," Cramer says, "are the ones who make it."

"To work well with Danielle Steel you have to fit into her schedule," explains a business associate.

The houses, of course, and the speed at which they are finished, reflect her passion for organization as well.

Keeping a positive attitude is the only thing that keeps her energy level up.

"I see her all the time when she's writing," says John Traina. "She has her office that she feels comfortable in . . . she's there in her track suit usually . . . [and] she posts her research on the walls. . . ." Danielle has discovered a researcher who can work at her pace, and the information she needs about the dates of a war, the style of fashion in World War II, or the sort of pens the Czar's family might have used before the Revolution is all at her fingertips—on the wall.

The reality, she pointed out to *California* magazine in 1991, is that you have to be ruthless. "You have to be terribly, terribly organized, and you have to be ruthless with your time . . . I'm ruthless about anything that interferes with my children or my work.

"I work ten hours a day and I spend ten hours a day with my kids, and that leaves me four hours a day to sleep." These inhuman work hours, it must be pointed out, only occur once every nine months or so, when she takes her nine days, her two weeks, to write a first draft in one fell swoop.

"[Organization] is something that is innate. One is, or one isn't. People either have it or they don't," explains Danielle. "And I'm terribly organized . . . my father was the most organized man I've ever met. He was German.

"I have a big appointment book," she explains, ". . . every night I make notes from the big calendar for what I'm doing the next day, so I run around with a piece of yellow paper with my list for the day.

"Without the list," says Danielle, "you can cash in my day, because I don't remember what I'm supposed to do. I end up with two hours of sleep to five if I'm lucky, and often four. And there just isn't a spare piece of meat in there.

"If I'm not working on a book . . . I work from around 7-8 o'clock at night to about four in the morning," she claims.

"If I'm working on a book I work pretty much around the clock. Every 20-22 hours, I take a 2-3 hour sleeping break, then I go back to it. But I only do that for, like, four weeks.

"I blast out a book in, oh, roughly two-and-a-half years. It takes me roughly a year on the outline, then I have a 100-page highly detailed outline . . . then it takes me four weeks of me sitting there 20 hours a day to do the first draft. And then I spend another year to year and a half on the rewrites.

". . . The outline is very long and laborious and the rewrite is very long and laborious but that middle part—it's sloppy and it's a mess and there are big pieces that will go, but it's just getting it on canvas—and then I can work with it and play with it. I only do that about twice a year. . . ."

Sometimes this crash two-week program of writing leaves Danielle physically exhausted. "I just finished one [recently] and it's not the first time it happened, but it was so obvious.

"I just fell apart afterwards," she explains, groaning.

"Every kind of ache and pain and problem."

During the mid-eighties, while she was having the five babies, she was able to work out at home, in the basement of John Traina's old mansion where she had a gym installed.

Recently, she's said, she goes to aerobics classes three times a week.

Given the problems she's had with her typewriter, and the physical demands of typing on a manual typewriter, she must be a woman with an extremely strong right arm, from those hundreds of thousands of carriage throws, and strong wrists and fingers, from all those millions of words. Just think of throwing a carriage on a manual typewriter twenty-five or thirty times per page, for over six hundred pages: That's eighteen thousand times per book. Let's hope she's had it made into an electric throw. Or that by now she's seen that you *can* use a computer as simply as a typewriter, and that it doesn't put you in the hospital with popped tendons from "hammering on cement."

"You always worry that this book is going to be as interesting as the last one," she says. "Especially after I've done a big book, I think 'oh, I'll never be able to do something like this again,' and then suddenly, there it is."

Is she a martyr? To take a night off with her husband after the children fell asleep and return the following afternoon took this schedule, she explained: "a day that started at seven in the morning, with three hours of sleep under my belt, and didn't end until four o'clock in the morning with every single minute of the day accounted for."

No time for gazing out the window, riffling through a copy of *Vogue*, or chatting on the telephone with a girlfriend. "I mean you HAVE to keep going," she explains. "And that's difficult.

"It's awfully hard when you work a day like that to go out and be charming and sit at a dinner party, and about 50% of the time when I go out, I KNOW I've got three or four hours of work sitting on my desk when I get back. OOOOOOH!"

But husband John Traina told a reporter "we're both used to the business world and a busy life. Danielle has her career and I have my career, and we probably approach things well together because of that. I like having a working wife, I think it's fine. She's far more organized than I am, however. . . .

"The nice thing about writing," Traina continued, "is it's not something you do day in and day out.

"She does it at certain times," explains John Traina, "and she plans for it, and before she starts, she clears the deck . . . and then she gets it done. . . .

". . . and then she goes back to being a housewife again. It's a nice thing for her to do.

"[When] she's doing her intensive writing it's almost around the clock," John Traina confirms. "That can go on for about four weeks. . . ."

Her husband has tried over and over to get her to at least consider the idea of a computer or a little laptop. "She's never gotten near a computer," he said in 1990, "nor an electric typewriter or anything modern. She's only comfortable with her 1947 Olympia." (Danielle seems to say her typewriter is a 1948, and her husband says it's a 1947: only her typewriter repairman knows for sure!)

But when the string of "Danielle Steel Presents" movies of the week started with producer Doug Cramer, the television productions (and, one guesses, the entertaining associated with them) were eating up even more of her time than the writing.

"I've gotten it to the point where if I JUST do the books," explains Danielle, "I've gotten it down to a dull roar that I can handle extremely well.

"Adding the TV thing, which I just did out of curiosity," Danielle continues, "has crunched up my time something tremendous," she told an interviewer, "and I'm trying to uncrunched again. But that's what has changed the balance."

Her time had gotten so tight in the early 1990s with the group of nine children, the house in the city and the compound in the country, the trips to New York and Beverly Hills and the vacations in Hawaii, that she seemed to be feeling overworked. Something had to go. And since she's always felt uncomfortable doing her glamour author photos, doing her introductions to the "Danielle Steel Presents" series made her even more nervous. So ultimately, that went.

"I'm sure I am [a workaholic]," Danielle answered a reporter. "I'd like to uncrunch [my time] again. I don't want to work that hard, and I really want to have more and more time with my family.

"But I do want to keep working," she added, "because eventually they all grow up and go away. And then what am I going to do? I mean, I wouldn't want to do nothing. But I'm doing more than I want to do. Actually."

But how can Danielle survive under all the pressure? Her husband John Traina explained to a reporter: "The one thing that affects it is that Danielle is doing what she loves to do and she's good at it. And that's a very satisfying thing. And a very lucky thing. To like what you are doing and to do it well."

Chapter Twenty-two

Heartbeat

"I never, never get to go shopping."
—Danielle Steel

A San Francisco socialite tells the following story: They were among the twenty guests at a chic dinner party where couples, including John and Danielle, were seated at separate tables.

In the middle of dinner, Danielle arrived at the table where John was seated with her mother, and said she was leaving. John and her mother said they'd leave as well. "No," insisted Danielle. "Someone here will take you back."

I asked Danielle why she had to go back "How do you think I feed all these people without going back home to work?" she said privately. It was typical of her. She gives the orders.

In reality, she certainly doesn't need to go home every night to work, to feed all the mouths, even to make the house payments.

But it seems there's something inside Danielle herself, some high-speed motor, that drives her on to work into the night, every night.

So when you hear that she buys things, enjoys picking out presents for people, and has a love for jewels, that John gives her wonderful sparkling gifts, you want to cheer her on. Someone needs to encourage her to have more fun with the money she's worked so hard for.

But you have to remember that to Danielle, the sheer act of writing herself into that dream world every nine months, may probably be more fun than any afternoon on a spree with a credit card at Tiffany's.

At one point after the birth of her daughter Zara, Danielle was asked if she was planning to have more children. This was after she numbered Beatrix, Trevor, Todd, Nick, Samantha, Victoria, Vanessa, Maxx and Zara in her brood. She laughingly told a reporter, "I'm not having any more children because it would be dangerous to my health—my husband would kill me!"

One reporter caught her running around San Francisco wearing designer jeans and a T-shirt that read "O-O-O-PS . . . I forgot to have children!" printed in bold letters above a biological time clock.

"Baby Zara was nursed by Danielle Steel at Denise Hale's penthouse luncheon," said the newspaper.

Danielle also nursed her child Maxx at a dinner party at the Gettys'. "Two nannies in gray and white uniforms stood by, ready to take over if needed," said the newspaper. "Afterward, Steel, elegant in a pale yellow Chanel suit, departed with her entourage in two blue Mercedes station wagons."

Reports on the size of her household staff vary. One reporter had it at eleven, with a chauffeur that doubled as a bodyguard, a gardener, a research assistant, social secretary and secretary, cook, housekeeper or two, and two or three nannies. In 1981, Danielle had ticked off seven. And that didn't include the new cook and his wife, soon to come.

But when asked if she had a nanny for each of the five young children, which was the gossip around San Francisco society, she countered by saying she only had the nanny and the nursemaid. "I have ME for each of the children."

When they travel to Napa, according to a friend, they make up a minimum party of twenty-one or twenty-two. Of course, that may include the sweet little Vietnamese pig and perhaps Swee' Pea the dachshund, some of the other dogs, the five to nine children, and their friends.

Danielle posed for a magazine in 1979 trying on a fox fur coat in a San Francisco fur salon, admitting to being a "compulsive shopper" who almost never goes out of the house without a hat.

The hardworking heroine of *Once in a Lifetime*, probably her second book in the marriage to John Traina, was a tiny, successful novelist often wrapped luxuriously in mink.

Her 1978 novel *Now and Forever*, perhaps modeled on soon-to-be-husband Dan Zugelder's rape trial, featured an entrepreneurial high-fashion woman, Jessica, making seasonal buying trips to the New York garment industry to stock her cutting-edge boutique in San Francisco.

Fine Things, a 1987 book, featured a male character who was a merchandiser in one of New York's top stores (a Bloomingdale's or a Saks) before taking over San Francisco's most fashionable specialty store. By the denouement, he and his wife chose to start a small, personalized boutique in the Napa Valley.

A writer should write about what he or she loves. Danielle herself is clearly a woman who appreciates fine things, and likes to let her readers in on the fun with her author photos on the back of each new hardcover.

Women's Wear Daily, the trade journal of the garment industry, interviewed her in the summer of 1986.

"I have to laugh," said Danielle, as she was getting ready to have her picture taken, putting on diamond-trimmed gold bracelets. "In real life I never wear makeup and I wear my hair in a braid down my back. This is a whole other side . . . I'd carpool in my flannel nightie if I could."

Occasionally, she loves to dress in expensive couture and pull out all the stops. Why keep such a spectacular figure otherwise?

For a *Los Angeles Times* interview, she wore a rich fox turban and a lush scarlet cape and skirt ensemble. This outfit was the sort of thing you'd expect a movie actress to wear when impersonating a romance novelist. It was everything that Kathleen Turner was not in *Romancing the Stone* with Michael Douglas.

Danielle has played directly into the glamorous woman writer stereotype. Perhaps she thinks it's good for business. But most probably because she's just being herself—truly in love with beautifully cut and beautifully fabricated couture clothes, with creative pieces of retro 1930s jewels, with luxury furs for foggy evenings in chilly San Francisco, with good leather luxury liner luggage for her occasional trips to New York and Los Angeles, and with Hermès bags.

Anyone who writes of the great French liners plying back and forth to Europe in the 1930s and 1940s would have a soft spot in her heart for the props of that life, the baubles from rue du Cambon and the deluxe boutiques with their tempting windows in the Ritz.

A friend who knew her in the mid-sixties when she married Claude-Eric Lazard says that she hasn't really changed. She's always loved buying things, she's always loved jewels, and she's always been adorable—terribly nice and sweet.

By the early eighties, she could buy clothes rather than design them in her imagination. A reporter noted that though she didn't finish her course of studies at Parsons School of Design and become the "new Coco Chanel" as she'd hoped, she was addicted to "buying exotic additions to her own wardrobe." She gave a discotheque party

for friends, said the report, and wore a lavender
lamé and red-sequined designer number from
Paris.

At a party for the famous *Vogue* photographer
Richard Avedon, she wore a classic 1950 Balenciaga
original, reportedly scheduled to go to the Costume Institute of the Metropolitan Museum of Art
in New York.

"I have a . . . secret passion for antique cars,"
she told the reporter then. "I now drive a Ford
Opera Coupe Deluxe, and have a 1940 four-door
sedan for the family." By the mid-eighties, the car
collection included fifteen, according to a newspaper report, including a beautiful 1950 Rolls-Royce.
"I think these are fantasy fulfillments," her agent
Mort Janklow was quoted as saying.

She also collects beautiful clothing. "I have a few
antique clothes," Danielle later told a reporter.

"They don't really hold up that well. My husband was related very distantly to Teal Traina . . .
when I find old Norell stuff with labels [I collect
it]. But no matter how pretty it is, it always looks
like old stuff, you can't really wear it."

In her country compound in Napa, she's used
antique Victorian whites as accessories in the guest
bedroom.

"I just like clothes, I've always had a real fasci-
nation with them," explains Danielle. "I'm fasci-
nated very often by the construction, which bores
everyone to death." (Although she's said she was
very happy to be getting away from cutting darts
all the time when she left Parsons Design.)

"I still love Chanel," she confessed in 1990. "And I think Gianfranco Ferre is *the* great designer . . . he's always been immensely talented, but the stuff he's doing for Dior is just extraordinary. There's that kind of wonderful, toned-down, throwaway chic. There are a lot of talented designers out there, but he really knocks my socks off.

"But I probably only go shopping for myself, in a browsy way, oh, maybe once or twice a year," said Danielle, "for a couple of hours."

She doesn't have the time to actually fly to Paris or New York to watch the couture collections.

"I don't go to the collections," she explains. "The collections send me tapes, and stores send me collections that come through town."

The local specialty stores treat Danielle Steel quite well, since she wears their clothes so well. "They're very sweet about it, they'll send the trunk show to my house and I'll look at it at three [in the morning] when I'm finished with my work, or I'll buy things from photographs."

Danielle, the "compulsive shopper," revealed, "I never, never get to go shopping." Perhaps she's shifted the shopping focus to her children and those special gifts for her husband, like gold cigarette cases to add to his collection. "That's a sacrifice I make for having nine kids, and for me, it's worth it. If you want to have that many kids, you have to sacrifice your own time."

These wonderful clothes she collects are night-out clothes, and the funny thing about Danielle is that she says she prefers to be home working. But since her husband is such a people-person, and has such a great time seeing his old friends in town, she says, "I go out for him and enjoy being out with him."

A friend had lunch with them in San Francisco and Danielle said she'd be wearing jeans. "But if you SAW the jeans, the jewels, matching, and he was dressed the same way. And the CAR," said the friend, describing a scene of unbridled luxury, almost *Dynasty*-like.

On May 15, 1988, one of Danielle's lushest novels was reviewed in *Publishers Weekly*. *Zoya* brushed across a canvas sweeping from the Czarist court in St. Petersburg to Paris devastated by World War I; and into the Roaring Twenties in Manhattan; followed by the struggle to survive in the Great Depression. And finally, on to the winning spirit of victory in the Second World War.

Danielle was again working very closely with a masterful researcher, who supplied her with the intimate details that breathed life into her historical settings. Here's the review:

> With the emotional panache that pleases her devotees, Steel (*Kaleidoscope*) portrays Zoya Ossupov, a courageous young woman of Imperial Russia who experiences both ecstasy and trauma.
>
> Daughter of a count who is a cousin of Tsar

Nicholas, Zoya enjoys a privileged, cloistered existence. Zoya, whose name means "life," is on intimate terms with the tsar's family. All of them, of course, are endangered by the Revolution.

The insurgents slaughter the tsar and his kin, and cause the deaths of Zoya's parents and brother, forcing her to flee to Paris with her aged but indomitable grandmother. Suffering in unaccustomed poverty, they are sustained by Zoya's wages as a dancer with the Ballet Russe.

Romance brightens her life following a chance encounter with an affluent New Yorker, Capt. Clayton Andrews. Enchanted by Zoya, Andrews eventually brings her to Manhattan as his bride, never imagining the tragedies that will befall them both.

Steel evokes the final days of Imperial Russia with characteristic bravura. As always, she offers a carefully calculated mix of picturesque locales, remarkable events, and appealing characters.

Herb Caen's column in *The San Francisco Chronicle* blurbed in mid-May that "I . . . note with incredulity that the 23rd and latest novel by S.F.'s Danielle Steel, out only two weeks, is already the No. 1 bestseller in the nation. Titled 'Zoya,' it vaulted immediately over Robert Ludlum's and Gabriel Garcia Marquez'(s) latest works, and these guys are considered heavy hitters whereas Danielle is reviewed lightly, if at all. It's a wonderment. I would have to guess that Danielle Steel has sold more books than every San Francisco writer put together."

"They have one of the most enviable marriages," says a friend who sees them at the San Francisco Opera. They had fun collecting together, and finding the perfect gifts for each other. He collects those antique jeweled Fabergé cigarette cases. And she collects those jewels and new diamonds.

Danielle talks nowadays as if she's never really worked, that she's always been a lady of leisure. But of course she started working in 1968 and seems never to have stopped! ". . . with the background I had as such, I've always felt it wasn't really OK to work," she told a reporter years ago.

The Nazis had forced the entire Schuelein family (her father was then only around twenty) to leave their elegant home and very rich lifestyle in Munich for the life of immigrants in strange foreign countries.

Perhaps the Schueleins didn't feel writing romance novels was a very useful work.

"It was even less OK to be a success," continued Danielle. "I have a real conflict within myself. I'm afraid to let it all hang out and say, 'Yes, this is what I am and what I do.' and 'Yes, that is me who is No. 1 on *The New York Times Best Seller List,* ' because it means you've flopped as a woman.

"So I think that to atone for the sin of being successful . . . I always kind of back off and hide it. I'm very much in the closet with my work."

When she gets her author photos taken, the glamorous Danielle, the Danielle image designed for public consumption, emerges.

She told *The New York Times* in 1989, "I feel I'm expected to look glamorous as an author and I'm a sort of retiring person," she said. "The photo session is a huge pain in the butt, if you want to know."

Readers have seen her evolve over the years, from the beautiful doe-like creature on the back cover of *The Ring,* to the classic white-shirted lady on the back cover of all the paperbacks, to today's strong woman on her latest hardcover, *Accident.*

Roger Ressmeyer's black-and-white photograph of Danielle on the back cover of *The Ring,* her first hardcover, shows a wistful, perfectly shaped Victorian face, and large dark eyes. Her thick hair is swept up and back. Her ears are adorned with large pearl ear clips. Around her neck, a Victorian-style choker which appears rather old, with a moon and stars, dotted with quiet little jewels . . . probably a moonstone to go with the theme.

Remembrance, the 1981 book with the first dedication to new husband John Traina, is backed with another black-and-white Ressmeyer photograph. The *Remembrance* jacket gives a more glamorous, happily-in-love Danielle, with backlit, full hair swirling around her shoulders. Again, she looks as beautiful as a model. And she is wearing the matched diamond earrings—the size of robin's eggs or maybe quarters—little makeup, and no necklace. Knockout diamonds.

About five years later, the *Wanderlust* jacket photo is again by Ressmeyer. Her jacket lavished with embroidery, her body lavished with jewels. On one finger, a large square ring that seems to be tiered with two rows of diamonds, and what seems to be those magnificent pearl earrings again from *The Ring*. Oh, and a Victorian choker of six or seven strands of rich pearls. Her glowing hair is spread out richly over her shoulders, and she's smiling at the camera, chin in hand, looking happy and in love.

For *Fine Things* and another Ressmeyer shot, she's been photographed in color, on a hot-pink background, wearing a white suit. The diamonds get a little carried away here, but it's great fun for her readers to take them all in. After all, the photograph of the author is, as one writer says, a gift from the author to the reader, telling her just a little bit about the writer whose world she is buying into.

In *Fine Things*, the reader is apparently buying into a world studded with diamonds. On her ears, sparkly diamond and gold ear clips. Around her neck, a fat gold-and-diamond spiral. Her nails are manicured a strong red, her lips a ripe reddish-peach. And on her right hand, a glimmer of what looks like three gold and silver and platinum bands from Cartier, and a signet ring of some sort on her pinky. Around her wrist, a heavy gold bangle. Another heavy gold bangle. Another gold bangle. And what's definitely more than a tennis brace-let—a wide strip of diamonds, unless it's part of the couture shirt. There are more diamonds on her lapel . . . but again, it's unclear, perhaps they're attached to one of the bangles. What we have here is a plethora of diamonds. On her other hand, a gold ring with a stone.

Bottom line: Diamonds are a girl's best friend. Her hair is, again, down, longer past her shoulders, and mixed colors showing touches of gray in with the rich warm browns. Her eyes are a greenish brown.

For *Zoya,* she is swathed in fox, both in the turban and around her neck . . . and on her ears, a pavé diamond ear clip is crossed with gold bands. It's a Ressmeyer 1988 portrait.

On *Star,* the photograph is copyrighted 1989 by Ressmeyer, and again Danielle is dripping in diamonds. She had told interviewers that writing *Fine Things,* which dealt with the death by cancer of a friend of hers, had led to her crying at her typewriter. She purposely set off to write *Star* as a more lighthearted entertainment, and her photo reflects that mood.

She glows before a romantic midnight-blue background spangled with stars, arms crossed on bare shoulders, with one hand bare, the other hand wearing a diamond that glitters from knuckle to knuckle on her wedding-ring finger. Around her neck, a heavy gold-and-diamond necklace of precious stones. On her ears, the magnificent matched diamonds.

Star was reviewed, along with *Zoya* and *Daddy,* in 1988. For some reason, Danielle's writing output was back at the speed of her early days with the paperback originals. Here's what *Publishers Weekly* had to say about *Star:*

Though Steel's (*Zoya*) novels showcase glamorous settings and turbulent romances, she writes convincingly about universal human emotions.

Her latest book begins in California just after World War II. At age 14, Crystal Wyatt's radiant beauty and singing talent have already aroused hostility in her narrow-minded rural community.

When Spencer Hill meets Crystal at her sister's wedding, an unlikely yet magnetic attraction binds them. Spencer, 13 years Crystal's senior, comes from a distinguished Eastern family that is forcing him to shoulder his deceased older brother's political aspirations. Though he yearns for Crystal, Spencer enters into a loveless but socially and professionally advantageous marriage with Elizabeth Barclay, daughter of a Supreme Court justice. Soon he implores her for a divorce, but Elizabeth vehemently insists on maintaining appearances.

Meanwhile, Crystal has achieved stardom in Hollywood, but her brutally possessive manager threatens violent reprisals if she ever tries to see Spencer. In her portrayal of the reunion of this star-crossed couple, Steel displays the dramatic flourishes her fans savor.

Message from Nam is a more conservative shot by Ressmeyer, showing not only the author, but the beautiful kind of metal-body manual typewriter she works on. In this photo, her brown-russet hair is up, her eyes are brown, and her lips are a red to match her manicure. On her right hand, she wears a gold signet ring, and on her third finger, what appears to be a pavé diamond and platinum ring that extends from one knuckle to the next. Her ear clips seem to be heavy cabochon ruby, set in gold, and centered with diamonds.

Her *Mixed Blessings* photograph is, of course, the most famous, because it has gone onto the back of all her paperbacks. Her hair is slicked back, her makeup is light, her eyes are hazel, and she is wearing only those large diamond studs on her ears, a white shirt with the collar turned up, and the tiniest gold chain barely visible against her lightly tanned skin. Here the author appears centered and calm, at peace with herself. It is as if she doesn't need to dress for the fantasies of her readers any more, and is able to dress in her own definition of glamourous.

While she's living the life of Danielle Steel, writer and harried mother, she's often dressed in jeans and T-shirts, ferrying kids from place to place wearing her beeper.

But in the evenings, when she and John have a formal night out, she's able to pull out all the high-wattage glamour without the nerves that always accompany the photo sessions. "Danielle and John Traina were seen kissing in an opera box at the San Francisco Opera," reported a magazine.

And they are friends with some of the most glittering folk in the City by the Bay, like Ann and Gordon Getty.

During the high social season, Danielle and John Traina can go to as many as three black-tie dinners a week at mansions in their Pacific Heights neighborhood. If there's an auction with antique jewelry, count on them to be interested. Or someone selling an antique car? Again, you may very well find them in attendance.

At some time during this wonderful year of having fun, Danielle has devoted concentrated time to her typewriter, for yet another book is reviewed by *Publishers Weekly*. First *Zoya* in April, then *Daddy* in December, a decidedly contemporary novel. With

Daddy, Danielle probably had no need for a researcher. She's writing about topics she may have discovered swirling about her when she remarried her own "Daddy," to whom the book is dedicated. Here's the review:

Steel's captivating 25th novel will send her rocketing past the 125-million mark for books in print and satisfy avid fans with its splashy sentiment, loudly plucked heartstrings and boldly drawn, if superficially developed, cast.

Oliver Watson is a successful, rather stolid, advertising executive with a beautiful wife, Sarah, three children, Ben, Melissa and Sam, and a house in suburban New York.

But his paradise is teetering over an abyss: Sarah, who never wanted a conventional life, coldly abandons husband and kids to "find herself" by pursuing a master's degree at Harvard.

Then Oliver's mother dies of Alzheimer's disease, leaving his 72-year-old father bereft, and 17-year-old Ben fathers a child and drops out of school.

Oliver blames unremittingly icy Sarah for every sorrow, yet initially refuses to get on with his life, even when his father points the way by finding a new love.

Steel (*Star; Zoya*) is at the top of her bestselling form as she steers Oliver through a fearsome new world of single parenthood, modern women and radically changed sexual mores before winding up with a paean to family life and romance.

Danielle and John were awarded "Best Entrance" at a Fine Arts Museum fund-raiser during the Christmas season. He was wearing a wonderful old overcoat; she was wrapped with fox. During the evening, she was beeped when it was time to feed baby Zara, who arrived by limousine and was met by Danielle at the party, according to *The Chronicle*.

She spent a reported $300,000 for her daughter Beatrix Lazard's coming-out party. Danielle's mother and father could never have had the money to carve out a place for her in old New York society. But she and Claude-Eric Lazard were a mother and father who could afford to carve out a place for her own daughter, Beatrix Lazard.

In the late eighties and early nineties, San Francisco was focused on the domestic doings of the Traina family. Were they moving from the mansion that Danielle had put so much work and love into? Would they buy the Spreckels Mansion? Would it be landmarked?

In April 19, 1989, Herb Caen noted that "Bestselling novelist Danielle 'Star' Steel and her husband, John Traina, have had their Jackson St. showplace on the market for $5.6 million and are searching for larger quarters to house their gaggle of offspring—nine at last count—and staff. If they can't find anything here, they might move, gafahbid, [sic] to Lozangeles. [sic] They've already taken a house in Malibu for the summer. . . ."

By summer and fall, San Franciscans were starting to gossip about the fabulous Spreckels Mansion, about to come on the open market for the first time ever. And a battle erupted over a change of ownership, and the changes that might bring to the grand old place.

The house, completed in 1913, was designed by George Applegarth, a student at L'École des Beaux Arts on the intellectual Left Bank of fin-de-siècle Paris. Applegarth possessed exactly the sort of classic French architectural panache that Danielle reveled in.

Specifically, noted *The Chronicle,* the Spreckels heirs had accepted a bid on the property from Danielle and John Traina. The Trainas had planned to help reduce the $13-million price by selling off some of the very expensive Pacific Heights backyard area to a developer, who would in turn build houses.

The neighbors were up in arms. The only way they could keep the "parklike estate," and the wonderful views, free from new construction was to have both the mansion and the entire park declared a historical landmark. It turned out that the City had already been considering landmarking the Spreckels Mansion before John Traina's land development became a hot issue in Pacific Heights.

Concerned residents included the descendants of George Applegarth, the architect of the mansion. In September they went before the Planning Commission, which recommended landmark designation, if the Board of Supervisors would agree.

And the Planning Commission seemed to make a recommendation which made both sides happy: the house's becoming a landmark would not preclude John Traina from selling the land for development, but the neighbors said any development or alteration to the house would have to be approved by both the Planning Commission and the city's Landmark Preservation Advisory Board. The next step was a public hearing in November to hear public testimony.

Yet in late October, Herb Caen noted that Danielle and John Traina had decided not to buy the Spreckels Mansion.

And as Christmas got closer and closer, Danielle's heart turned to thoughts of Christmas. She and her husband popped by Celebrations, to see the show of Christmas decorations and tables by San Francisco socialites.

For the symphony opening of 1990, Danielle decided to wear a gray glen plaid Christian Dior haute couture ball gown designed by Gianfranco Ferre, something she intended to wear to the opening of the opera as well. With a bouffant wool skirt and matching shawl, it featured a caviar-beaded

long-sleeved top with a bustle of silk flowers. "I
like it," she said, "it's so quiet."

Gordon Getty, also at the opening, said "any
night at the symphony is special. But on opening
night, I have to get on the soup and fish instead
of my regular clothes," referring to his formal evening wear. Ann Getty, his wife, was wearing a lavender dress and a knockout six-inches-wide
jeweled brooch by JAR, a chic jeweler in Paris, en-
crusted with emeralds, diamonds, and other precious gems set as flowers and fringe. "It reminds
me of when you're a little girl looking in the windows of Woolworth's [sic] at all the colored glass,"
she told a reporter.

Denise Hale, another friend of Danielle's, also
wore what she'd planned to wear to the opening
of the opera: a white haute couture bustier by
Gianfranco Ferre.

On October 14, *The San Francisco Chronicle* in-
formed readers that word was going around—
again—the Trainas had bought the Spreckels
Mansion. When asked about it, John Traina joked,
"Sure, we're buying two."

On October 9, Caen wrote in *The Chronicle* that
"Everybody involved in this deal is clamming up
as though it were the Iraq invasion date, but it's a
decent bet that author Danielle Steel and John
Traina are buying the huge but decaying Spreckels
mansion for around $8 million, which'd make it

the most expensive fixer-upper in local history. . . ."

Pat Steger, in her October 12 social column, had the latest rumor: Danielle and John had just closed the Spreckels Mansion deal. She also mentioned that Paloma Picasso and her husband Rafael Lopez-Sanchez, friends of Danielle's, were in town to attend the November Opera Ball/Fol de Rol.

October 18: "Latest poop from Le Group," writes Herb Caen, about Danielle and John buying the Spreckels mansion . . ." they 'stole' it for $6 million, another milestone in the history of affordable housing. The huge garden on the Jackson side reportedly stays with the Spreckels clan, which hopes to develop it before the neighbors go bananas."

October 19: Columnist Pat Steger reported Danielle and John had a wake-up call from NBC-TV chairman Brandon Tartikoff to congratulate her on the Nielsen ratings for the Monday Night TV movie of her book, *Kaleidoscope*. He called again Wednesday to congratulate her on the high ratings of TV movie "Fine Things."

Brandon Tartikoff and his wife Lilly were planning to fly to San Francisco that Sunday for the premiere of an opera with costumes designed by Gianni Versace, and the Italian Consul was planning a black-tie dinner.

Some of the scenes in "Fine Things" had been shot on location at the homes of friends. The party scene, for instance, was filmed at the home of Lu-

cinda and Charles Crocker, who'd just returned
from a $1,000 two-room suite at Italy's Villa d'Este,
according to Steger. Claude and Patty Rouas, who
have the Piatti restaurant in Napa, had allowed
filming at their Auberge du Soleil for a scene in
"Fine Things."

On October 24, Herb Caen wrote that the Trainas had decided NOT to buy the Spreckels Mansion.

October 31, 1990. Pat Seger wrote about Pat Con-
roy, author of *Prince of Tides,* moving with his wife
Lenore from Atlanta to Pacific Heights. Already,
they were serving on the honorary committee for
the Children's Hospital ball, the sort of volunteer
work that Danielle was known in San Francisco social circles *never* to volunteer her time for.

John and Danielle Traina were spotted at the
school fair with their children. And regarding the
Spreckels Mansion flap, antiques dealer Bob Her-
ing said, "I think they should be applauded [for
buying the Spreckels]. They're the only ones who
can do it right."

By spring, major moves were afoot. Pat Steger
reported that Robin Williams and his family had
sold their house in Sea Cliff and would spend a
year in Los Angeles working on films.

But when he moved back to San Francisco,

Robin Williams was rumored to be interested in buying Danielle and John Traina's house.

"However, Danielle said that their children were so upset about selling the house that they've taken it off the market."

Another rumor was that the couple would move into the Spreckels Mansion, which they'd still never officially said they'd bought, in September when renovations were to be finished.

In May, Herb Caen wrote that the Trainas would move into the Spreckels Mansion in October, and their old Jackson Street house would be sold to Robin Williams.

Two days later, Danielle and John showed up along with a crowd of about six hundred for the Project Open Hand second cocktails and auction. Car collectors John and Danielle Traina went home with a 1956 Chrysler New Yorker. But the major question among San Francisco socialites was just WHERE would they park it.

In July, three months earlier than the newspapers had estimated, the Trainas completed the move into their new house. Like the transformation wrought at the "old mansion" and the construction and transformation at the "country compound," Danielle had forced the contractors to meet her schedule. Anyone who's ever worked with contractors knows the miracle this entails.

A moving man from Kennedy Movers told a reporter, "We've done some big jobs, moving offices, but I guess this is the biggest household job we've ever had—except maybe when the Hearsts [Patty Hearst's parents] closed their house in Hillsborough."

Neighbors near the old mansion and the new mansion told a tale of a ten-day move . . . and that didn't count packing up inside the house before the move actually started.

Before the house was emptied, they made a room-by-room video of it for prospective buyers, like Robin Williams.

By September 1991 Danielle threw one of her famous birthday dinners for John and fifty or so of his closest friends at the new Spreckels Mansion.

And by October 3, 1991, they hosted their dinner-dance in the newly gilded ballroom—for eighty guests—to show off their new mansion.

And in December Danielle attended a dinner-dance at the Hearst Court of the M. H. de Young Memorial Museum, "looking like a heroine from one of her novels . . . a classic Christmas beauty." Apparently, moving for ten days and throwing a party for fifty and a party for eighty hadn't broken her social stride.

Danielle was wearing a deep red satin Valentino evening gown with short sleeves, a bouffant skirt, and a sexy V-cut back.

And she was about to celebrate her very first Christmas in the Spreckels Mansion, which had been built by Alma Spreckels, the woman who had organized San Francisco society to construct the de Young Museum itself, where she was dancing under the stars that evening.

When the Spreckels Mansion was sold to the Trainas, San Francisco property records indicate that it was valued at over one-and-a-half million dollars. Of that, the land was valued over a million. So that vast hulk of a house was being taxed at a rate of a three-bedroom split level in the more desirable areas of Los Angeles.

Perhaps Herb Caen was correct when he called it one of the most expensive "fixer uppers" in Pacific Heights. (The Trainas' old house, at 2510 Jackson, was probably more valuable on the current real estate market, because it was welcoming, not stern, and much less terrifying to potential owners.)

Papers filed with the City of San Francisco on the property show the past owners of the Mansion "still have interest". Dorothy Munn—now living in Palm Beach, Florida—the daughter-in-law of the redoubtable "Big Alma" Spreckels, who built the place; the Wells Fargo Bank, trustee, Joan de Bretteville Spreckels; trust, Adolph and Charles Rosekrans (also Spreckels family children). Dodie Rosekrans first lived in the Mansion as a young bride in the sixties.

Initially, Danielle Steel was listed as an owner of the Mansion. But recently Danielle's name was removed, and John Traina receives the tax bill now as the sole owner.

Another grand San Francisco opening, the Fall Antiques Show was up and running the following month, and *The Chronicle*'s reporter ran in just as Danielle and John Traina ran out. With the huge Spreckels Mansion to refurbish, they were probably in the market for some world-class antiques from the best dealers from London, Paris, Germany, and Holland, in town for the festive show. At Shirley Rendell's autograph section, a bit of writing in French by that other American Francophile and novelist, Edith Wharton, was selling for $4,750.

Several days later, Danielle and John were also guests at a small lunch hosted by Denise Hale and Sotheby-San Francisco's Deborah Hatch. Among the other guests were Lady Victoria Leathan, who lives in a 240-room English country house called "Burghley House," and sells reproduction antique jewelry on Home Shopping Network; Harry and Margot de Wildt, chairman of the Antique Show.

John was wearing, according to the *Chronicle* reporter, "a fading tan," and Danielle was wearing, "powder blue set off in aquamarine gems. The gems included a necklace of antique rectangular stones, perfectly matched; a huge stone set in a three-inch-wide gold bangle; assorted rings and pin; plus an arm load of her antique diamond bracelets. This girl has a Jones for jewels."

On November 21, 1993, the paperback of Danielle's novel *Mixed Blessings* had just hit the *New York Times Best Seller List* at number seven. The next week it was number one.

And Danielle was basking in her usual place in the sun, riding at the top of the best-seller list, having just moved into the grandest old fixer-upper mansion in San Francisco.

Chapter Twenty-three
Star

"She can do anything."
> —Douglas S. Cramer, producer of
> "Danielle Steel Presents"

1990: Danielle Steel and John Traina made a hot couple as they danced that sexy Brazilian *lambada* at a very private dinner given in their honor by Tommy and Patti Skouras (Skouras is the nephew of the famed mogul who ran 20th Century Fox). Among the guests was Danielle's new producer Doug Cramer.

Danielle and John were nesting during their visit at the luxurious five-star hotel, the Beverly Wilshire, conveniently located at the foot of Rodeo Drive, the famed shopping street in Beverly Hills.

Now in 1990, together with NBC, producer Doug Cramer had finally started the deal to translate Danielle's novels to the television screen.

The movies on "Danielle Steel Presents" would be personally introduced by Danielle. "The way Loretta Young used to do," Doug Cramer told a reporter. "She's been involved in every aspect of the project. She can do anything."

A couple of days later, Doug Cramer, now their business partner, gave a Beverly Hills lunch for Danielle and John, along with the then-head of NBC Entertainment, Brandon Tartikoff.

Doug Cramer had first met John Traina in the early eighties, when he used Traina's expertise and the Pearl cruise line for the "Love Boat in China" show. Cramer used to have Saturday night tickets back then to the San Francisco Opera, and Doug Cramer would see Danielle and John there socially.

How did Danielle happen into this television contract? In 1989, not one but two of Danielle's novels were among the year's top five best-sellers: Tom Clancy had number one, Stephen King had number two, Danielle had three and four with *Daddy* and *Star.* Amy Tan was also among the top twenty best-sellers that year. But Amy Tan's *Joy Luck Club* has now been made into a fine movie, produced by Oliver Stone. Danielle's have not.

Danielle Steel's novels were simply not the subject of much excitement among Hollywood film producers. In 1988, her publisher was printing one million copies of *Kaleidoscope* in hardcover—$20,000,000 worth if they all sold, not to mention the much larger paperback printings—and yet producers weren't bidding for the rights to make the movie.

In August of 1988, the year *Kaleidoscope* came out, Danielle and John rented a house in Malibu's Trancas colony, hoping to meet up socially with studio chiefs.

Revealing her publicity background, Danielle told a *Los Angeles Times* reporter that year that the headline of the profile she was writing on Danielle should be "Why Haven't Danielle Steel's Books Been More Commercial in Hollywood?" *Crossings* had been made as a TV miniseries, and a couple

more books had been optioned for TV, but
Danielle had said she really wanted to walk into a
theatre and see them on the big screen, (perhaps
like her early inspiration Jackie Susann's *Valley of
the Dolls*).

By the time 1990 rolled around, Danielle may
have given up on her big-screen dreams. Because
she made a sweeping deal to translate her books
into TV movies-of-the-week.

A *California* magazine article sketches in the outlines of her relationship with television producer
Doug Cramer.

Doug Cramer and Danielle had first met with
NBC's Brandon Tartikoff in September 1989.
"[Tartikoff] was captivated after meeting her and
wanted to make the deal," Cramer says, "but it
wasn't done until the end of March [1990] because of her batteries of agents and lawyers and
papers spelling out *exactly* what she does and
doesn't do."

In the sixties, Cramer had helped develop the
series *Peyton Place, Batman,* and *The Brady Bunch,*
as well as *The Odd Couple* and *Love American Style*
in the early seventies. Even as a kid he was in
love with show business—he had summer jobs at
Radio City Music Hall, the MGM script department, and Cincinnati Summer Playhouse, in the
city where his mother worked as a reporter. In
the sixties, Cramer was with ABC, Fox, and Para-
mount, and by the mid-seventies moved into producing.

With Aaron Spelling, he co-executive produced

The Love Boat, Hotel, The Colbys, Matt Houston, and, of course, *Dynasty.*

Both Doug Cramer and Danielle Steel had battled the monster of alcohol and drug addiction in their mates: Danielle had Bill Toth, and Doug Cramer had been married to Joyce Haber, the once-powerful gossip columnist for the *Los Angeles Times.* They divorced in the mid-seventies, and after repeated bouts with cirrhossis of the Liver, Joyce Haber died in 1993.

Doug Cramer's movies and miniseries included "Hollywood Wives," from the book by Jackie Collins, and "The Users," by his former wife.

He was immediately impressed with Danielle's organization and self-discipline. "I was married to a writer," says Doug Cramer, "and I ran her life—she wasn't organized. The ones who are organized are the ones who make it. A lot of successful actresses are like that. Jaclyn Smith [who has played in Danielle Steel's TV movies] has it written in her contract that she has breakfast and dinner with her kids, and if possible, lunch with the kids on the set. No overtime. The women who are able to [have both a career and a family] are VERY organized."

With Aaron Spelling, Doug Cramer had been producing *Dynasty,* creating the glittering world of high finance, stretch limousines, and greed that defined the Reagan era.

In 1986, Doug Cramer and Aaron Spelling had been the producing team on Danielle's first miniseries venture, "Crossings." She had very little involvement with that," he said. "I'm not sure she read the script."

Lilly Tartikoff, Brandon's wife, was an old friend of Doug Cramer's. They worked together on the American Ballet Theater. Doug knew how fond Lilly was of Danielle's work, that she'd read all her books.

So when Doug Cramer met for lunch with Bob Iger, of ABC; with Kim LeMasters of CBS; and with NBC's Brandon Tartikoff and suggested to each of the men individually the idea of the Danielle Steel movies, he was not surprised that Brandon immediately said, "Will Lilly love that!"

His wife Lilly used to stay up in bed with the network chief, reading Danielle's books, and was a long-time fan.

"Brandon immediately knew what it was about— no question that NBC was where she should go," Cramer told a reporter.

And in 1990, Danielle agreed to Doug Cramer's bold request that she go on television and personally introduce each episode for NBC. Speaking in a voice tinged with the New York accent of her youth, and just a tad nervous, she wears luscious clothes and looks as gracious and beautiful as Loretta Young in the heyday of her show in the 1950s.

For these taped appearances, Danielle dresses in fashions purchased from stores like I. Magnin and Saks Fifth Avenue. She doesn't have to go down to Union Square to visit the stores: The stores come to her. They send the designer's trunk shows to her house, and she looks at them when she's finished with her work. She also sparkles on the show in jewels from her extensive private collection.

Publishers expect their star writers not only to produce but also to promote. Danielle Steel's introductions to the TV movies are her nod to promotion. Jackie Collins was appearing on every TV talk show in the country when Cramer signed Danielle. "She [Danielle] won't even do the affiliates meeting for NBC. NBC even offered to send a crew up to her house in San Francisco [but] the TV people just wouldn't do the security pledges and sign the documents." Those were the most serious disagreements with Danielle over the TV movies—fighting against Jackie Collins movies on another channel, while he was fighting to get an audience and make the show.

They survived five months of negotiation from early November to late March. Why did negotiating the final deal take five months? According to Cramer, at first Danielle's lawyer Lou Blau had it—only a month. Then ICM [her old TV agents], where she worked with Alan Berger. Then Mort Janklow had it another two or three months. Then Danielle asked Doug Cramer who the most knowledgeable television person in town was. She hired Ken Ziffren on his recommendation, at Ziffren, Brittenham, Branca in Century City, and the deal was finally finished in March after a November start.

The NBC network selects the books and the order they want to present them in; and NBC has the rights to all Danielle's books, past, present, and future. On their side, NBC has to promise a certain number of hours a year be committed to her movies.

Brandon Tartikoff, then head of the NBC network, had such a belief in her drawing power that he went ahead and put up the money for getting the first script written, according to Cramer, even though the deal wasn't signed yet. "Come on," said Cramer to a reporter, "we all know writers come cheap. But a quarter-million [dollars for a script] isn't nothing to a network these days."

There were two different writers on "Kaleidoscope."

"To work well with Danielle Steel," explains the producer, "you have to fit into her schedule. To shoot the introductions to 'Daddy' and 'Changes,' we scheduled on the 30th of November for the 4th of January, and she only gave us three available dates for January before the air date for the movie." She was "a bit piqued" according to Cramer, "because we didn't select the hotel suite where it [was] shot [fast enough] . . . she feels there's no time for her to select clothes to go with the coloring of the suites," he told a reporter.

Her hair and makeup people for the shoots come up from Los Angeles. They're Union members, sworn to secrecy. They also do her makeup for his annual barn dance at his Santa Ynez ranch.

And in the midst of all this high-level negotia-

tion for televising her books, Danielle Steel had
time to write yet another novel. She has always
talked about appealing to men as well as women,
and *Message from Nam* was a daring attempt to do
just that.

In 1990, Danielle set out to break the mold her
readers expected of her. She wrote a novel that
placed her characters in the center of the Vietnam
conflict, something that had swirled about her in
real life when she first moved to San Francisco in
the early seventies, a city extremely politicized
against the war.

Visiting the Presidio, where Dan Zugelder was
probably undergoing the calcium tests for the
space program, she probably met other prisoners
in the experimental group. These others were
probably conscientious objectors. The doctors who
ran the test programs felt the COs made the very
best subjects to work with.

Publishers Weekly reviewed the novel on April 13,
1990. Here's what they wrote:

> An audacious—and ill-conceived—departure
> from her usual glitzy settings, Steel's (*Daddy;
> Star*) 25th novel focuses on the Vietnam War,
> though it merely skims the surface of that tur-
> bulent era. In an attempt at seriousness, Steel
> awkwardly shoehorns in a veritable almanac
> of historical facts and such painful milestones
> as the assassinations of JFK and Martin
> Luther King Jr.
>
> Her heroine, feisty Savannah native Paxton

Andrews, disdains the role of a Southern belle and flees to UC Berkeley, where she pursues a journalism major and instantly falls in love with law student Peter Wilson, son of a newspaper tycoon.

When Peter is killed in Vietnam, grief-stricken Paxton wangles a ticket to the front as a journalist, where, with an initial boost from a tough, fatherly AP correspondent, she knocks out an acclaimed column for seven years.

Steel's undemanding style is too often marred by gushing, breathless prose that trivializes serious events. While the best-selling author isn't at the top of her form, her fans will enjoy the emotional firestorm as Paxton reels from a series of tragic blows, some concerning her hotheaded lover, Sergeant Tony Campobello, a POW.

After reading *Message from Nam*, *Boston Globe* columnist Ellen Goodman wrote, "I remain bewildered by the popularity of Danielle Steel; the only explanation I can think of is the sheer power of marketing. As far as I can read . . . Ms. Steel is . . . a speed-writer of fiction, so breathless to get to the finish line she doesn't even stop for character development or for rewriting. [Her] stream-of-consciousness writing style [is] allowed to pass unexpurgated, unedited, from author to reader."

Danielle herself described the book as "a very

serious, heavy-duty story about the war in Vietnam."

Danielle may have been disappointed by the inability of *Message from Nam* to battle its way to the top of the best-seller list, but she didn't let it slow her down. She continued writing, and The Cramer Company, Doug's television production company, was now producing her television movies at an even *faster* rate than she was producing her books.

"There's something wonderful about doing something, completing it and letting it go," explained Cramer about making the TV movies based on Danielle's novels. "There's such a tremendous grind that goes along with a series [like *Dynasty*]. And when *Dynasty* went off the air, I think each episode was costing us about $1.6 million, which is very expensive even by today's standards."

Doug Cramer assured the magazine *Broadcasting* that "There won't be any *Dynasty* in these movies. In fact, I think the only tuxedo seen in 'Kaleidoscope' is at the end of the movie."

Cramer also explained that the average movie on television has about eighty to one hundred scenes. "Kaleidoscope" would feature two hundred, and the longer "Fine Things" will use three hundred, which makes Cramer's TV films look much richer. They won't be sharing the world of Judith Krantz's, Harold Robbins's, or Jackie Collins's jet set/romance tales, but continue the

Danielle Steel tradition of realistic, gripping emotions and situations, from which her characters learn and grow.

Jaclyn Smith stars in "Kaleidoscope" as Hilary Walker, an ambitious, workaholic network news executive who is haunted by her turbulent childhood and flashback nightmares of murder.

"Danielle Steel's popularity speaks for itself," says Jaclyn Smith. "All the Steel books I've read are entertaining, romantic, highly emotional and convey a sense of history. They have so much going for them that you can't put them down. Once you start one, you're hooked!

"Hilary is the quintessential Steel creation," Jaclyn Smith continued. "She has had a very sad life. Orphaned, she was separated from her two sisters at a tender age and then left to fend for herself. She tries to forget and negate her childhood by burying herself in her work, where she is strong, driven and highly competitive. But her weakness is a past she wants to forget.

"When she finally is reunited with her sisters, it's like primal therapy. She is forced to confront all the dark recesses of her life that she has tried to avoid. What actress could resist a part like that?"

Perry King, who played opposite Smith as John Chapman, a private detective hired by a rich businessman to find Jaclyn Smith and her sisters, studied differently for his role.

"I did not want to read the book before acting this part," said King. "A kind of sixth sense told me to fly by the seat of my pants—to play this role instinctively rather than read the book and come to the film set with preconceived notions."

Perry King told a reporter that he was especially attracted to the "Kaleidoscope" role because the plot involved child abuse, an interest that takes up a lot of his time when he isn't working in a film.

"I am very involved with a child abuse clinic in Orange County, California," explains King. "I feel lucky to be a working actor and I wanted to give something of myself to a worthy cause—and child abuse is one of the worthiest causes I know. Treatment of child abuse is the fastest growing business in southern California," continues King. "That tells you how dangerous and out of control this problem [of child abuse] has become.

"A strong plot element in 'Kaleidoscope' concerns the abuse of Jaclyn Smith's character as a child," says King. "Although her character gets away from an unhealthy foster home and eventually becomes a big success in business, that terrible experience as a child taints her entire life. It's difficult for her to love or really connect with anyone."

And Jaclyn Smith agreed that the characters were as fascinating as the plot. "You don't have to be a Danielle Steel fan to enjoy 'Kaleidoscope,'" she says. "Watching this character go through horrendous events, overcome a tortured life and then come out ahead represent universal themes that everyone will relate to."

The airing of "Kaleidoscope"—the network's very first experiment in the Danielle Steel series— was a triumph for NBC. They grabbed their top Monday movie rating in a year.

"Fine Things" was the second of NBC's double-header movie event. It starred recent mom Tracy Pollan, the adorable wife of Michael J. Fox. The male lead was D.W. Moffett, and Oscar-winner Cloris Leachman played the mother. The movie was about a high-powered executive who juggles his work and family after his young wife dies, only to have tragedy strike again when his stepdaughter's natural father surfaces, demanding custody in an attempt at extortion.

An element in the plot which sounded like a distant echo of Danielle's real life was when Liz confides to Bernie, her new husband, about her first marriage to an out-of-work man who abandoned her after her baby was born. The child was then told her father had died. And the father then showed up and demanded money . . . and even child custody. The father kidnaps the child and abducts her to Mexico, outside the court's jurisdiction. But Bernie stops at nothing to get the young child back safely.

Actress Tracy Pollan wanted to go back to work right away after having her baby, she told a reporter, but didn't bargain on the work involved with "Fine Things." Since her character dies of cancer before the third hour of the three-hour movie, she thought she could handle it.

"Then the night before I started shooting I saw the call sheet listing scenes to be played the next day," she said. " 'I've made a terrible mistake!' I thought. It was the actor's nightmare:

Scene 1: I give birth.

Scene 2: the doctor tells me I have cancer. 'I'm sunk!'

The next morning I get to go to the set. They introduce me to the producer and say, 'Get onto this table. Put your feet in the stirrups. . . .' "

Brandon Tartikoff, head of the NBC network, watched both of Danielle Steel's new television movie projects with his wife, according to Doug Cramer. "Brandon took home the unfinished film [of 'Fine Things'] to watch with Lilly,"—a film that didn't yet have the score—"saying he'd just watch an hour or so, and watched the whole thing with Lilly," Cramer told a reporter.

"And again with 'Kaleidoscope,' " said Cramer, Tartikoff and Lilly started watching the broadcast, and "next thing he knew, it was 11 o'clock. Both of them were caught up with the movie, and it got phenomenal numbers. He was on the phone [to Doug Cramer] the next morning at 7 A.M."

It was the highest rated TV movie of the *year* to that date.

And it got the highest numbers ever, opposite the *opening game of the World Series.*

So NBC then made the decision to put "Changes" up against the NCAA basketball finals, and history was made: Danielle Steel representing the women against all the major CBS sporting events, one or two in the fall, one or two in the spring. The programming decision jolted cocksure CBS in the midst of their macho sporting lineup.

Changes was a twenty-nine-week best-seller in 1983 and 1984, and now appeared on the home screen starring Cheryl Ladd as Melanie Adams, network correspondent for *The Morning Show.* Mel flies to L.A. for a story about a heart patient and falls in love with her doctor, Peter Hallam, the world's most famous heart surgeon. She finally moves to L.A. with her teen twin daughters to marry Dr. Hallam and live in his Bel-Air mansion. But as she settles into the mansion, she runs across serious complications trying to balance family life with her new career in local TV.

John Carman, in *The San Francisco Chronicle,* notes that "Changes" is an "impossible hybrid of *Rebecca* and *The Brady Bunch*" and complains that Mel and Peter (played by darkly handsome Michael Nouri) only cook themselves up to a lukewarm, compared to the famously hot love scene between Cheryl Ladd and Lee Horsley in her earlier miniseries, "Crossings." But he admits that with 130 million copies of her books then in print, Danielle Steel is obviously on to something.

"Changes" was Cheryl Ladd's third Danielle Steel role, after the Australian movie *Now and Forever,* mentioned in an earlier chapter, and the 1986 "Crossings."

"Changes" was sent out by NBC as its secret ratings weapon in overcoming the NCAA basketball championship on rival CBS.

Once again NBC threw Danielle Steel's movie up against a big sporting event. "Daddy" was against ABC's "Monday Night Football," "Palomino" was against CBS's baseball. Sports for the men, romance for the women. It seemed to work.

"Miss Steel is a force," said the New York Times critic John J. O'Connor, "and not only on the best-seller lists. . . ."

"Palomino" was the story of a successful woman photographer, Samantha Taylor (Lindsay Frost) who travels to the sumptuous California ranch run by her old friend Caroline (Eva Marie Saint) after being thrown over by her anchorman-husband. On the ranch she meets the cowboy of her dreams, falls in love, and has a riding accident that leaves her paralyzed.

According to the *St. Petersburg Times,* statistics from the Romance Writers of America show that paperback romance novels have twenty-two million readers. This number is quite interesting because an average of seventeen million viewers—almost all women, according to NBC—tuned into the three

Danielle Steel movies last year when NBC put Danielle up against sports.

Newsday's critic Marvin Kitman wrote that he preferred Jackie Collins, because "Steel is too heavy for me, with her psychological studies and plots which rely on aspects of characters' motives, feelings, life goals. Also, she's too realistic. Her stories are often about real people, not just the rich and famous, the fake make-believe world of passion, power and greed, superficiality and glitz that characterized the golden age of TV literature, the Judith Krantz epoch of the 1980s."

Marvin Kitman, reviewing "Daddy" in *Newsday*, called it "Steel at her best doing a story about marriages, careers, choices, changes." The stars were Patrick Duffy, Kate Mulgrew and Lynda Carter.

Duffy played Oliver Watson a successful ad executive in Chicago with a happy eighteen-year marriage blessed with three children.

But Duffy's wife, Kate Mulgrew, had always wanted to be a writer. Now she's accepted in the writing program at Michigan (a change from the book's original Harvard). And she takes off.

Her husband is devastated. And so are the children. "As she goes for it," says Kitman, "the family falls apart. But it is rebuilt, according to the wonderfully predictable and satisfying Steel formula."

"Maybe my brain is getting soft . . . but I actually found this condensation of a mini-series an interesting two hours. Not in the same class as the

Dominick Dunne novels (An Inconvenient Woman, The Two Mrs. Grenvilles) and the general way they did novels at NBC under Brandon Stoddard. But 'Daddy' is equally as involving as a World Series game, which, after all, is often a bunch of men standing around, hitting foul balls, spitting and whatever else they do in baseball."

The Chicago Tribune's television critic, Rick Kogan, like Marvin Kitman at New York's *Newsday*, had finally given in to the undeniable success of Danielle's television movies. He called it "unreality programming" to counter the NCAA basketball finals. He admitted he'd be watching the basketball himself, but "many others will be drawn to bestselling author Steel's special—and amazingly successful—brand of silliness. For the last couple of years, NBC has craftily counterprogrammed adaptations of Steel's novels against such muscled offerings as the World Series and 'Monday Night Football.'"

The previous three Steel movies—"Kaleidoscope," "Fine Things," and "Changes"—had all proved ratings winners, ranking among the top six made-for-television movies of the 1990-91 season.

"Jewels" was a two-part miniseries that began at eight on Sunday and nine on Tuesday up against the World Series on CBS, with Danielle introducing the story and then reprising it for her millions of viewers.

The *Washington Post*'s Rod Dreher, in "Danielle Steel's costume 'Jewels': All that glitters leaves you cold," wrote "Incorporating an author's name into the title of a film version of one of her novels can mean . . . in the case of 'Jackie Collins' Lady Boss' last week and 'Danielle Steel's Jewels,' which debuts tonight . . . [that] . . . The gloss here consists of Tinseltown trash-glitz (Miss Collins) and shiny-jacket, jet-set romance (Miss Steel). 'Danielle Steel's Anything' is bound to be torrid, shallow and as pulpy as a fresh-squeezed orange."

As usual, the male TV reviewers couldn't understand the appeal of Danielle Steel, for yet another saga, "Jewels." "Jewels" is the story of Lady Sarah Thompson Whitfield, matriarch of a jewelry empire, who discovered such a cunning way of helping postwar refugees fleeing Germany that she raised the hackles of *The Wall Street Journal*. The "extraordinary Lady Sarah" starts as a young American socialite (Annette O'Toole) who recovers from a horrible early marriage, travels with her parents to Europe, and there falls in love with William, Duke of Whitfield (Anthony Andrews).

By the fall of 1992, Danielle's press kits were noting she was today's best-selling writer, with twenty-nine books published in twenty-nine languages, and an annual income estimated at $25 million.

For the television adaptation of *Heartbeat, Washington Post* critic Tom Shales, another male reviewer, said, "Join us now for another installment of 'Love Among the Very Dumb.' . . . Surprisingly, though, 'Danielle Steel's Heartbeat' is appreciably less insipid than previous Steel-driven films."

The men were starting to come around.

Hollywood Reporter columnist Laurence Vittes came out on the side of "Star," up against the season's opening hit shows on CBS.

"Starring Jennie Garth as a California country girl and Craig Bierko as the Galahad-on-a-white-horse lawyer she loves but cannot totally have, the tearjerker is a beautifully produced, well-paced and superbly cast tribute to the very good and very beautiful . . . Garth does an impressive job of capturing her character's painfully intimate joys and sorrows without laying it on too thick.

"As an impossibly sensitive hunk," continues Vittes, "who just can't say no to the not-so-wicked East Coast witch who sort-of loves him (Terry Farrell), Bierko never does seem to age—but who cares, when he's so noble.

"The photography is lovely, the musical score sheer poetry, and the direction appropriate languid. All in all, a sweet treat for all viewers who can't deal with any remotely reality-based programs."

Tom Shales of the *Washington Post* went up to bat again against Danielle's latest four-hour miniseries.

"Latest in a long line of Steel traps," he wrote, ". . . [it] is a rambling and preposterous miniseries that uses the tragedy of the Vietnam War as backdrop for four hours of melodramatic hokum."

The *Seattle Times* TV critic John Voorhees wrote, "The ultimate vulgarization of the Vietnam conflict has been achieved: It's being used as a kind of backdrop for yet another of Danielle Steel's tiresome potboilers. . . . As always, a headstrong young woman is at the center of Steel's saga, only instead of the battle for a career and its effect upon the heroine's love life, this time it's the war in Vietnam that gets in her way."

Danielle and John managed to give dinner parties in their home-away-from-home by using the L'Orangerie restaurant, one of the most elite, expensive, and very French dining spots in Beverly Hills.

To start, Danielle has L'Orangerie's scrambled eggs, in the shell; topped with Beluga caviar.

Not only does Danielle enjoy her meals at L'Orangerie, but she is able to write them into a book, in this case, *Mixed Blessings*. Diana Goode and her husband Andrew Douglas have been trying to get pregnant; she finishes her meal, goes to the ladies' room, and finds the "telltale sign, a bright red rush of blood" that announces to her that, despite her recent attempts, she's still not pregnant. She starts to get dizzy as the room swirls around her.

* * *

In the fall of 1993, after the Danielle Steel TV-movie production schedule was firmly in place, Danielle and John gave yet another of their many Beverly Hills dinner parties in the courtyard at L'Orangerie. They invited several dozen of their closest friends as guests.

Why were they in Beverly Hills? A combination of business and pleasure, according to George Christy's interview in the *Hollywood Reporter.*

Shopping: Danielle loves Fred Hayman's shop on Rodeo Drive—Giorgio's successor, the store Judith Krantz built her first novel *Scruples* around.

Pleasure: They find the French cuisine in L.A. better than in San Francisco. "You can't find French food there like we're having tonight at L'Orangerie," John Traina told George Christy. (Their favorite restaurant in San Francisco belonged to a Los Angeles chef as well: Wolfgang Puck's Postrio.)

For her Beverly Hills dinner party, Danielle was dressed in an impeccable Galanos outfit—he's the Los Angeles couturier whose creations ran over $10,000 and were favorites of the Mrs. Reagan/Mrs. Annenberg/Mrs. Bloomingdale 1980s set. A black silk blouse floated pristinely above Danielle's black broadtail pants (broadtail is the fur or the skin of a very young or premature karakul lamb; the flat wavy appearance of the skin resembles moiré silk). John looked equally dashing in a navy Brioni suit and Gianni Versace necktie.

Bulky Marvin Davis, former owner of 20th Century Fox (who once appeared as a guest on Doug Cramer's *Dynasty* with his wife Barbara) sat at John's table, where he told CAA agent Bill Haber's wife Carole that his daughter Nancy had met a marvelous NY investment banker skiing in Aspen and would soon marry. Carole Haber and her agent husband Bill—who represents Danielle's Hollywood television deals—have a farm, some call it a "château," near Paris.

Mrs. Davis, wearing Tyler/Trafficante, discovered Jackie Collins, the author, seated at her table, yet another client of Danielle's superagent Mort Janklow. Also there, Danielle's lawyer Lou Blau, thanked by Danielle in one of her early novels, whose firm now handles Kevin Costner as well as Danielle.

One of Danielle and John's nine children—John Traina's son Todd came with his boss Kostas Iannios and Mr. Iannios's publicist wife, Nancy Iannios. (Todd is now working for Mr. Iannios's Big Rock Productions in Los Angeles.)

But the man with whom Danielle may have spent the most amount of time gossiping with later was James de Givenchi, the West Coast jewelry specialist for Christie's auction house, which runs neck-in-neck with Sotheby's for the really glorious diamonds that come up at auction.

The wines? A Meursault, Château Beychevelle and the Rieussec sauternes.

And so it goes in Hollywood. An endless round of the best wines, caviar in scrambled eggs, and source material for more novels. And while the word in San Francisco is that Danielle has grown tired of the Napa compound, she hasn't seemed to tire of Los Angeles and the glittering life to be found there. Perhaps John Traina and Danielle Steel will soon find themselves owners of a charming house in Bel-Air, perhaps something like the Bel-Air house she rented in fiction as the successful novelist (Lindsay Wagner) with a deaf son in "Once in a Lifetime," the small-screen adaptation of her novel in 1994.

Chapter Twenty-four
Secrets

"America Reads Danielle Steel"
—Publisher's slogan for more than a decade

In late 1989, one page of *The New York Times Book Review* section advertised Danielle Steel's twenty-fourth novel, *Daddy*, under the headline her publisher has been using for a decade: "America Reads Danielle Steel." Her author photo was sexy: She wore luscious red lipstick and a shirt with the collar turned up.

But farther back in the same issue was an ad for Danielle Steel's Max and Martha series, six books she'd written for the children's market. Here a more motherly Danielle was photographed reading to four children. She was wearing a sweater, and her hair was tucked up into a bun. This time the headline read: "Young America Reads Danielle Steel." Danielle, mother of nine children, was writing books to appeal to her favorite intimates: children. The books have not been a major success.

Danielle's new Max and Martha books—Max lives in New York and Martha in San Francisco—were reviewed before Christmas in *The Chronicle*. ". . . as in Steel's adult fiction, emotional issues are foremost; the ones here are appropriately scaled down to one transient issue: Mom remarries, a best friend moves away, Dad is injured . . . a new baby comes to the house."

And meanwhile her children were getting out on their own in San Francisco and New York.

Todd's twenty-first birthday was celebrated with several parties around town in December.

1990 was the year both Beatrix and Trevor graduated from Ivy League Princeton University in New Jersey.

So Danielle and John threw a party for them in the "old" mansion one Monday in July to celebrate. The house was decorated with Princeton's colors—orange and black—and full of oodles of orange-and-black balloons.

The next night, John and Danielle took Star's private room to throw a cast dinner for the group in San Francisco shooting "Fine Things"—Doug Cramer himself was up in Toronto, shooting the book *Kaleidoscope*.

On August 4, Danielle and John and "the family" drove down in the "land yacht" to Doug Cramer's annual barn dance at his Santa Ynez ranch.

Just before the barn dance, Trevor, who was off to graduate school at Oxford University in England, and his brother Todd, a student at Connecticut College, threw a party for a couple of young things visiting from London, one the stepdaughter of the Heskeths, who have a big old family estate in England; the other the daughter of the well-known Hoare private banking family in London.

* * *

On February 20, 1991, the San Francisco Landmarks Preservation Advisory Board met to consider a "certificate of appropriateness" for the new gates Danielle and John wanted for their new house, Landmark Number 197. They wanted to install copies of the original gates which had been removed years ago, all to be painted an antique bronze, the original color. The request was filed on Valentine's Day.

One of the board's members—absent in Nepal. Only in California. . . .

The gates were designed by Jensen's ironworks in Napa, and were adapted from the original drawings for the mansion going back almost a century. The work was approved, and the gates were in place for the big dinner-dance celebrating their new mansion.

Another building permit that had gone through the city bureaucracy at that time was to remodel the kitchen and put in new electricity and plumbing. Another was to remodel the nonstructural partitions—knocking down walls and rebuilding them, as Danielle had so successfully done in their previous mansion, where she divided the second floor into apartments for the teenagers, and apartments for the newly married couple. Reinstallation of the iron gate was approved in November; and here in major earthquake country, they worked out a way to brace and secure the mansion's parapet so it wouldn't fall and crush anyone.

And just before the Landmarks committee met to consider the security gates for Danielle's new mansion, *Publishers Weekly* brought news of yet another Steel novel, *Heartbeat.* The small article about the book, with Danielle's author photo from the book jacket, was in a group of reviews by authors: Alan Dershowitz for *Chutzpah;* Robert B. Reich (President Clinton's Secretary of Labor) for *The Work of Nations;* Mickey Rooney for *Life Is Too Short;* Mark Helprin for *A Soldier of the Great War,* and more. Here's a taste of the review of Danielle's twenty-seventh novel, *Heartbeat:*

It's an unorthodox modern love story. . . . It opens on a happy young couple . . . and when she gets pregnant, the idea of having children reminds him of the squalor he came from. But . . . she keeps bumping into a man who writes the most successful daytime soap. He's into sexy starlets, but he falls in love with the pregnant woman next door. It has a nice comic touch.

But *The San Francisco Chronicle*'s review of *Heartbeat* by Patricia Holt, noted that "Steel, who wishes to be considered a serious novelist . . . shovels out fiction as though she were digging to China, and her public carts it away just as fast. With more than 150 million copies of her books in print, Steel's tales of heartfelt (offstage) couplings constitute the most successful literary career in history."

* * *

Doug Cramer, Danielle's TV producer, took Danielle's first child, daughter Beatrix (or "Bede") Lazard, to the opening of the San Francisco opera and the $400-a-person Opera Ball on September 7, 1990.

Beatrix and Doug Cramer were a couple again at the opening of the opera the following year: "The [opera] opening reminds me of *Dynasty,*" he told a reporter, "but with more class and style."

The next month, Bede was helping John Davies—after whose family San Francisco's Davies symphony hall is named—organize a black-tie dinner-dance for Beau Giannini—that's Bank America—and his fiancée in the garden of Davies's parents house at the Schramsberg Winery.

Around Christmas, *The San Francisco Chronicle* ran a story headlined "a New Generation Makes Its Mark: Society Kids Take Up Endeavors Outside the Expected Realm."

Bede, along with several others, went into what the newspaper called "the rag trade." She went into a training program at The Gap's Banana Republic division working for Bob Fisher, the President of the division, and grandson of The Gap's founder, Don Fisher.

That year, Bede's mother Danielle had been no slouch either. After readying *Heartbeat* for publication in March, she had continued on to her twenty-eighth novel, *No Greater Love. No Greater Love* is a story of romance on the *Titanic. Publishers Weekly* reviewed it on October 18, 1991:

Steel (*Heartbeat*) shamelessly plucks her readers' heartstrings in this predictable sentimental novel. In 1912, during a harrowing Atlantic crossing, 20-year-old Edwina Winfield loses her parents and fiance in the sinking of the *R.M.S. Titanic*.

She bravely shoulders full responsibility for her younger siblings—sensible Philip, wiseacre George, angelic Alexis, and toddlers Fannie and Teddy—and resigns herself to spinsterhood, certain she will never wish to marry.

Financially if not emotionally secure in San Francisco, she ponders the fate of their father's newspaper business, capably mothers her brood and politely declines the amorous advances of a family friend.

Additional tragedy awaits in the form of WW I and again, tears are shed, but the indomitable Winfields prevail, eventually gaining access to glamourous 1920s Hollywood.

As George develops a career in the movie industry and stunning blond Alexis dreams of stardom, readers will begin to suspect that long-suffering, virtuous Edwina might have another chance at happiness (read: true love).

Steel can never be accused of subtlety, but fans of her brand of romance won't be disappointed.

Danielle Steel hadn't made an author tour for a long time. But both she and her publisher must have been shocked when *Message from Nam* failed to hit the number one spot on *The New York Times Best-Seller List.*

Hitting number one had become her regular routine. Getting second best must have been devastating.

Here's how she explained not hitting the top of the best-seller list to *California* magazine:

Was the unexpected seriousness of the title *Message from Nam* partly to blame?

"I'm sure."

"But it was our stupid timing [Delacorte Press, Mort Janklow, Danielle Steel]," said Danielle. "They [Delacorte] brought it out right with Scott Turow. He was on the cover of *Time* magazine and he had his book out and his movie out at the same time."

"His [Scott Turow's] hardcover," continued Danielle, *Burden of Proof,* "came out the same week as his paperback and his movie [*Presumed Innocent*], which was on the cover of *Time.* . . ."

"That," she continued, "was an unbeatable combination.

"And it's not terribly fair," continues Danielle. "You know, *Time* gave him all sorts of raves and put him on the cover. But they also happen to own his publishing company [Warner Books], which people don't realize.

"People are always calling me to make sure when we're coming out," says Danielle, "to make sure books don't bump into each other. In most cases, it's okay, because Mort [Janklow] represents most of them. But he doesn't represent Turow," continues Danielle, "and . . . it took us by surprise. All of us. We ran right into them."

No, it wasn't a birthday party with cakes and balloons and that sort of thing. This was a very grown-up birthday party for a very grown-up young lady, the first of the family of nine children to turn twenty-five.

She had a black-tie dinner-dance at the Trafalgar Room of Trader Vic's—one can't imagine she could have paid for it on her trainee's salary alone. But as a Lazard, she probably had a little nest egg someplace.

But tonight, someone was footing the bill for the party. There were 120 guests.

Everyone had been asked to wear wigs. That included the waiters. That even included the musicians in the band.

Bede herself wore a "Lady Godiva" sort of wig, for her party, themed "Don't Flip Your Wig over 25."

The following year Bede Lazard was seen dancing to a group called Bare Foot and the Killer Whales, among four hundred others who'd paid $30 each for their tickets. Before the dance, benefiting the UCSF Pediatric cancer department, she and her date started the evening with a dinner for about 130 at Trader Vic's. Bede was the date of Art Muldoon, who was off to business school in the fall at Northwestern, outside Chicago.

A couple of months later, Bede was dancing to the New Orleans Radiators and the Aftershocks, now on the committee for the benefit, again raising money for the UCSF Pediatric cancer department.

John's son Trevor had a six-week 1991 spring break from Oxford. He flew home to see Dede and Al Wilsey, his mother and stepfather, by going around the world, stopping in Prague, Czechoslovakia, then making a few stay-overs in Asia, before arriving in Hawaii, where John and Danielle were holed up with the rest of the family at the Mauna Kea for a couple of weeks.

The following year, Trevor joined Seagram's as a marketing man in New York.

Danielle seemed to be the mother who was buying up the most presents in San Francisco: first she cut a swath through Hermès. But she then beat records by "forging ahead with a sweep through Tiffany," according to the newspaper.

But Danielle hadn't only been Christmas shopping and going to dinner parties. A big shipment of *Jewels,* her twenty-ninth novel, was hitting the bookstores in time for summer beach reading. *Publishers Weekly* reviewed *Jewels* on March 30, 1992. Here's what they wrote:

In the Steel collection, *Jewels* is merely a semiprecious gem. Set in the WW II era, the novel depicts the travails of its heroine, Sarah,

Duchess of Whitfield. The beautiful debutante daughter of a wealthy American family, Sarah has endured the disgrace attending her divorce of her caddish first husband.

Eventually she marries the charming and very rich Duke of Whitfield, who buys her a château in France. The rest of the novel follows the self-satisfied course of their usually happy union.

WW II offers Steel a chance to pump drama into this bland narrative, but she misses it. Sarah spends the war comfortably ensconced on the grounds of her château, looked out for by a solicitous German commander so polite she doesn't guess he has fallen in love with her.

Meekly, he leaves the moment Sarah learns her husband, the duke, has survived a Nazi prison camp. After she nurses William back to health, their idyllic marriage placidly resumes.

They are rich and envied. They eat well, dress well, live well, have children and open a jewelry store for amusement. The narrative's greatest conflict comes in the final chapters, when widowed Sarah has to deal with her unruly offspring.

Costume jewelry has more sparkle than this uninspired tale.

Seven months later, Danielle made another run for the number one spot on *The New York Times Best-Seller List*, this time with *Mixed Blessings*, a dra-

matic treatment of three couples desperately trying
to have babies, and the infertility depression that
each, in turn, faces and conquers. *Publishers Weekly*
reviewed in October 26, 1992, like this:

> The prolific Steel (*No Greater Love*) turns
> her attentions to a contemporary topic: infer-
> tility, and the desperate measures that couples
> resort to in the hope of biological parenthood.
> Steel's approach, however, is often maudlin
> and simplistic. Here, three California couples
> are married on the same day; none of the
> women proves able to conceive.
> The couples never meet, but Steel tracks
> their common fate with a vigor that rivals her
> characters' quest for children.
> Various partners consult fertility experts,
> and ultimately every conceivable aspect of re-
> productive medicine, including surrogate
> motherhood, is given its due.
> Steel explores the emotional strain on the
> couples: Diana and Andy, who previously led
> charmed lives; bubbleheaded would-be starlet
> Barbi and unexciting but wholesome Charlie;
> and 42-year-old Pilar, a successful attorney,
> and 61-year-old Bradford, a judge and wid-
> ower who has two children.
> Marriages founder, but conventionally good
> characters find their way to happy endings.
> While Steel sets up potentially complex family
> relationships, she forgoes developing them;
> just as it wreaks havoc on the characters, the

single-minded pursuit of babies damages the narrative.

In the summer of 1993, while Danielle had published three best-selling novels in the past year and a half, *No Greater Love, Jewels,* and *Mixed Blessings,* John Traina had just brought Trevor and Todd—along with their stepsister Bede Lazard—to check out the Fabergé goodies the Russians had on display at the Hermitage in St. Petersburg and the Kremlin. "We were wined and dined in high style," said John Traina, "but my Fabergé collection is better than theirs." Trevor, back in New York from Russia and still working at Seagram's, was flying off to San Francisco for the fourth of July, while his brother Todd, working for a Hollywood production company, was flying back East to be with his mother at Newport.

Trevor again returned to San Francisco in September for the opera opening. The grand City Hall rotunda was the site of the pre-opera sit-down dinner. As columnist Herb Caen tells it, Trevor, gazing about "at the fading magnificence" said, "It's just like home, only smaller." Referring, of course, to his mother's new acquisition, the landmark Spreckels Mansion. A Spreckels there for the opera managed to spill an entire glass of red wine down one of the opening nighter's several-thousand-dollar yellow-and-black dress. She asked for soda water and a tranquilizer. And what was Danielle wearing? "In deference to The New Austerity," Caen reported, "a famous lady novelist with acres of clothes showed up in a simple but eloquent white blouse and black skirt."

Danielle Steel, with all her nesting instincts, must have found it unsettling to move from the old mansion to the new house, the Spreckels. But she managed to organize the move in the smoothest, most calming way: By moving each room in its entirety from the old house to the Spreckels, there was a certain familiarity about the new house once everything was put in place.

Another thing they may have been upset about is the lack of a private gym—their schoolmates used to be quite impressed at the old house when they'd visit Danielle's gym and sauna in the bottom level of the house. Now all they have is a large pool at the top of Pacific Heights. It's an indoor pool, with lots of windows, where John Traina can swim laps.

Danielle Steel came to the black-tie dinner-dance for about 120 at Trader Vic's Trafalgar room for writer Paul Erdman's thirty-fifth wedding anniversary, along with Charles de Limur and Arthur Hailey.

After the big San Francisco earthquake in late October, people remembered the earthquake survival group that Danielle Steel had started years back on her block on Russian Hill. Her neighbor at the time, Monica Clark, told a reporter that the group still worked.

Flying from Spain to New York in her private jet, Ann Getty decided to continue on to New York after hearing about the quake, so she could be with her husband Gordon Getty. John and Danielle told Herb Caen they had decided NOT to buy the Spreckels Mansion, despite the fact that the sale seems to have gone through in the spring of 1989.

In a couple of weeks, Danielle was at a black-tie dinner with John. Her Bob Mackie gown was emblazoned with Danielle's zodiac sign, Leo, the lion, in rhinestones. John was wearing a leather trimmed dinner jacket.

A few weeks later Danielle and John went to Basil the bulldog's dinner party. Basil, who lives with Tiffany's Michael Barcun and decorator Ran Schwartz, sat underneath the table hoping for scraps of steak, while a Getty—Gloria this time—the Trainas, and others sat for dinner.

A couple of days later, Danielle and John stopped by to meet dermatologist Aljandro Cordero, up from Argentina, who claimed to be among the first to use Retin-A to erase wrinkles. Danielle was on her way to a dinner party at L'Etoile, given by the Chevaliers du Tastevin. Now that John Traina has been mucking about with the vines and the grapes, they keep up with the wine talk. The wine served at dinner, Villa Zapu, was from some Napa neighbors, Anna and Thomas Lundstrom. (Her father is the Swedish Ambassador to the United States, Count Wilhelm Wachtmeister.)

Meanwhile, Simon Critchel, Cartier's U.S. president, invited Danielle and John to a dinner-dance at the Ritz Carlton.

The previous week, John was asking jewelry designer Angela Cummings of Tiffany all about her work, because he's writing a book for Doubleday called *Extraordinary Jewels*.

Four months later, Cartier's Critchell sent out invitations for guests to sit at the two tables he'd bought for the September 4 gala opening of the San Francisco Symphony—the personal invitation was sent out on engraved sterling silver trays, delivered by a costumed page to, you guessed it, Danielle and John, among others.

By October, *The San Francisco Chronicle*'s Social Scene writer, Pat Steger, wrote: "There have been so many parties and openings in the last few days, it's like there's a show in town called 'Making the Rounds.' Some of the featured players were John and Danielle Traina, who went to two of three Tiffany openings, the Waltz Ball Saturday and still had time to give a little lunch at home Friday."

Danielle's thirty-first novel, *Vanished*, brought up themes that she wrote about in her early fiction. The character Charles seemed based upon the alcoholics and drug addicts she'd been so disappointed by. Her Delacorte publisher signaled their belief in the strength of her tale by ordering a one-million first printing for the hardcover, priced at almost $24.00. *Publishers Weekly* gave it the once-over on June 7, 1993:

Despite some redundancies and dimension-less supporting characters, Steel's 31st novel is a potent blend of romance and intrigue.

When Marielle Delauney marries New York steel magnate Malcolm Patterson in 1939, she does not tell him of her tragic past—neither the drowning accident that claimed her first child, nor the subsequent beating by her husband Charles that caused her to miscarry, nor the two years she spent recovering in a sanitorium.

But what does the enigmatic Malcolm already know? When they have their own child, Teddy, Malcolm, to all appearances, is an adoring father.

The still-vulnerable Marielle begins to gain self-confidence, even though she endures daily confrontations with a hostile and even sinister household staff.

Then the day after Marielle has a chance meeting with Charles, who drunkenly makes vague threats against Teddy, the four-year-old is snatched from his room, the nanny and nurse chloroformed and gagged.

The FBI is summoned, Marielle's past is exposed by a frenzied media and Charles is arrested.

But where is Teddy? The author of *Mixed Blessings* keeps her secrets well, and—the annoying reprises of critical scenes aside—presents a strong portrait of a tormented young woman moving toward stability.

* * *

Danny Zugelder is still sitting out his time in Colorado.

But he's been moved.

Moved to high security in this year, 1994. He's gone into a millennium kind of place, the high-security lockup.

Drive east from Denver, run about ninety-five miles along Interstate 76 toward the spot where the sun blazes from the horizon every morning.

Here, in the town called Limon, the head of Cartier jewelers doesn't send invitations hand-engraved on silver trays, delivered by a costumed page. Here, they don't wear matching emeralds. Or even many diamonds. There's no yacht club, no Trader Vic's. The town of Limon is surrounded by a dry, bleak prairie land with dead brown grass and tumbleweed.

This is ranchland and the land of poor farmers, struggling to hang on through this blistering recession.

In Limon, the New Austerity isn't a nineties version of Radical Chic, it's a reality. On top of the near-depression, God chose to batter this town with some of Colorado's most violent tornadoes a few years back, perhaps to test their faith. Trees impaled farmhouses like Trader Vic's swizzle sticks through a cherry.

And through this flat, quiet town are found some of Danielle Steel's fans. These are the women who long for the entertainment of her novels, the closeness they feel to her characters, the sense of caring she conveys. These readers need the emotional assurance that things will turn out all right for a good woman by the end of a Danielle Steel book. Even if it won't in real life.

These are some of the women who have helped build the career of Danielle Steel.

And in this town is a man who remains convinced that he helped build the early career of Danielle Steel by giving her a whole new world to write about. Danny Zugelder.

Drive south of town, past the dreary mobile home parks, the two sets of railroad tracks. Pass the feedlot, where the ranchers fatten up their cattle for the kill.

Here is Limon Correctional Facility. It doesn't sit on beautiful San Francisco Bay like San Quentin or share the rolling grasslands of the Vacaville's campus-like grounds. No famous intellectuals like Harvard's Dr. Timothy Leary have walked through its gates and enriched its psychology department. This place is the end of the line.

An American flag snaps smartly in the chilly early-morning wind next to its companion, the state flag of Colorado. A high lonesome guard toward stands watch. All around the perimeter, high chain-link fences topped with silvery, gleaming cold rolls of razor-sharp barbed wire make their point: no getting out of here.

The visitor first goes through a metal detector, then into a long outdoor walkway. High chain link on both sides. Automatic gates trap the visitor into a cage-like square for a minute, until an inside gate slides open. No one is in sight. It is like being in a dog pound. Or perhaps the neighboring feedlot.

The guard inside checks a visitor through to the visitor's room, through another two locked doors, buzzed open.

Once inside, a visitor comes up against what Hannah Arendt once called "the banality of evil." The visitor's room is like the lunchroom in any of a thousand offices around the United States, from Denver to San Francisco to New York. Formica tables, plastic chairs, fluorescent lighting behind panels, dead-white light.

The man behind bars has given up his secrets to parole officers and prison reports and court records going back over twenty-five years. When he gets out of prison, he says, he's going back to California. He's going to live with his sister and brother-in-law at a Christian camp.

But will he break out first?

Someone smuggled a gun into Canon City for him. He was planning to break out.

He'd been using a lot of drugs in prison.

So they moved him.

Limon, they say, has tighter security.